Vision to Execution

Marvin Covault

ISBN 1-59109-358-9

To order additional copies, please contact us.
BookSurge, LLC
www.booksurge.com
1-866-308-6235
orders@booksurge.com

Vision to Execution

TABLE OF CONTENTS

INTRODUCTION

Fear of the unknown is a natural human trait. Many people are uncomfortable going where they have not been or doing what they have not previously done; they prefer to remain in the comfort zone they have created over time. One of the ultimate human challenges is to motivate subordinates to explore new horizons. Those who initiate this and turn it into reality are leaders. Leaders command the present, advance ideas and shape the future. This is a book for leaders, leaders at all levels in every type of organization. It describes what leaders are and what leaders do. The basic assertion is that leadership is an art, not a science. The young leader reading this book can gain an appreciation for how extensive the subject is and embark on a lifetime of study, observation and learning. This is also a book for the experienced leader who is seeking innovative leader development techniques and ways to harness the efforts of large numbers of people in order to move the organization forward.

Organizations are comprised of leaders and those who aspire to lead. The principles, ideas and philosophies outlined in this book are applicable to every type of organization: government agencies, small privately owned businesses, Fortune 500 corporations, religious organizations, law enforcement agencies, institutes of learning, healthcare facilities, the military, non-profit organizations, etc. Because leadership principles are universal, anyone can take these lessons into the workplace and implement them immediately.

My background is as a practitioner of the art of leadership. Having spent my entire adult life being trained to lead, leading at numerous organizational levels and training others to lead, I gained perspective and insight on both highly effective as well as dismally ineffective leadership practices.

Helmuth von Moltke (1800-1891) was a prolific author and a brilliant military strategist. As Chief of the Prussian and German General Staff from 1858 to 1888, his successes on the battlefield changed the map of Central Europe. During his thirty-year reign as Chief of the Prussian and German General Staff, Moltke completely changed the training for military leaders. He recognized that technology (railroads) had changed the battlespace because large forces could be quickly transported long distances and adequately supplied by rail. Larger battlespace necessitated decentralized operations and, therefore, decentralized decision-making. Success was measured by how well subordinate leaders could make timely decisions on their own and work from an understanding of their senior leader's intent. Moltke came to the conclusion that one cannot rely on natural genius for the development of senior leaders. It is a powerful statement sending a compelling message about the importance of leader development and the overall culture of an organization.

From that assertion Moltke set about changing the training and development of his officer corps. Leaders are not appointed, leaders are developed over a long period of time through hard work, planning, resourcing and mentoring. He would plan and personally conduct elaborate staff rides where young leaders were transported to former battle sites and mentored through the operation, learning from past failures and successes.1 Moltke's army was successful because it was well led and as a result, he figures prominently in military history. However, his legacy has less to do with the number of battles he won and more to do with the leadership principles he instilled in his subordinate leaders. His greatest, lasting contribution was that of a thinker, not a warrior, which further proves that the lessons conveyed in this book are timeless and universal.

This is a how-to book. I want to take the subject of leadership and break it down into understandable parts.

Understanding leadership is a little bit like cooking an elephant. Do not begin by trying to find a pot big enough. The only way to cook an elephant is one part at a time. That is also how to learn about and understand leadership, one part at a time.

I am going to briefly describe the tools that are available to every leader. In that regard let me introduce a simple analogy, a theme that will carry on throughout the book. You decide to build your dream house and purchase the perfect lot on a golf course, by a lake, by a mountain stream or on Elm Street. You hire a general contractor, construction is about to begin and the contractor shows up with a huge truck and parks it on the lot. Curious, you look inside and find dozens of toolboxes, one for each subcontractor—the framers, roofers, electricians, plumbers, etc. Every tool necessary to construct the entire house lies within those toolboxes.

I have loaded up the leadership truck and am about to park it on your lot. Some of the tools in each box are common because there are a number of leadership principles that are enduring, common to every leader at every level and will never change. What I am going to do is open every toolbox and describe each of the tools available to you. After suggesting how each tool can be used and its benefits, you choose the tools that are right for the leadership challenges you face each day in the workplace and start using them.

This book is presented in two parts; the purpose of part one is to establish the context for leadership by describing the underpinnings. All leaders must have a base from which to work and they must also recognize that many leadership principles are enduring. Had I lived a thousand years ago or a thousand years from now, I could be writing essentially the same book. There are a few things that change: the environment in which leaders work, the amount of information available (currently at an all-time high), pace of play (also at an all-time high) and generational attitudinal shifts. Irrespective of these factors, sound leadership principles have endured and provide the underpinnings for what leaders are and what leaders do.

Part two describes how to use a framework for action

to move an organization forward. An organization with no commonly understood framework for action will be less efficient and less effective than it should and can be. The framework provided in part two will provide you with the ability to out-think and out-perform the competition.

It is my intent to:

- Provide a set of enduring leadership principles relevant to the challenges of the twenty-first century operating environment.
- Define the differing responsibilities among direct, operational and strategic leaders.
- Help senior leaders appreciate how using a chief of staff, kitchen cabinet, war council, or skunkworks can enhance their productivity.
- Establish that every leader's second most important responsibility is leader development.
- Explain why leaders must proactively shape their organization's culture.
- Substantiate that a time-proven framework for action is necessary in order to successfully navigate from vision to execution.
- Illustrate that leaders at every level have the means and the responsibility to create conditions for success.
- Describe every leader's role in character development.
- Present an example of how to apply all the leadership lessons during a crisis.

Let us climb on the leadership truck and look inside each toolbox.

To Deborah, Andrea and Casey for their encouragement and editing.

PART ONE

LEADING ORGANIZATIONS,

THE UNDERPINNINGS

CHAPTER ONE

LEADERSHIP FOR THE

TWENTY-FIRST CENTURY

While leadership Principles Are Enduring, A Changing Operating Environment Impacts On How Leaders Act And Function.

T he purpose of this chapter is define some special challenges facing leaders today and to set the stage for how to deal with them.

The days and weeks leading up to January 1, 2000 provided an opportunity for reflection. The media focused on change in culture, life styles, events of the millennium, person-of-the-century in every conceivable category and so on. Reflecting on the subject of leadership, entry into the twenty-first century also coincides with some significant changes in the organizational operating environment.

In one sense the passage of time (a generation, a century, a millennium) is meaningless because leadership principles are enduring. For example, the baseline for any leader is character. Can you be relied on to keep your word? Do you genuinely care about people? Does your reputation include integrity? As a test of one's character, these questions have not changed in the thousands of years people have been exercising leadership skills and they remain applicable in the new millennium. What does change is the operating environment and that impacts a leader's actions and functions. There are three critical issues confronting leaders as we transition into the twenty-first century, information availability, pace of operations and societal influences.

Information is one example of a constantly changing environment, how much there is and how we get access to it. Imagine being a business leader at the beginning of the last millennium. Generally, they were local and dealt with their suppliers and customers face to face. They made a few seasonal or annual decisions and could see their entire domain. They were concerned with turning information into knowledge, which would enable them to make sound decisions concerning growth, profit and future operations. However, the volume of information with which they were confronted was limited.

Information availability and accessibility has steadily increased through the centuries. Transportation systems advanced from caravans crossing South Asia to worldwide shipping, railroads, interstate highways and airplanes. Johannes Gutenberg, a fifteenth century businessman from Mainz Germany, saw the need for a rapid, inexpensive way to produce written documents and developed the printing press thereby making information available to the masses.2 Information began moving faster when Samuel Morse received government funding to construct a telegraph line between Washington, D.C. and Baltimore, Maryland. The first telegraph message was transmitted on 24 May, 1844 and read, "What hath God wrought!" Alexander Graham Bell was born in Edinburgh, Scotland and immigrated to the United States in 1871. In 1875, Bell developed the first version of what we would come to know as the telephone, taking information transmission to a new level. The first words heard on the telephone were spoken by Bell to his associate, "Mr. Watson, come here. I want to see you." A year later, Bell made a long distance call of 143 miles and in 1877 the Bell Telephone Company was established.3

Now we are in the midst of an information technology

revolution and the potential societal consequences are as yet undetermined. What is clear, however, is that the information environment for today's leader has been impacted more dramatically in the present generation than the sum total of all previous generations. Leaders today, as they have throughout history, seek to turn information into knowledge. However, massive amounts of information can be made instantly available and it must be recognized that the leadership equation has become more complex.

A second significant environmental change for leaders is the pace of operations. While change in pace is tied to the changes in how information flows, it is a force in and of itself and has important ramifications for leaders. Contrast the businessman of a thousand years ago with the industrialist in the late nineteenth century who could receive updates by telegraph every day; and today some leaders are receiving more email in a day than can be read, let alone acted upon. One outcome of this exponential increase in the pace of operations is that more and more issues appear to be a crisis or actually become a crisis. A senior executive of a major U.S. financial services corporation confided to me during a meeting in 2000 that his biggest problem on a day-to-day basis is getting people to compress time. He asserted that all opportunities are now time sensitive; solutions have to get downrange quickly. What I heard him saying was they do not have the mechanisms in place to deal with an accelerated pace of play and were therefore faced with crisis after crisis. Welcome to the challenges faced by the twenty-first century leader.

There is a third factor influencing twenty-first century leadership and it has to do with what society provides. As young adults, my parent's generation suffered through the Great Depression, fought and won World War II. Their generation survived because they genuinely cared for less fortunate neighbors and worked as perhaps the greatest team in history. The totality of the World War II effort transcended the fighting forces and included virtually every American. They worked hard and made personal sacrifices every day. In support of the war effort Rosie the Riveter turned out complete fighter aircraft in hours and war ships in days. Neighbors working together for the greater good was an early lesson in my life growing up in an Iowa farming community in the 1940s and 1950s. My contemporaries, sometimes referred to as the Silent Generation, (work hard, spend wisely, trust the government) were optimistic about the future and had strong moral values. The point to be made is that when my generation entered the work force in the 1950s and 1960s, we came with a strong sense of teamwork, loyalty and stability, factors our leaders could capitalized on. But generations change. For example, our society experienced a dramatic shift in the 1960s with the Baby Boomer generation (more fearful of the future and fairly socially liberal) as some participated in the anti-Vietnam, anti-government, anti-authority movements. Recently entering the work force, Generation X has been generally characterized as living for the present, looking for immediate gratification and individualism is more revered than teamwork. Next we will see the Millennial Generation, very technically literate, maturing rapidly, perhaps overly materialistic. 4 Of course it is not fair to paint every generation member with the same brush and the comparisons are not meant as a critical commentary, but it is a fact that every generation is influenced by a different set of factors and offer leaders different challenges. Leaders must recognize this and deal with it in some positive way in order to extract the best from subordinates who represent different generations.

With these three factors in mind – information volume, pace and generational change – what is it the twenty-first century leader needs to do to be successful? First they must recognize that how leaders deal with these issues and keep the work force focused is a multi-faceted problem. There is no single sentence that can capture what leaders have to do to confront the totality of their leadership responsibilities. Second, they must grasp that solutions come from several initiatives such as understanding and using the continuum of leadership, dealing with change, organizing for action, having a positive culture, developing leaders, building character and working from a framework for action. Having recognized the problems, there are a number of toolboxes available to do something about them and that is what the succeeding chapters are all about.

RECAP

1. The twenty-first century environment has complicated leaders' tasks because of:
    *   The volume of incoming information and greater emphasis on the leader's role of turning information into knowledge.
    *   The pace of play and young leaders acting on more far-reaching issues and making confident decisions.
    *   Shifts in generational attitudes and values.
2. To be successful, twenty-first century leaders must:
*   Know the generations and deal head-on with change.
*   Establish a moral baseline for their organization.
*   Have a plan to develop leaders.
*   Work within a framework for action in getting from vision to execution.

ENDURING LEADERSHIP PRINCIPLES

This is the first of the leadership principles that will emerge as we move through the underpinnings and framework for action. These are the principles that became important to me as my leadership experiences and responsibilities increased over the years. But these are mine; what is important is for you to develop your own as you work your way through the book. So take this opportunity to turn to the final pages of the book where space has been provided for you to begin recording your enduring leadership principles.

Great leaders:

Understand their changing environment.

CHAPTER TWO

DEFINING A LEADER

Once We Define What A leader Is, We Will Have Determined What It Is He Or She Does.

The purpose of this chapter is to assist you in finding a definition of leadership that you are comfortable with or provide insights to aid you in developing your own. A good definition will be a primary tool in your leadership toolbox as you pursue your responsibilities in getting from vision to execution.

In seeking a definition the first inclination is to look in a dictionary:

Leader n. A person or thing that leads; directing, commanding, or guiding head, as of a group or activity. 5

This is a start but a brief dictionary definition does not provide a sense of what "directing, commanding or guiding" is all about.

A person in a leadership position goes to work each day and the manner in which they perform can be charted along a wide spectrum. On one end of the spectrum some leaders work to clear their physical in-box of hard copy messages, delegate minor tasks, review documents and sign certain items. Additionally, they will be working to clear their virtual in-box consisting of email and voicemail. In doing so, they may make decisions and manage activities, most of which are either sustaining or reactive in nature. While they may be the designated head of a group or organization, if these activities consume their day, I will assert they have been captured by the tyranny of the mundane and are abrogating their leadership responsibilities.

At the other end of the spectrum, the head person views each new day, each new situation as a unique opportunity to move the organization forward, from out front, working toward a designated end-state. Out front means routinely taking responsibility for the actions of the organization, guiding and directing subordinates into heretofore uncharted territory. End-state represents a solution that is not within the current day-to-day routine of the organization. The end-state may represent a new order which embraces change to present-day procedures. It is all about anticipating the future and moving toward it in new and innovative ways.

On the first end of the spectrum, the leader was expending time primarily to end actions. This is a reactionary approach, a passive style, the management of ongoing systems, allowing what is sent to them by others to dictate their behavior day-to-day, task-to-task. While at the other end of the spectrum, the real leader is principally moving the organization towards an end-state while also completing routine daily tasks. The person who simply reacts to what is in their in-box does not appreciate that dealing with change, seeking innovative solutions and executing plans is necessary in order for the organization to have a future.

POWELL'S LESSONS

General (now Secretary of State) Colin Powell revealed in his autobiography *My American Journey* that he used a few simple rules to guide his professional life, and as a constant reminder, kept them on a scrap of paper under the glass top of his desk. He has expanded upon these rules and in a speech prepared as part of his Outreach to America program listed eighteen lessons. Several of General Powell's lessons have particular relevance to leadership. In lesson number one, General Powell says:

> **"Good leaders sometimes make people unhappy. Good leadership involves responsibility to the welfare of the group, which means that some people will get angry at your actions and decisions...... Ironically, by procrastinating on the difficult choices, by trying not to get anyone mad and by treating everyone equally nicely regardless of their contributions, you'll simply ensure that the only people you'll wind up angering are the most creative and productive people in the organization."6**

Several thoughts on leadership have been captured in this paragraph. First, being a leader is hard; you will be challenged and tested everyday. Second, a leader must work to build consensus, there will be dissenters and those dissenters will raise doubts, perhaps even in your own mind. Third, compromise is the tool of the timid soul who wants only to reach an end point. Too often compromise is the process of taking the best aspects of two conflicting agendas, mashing them together and ending up with the worst possible solution. A good leader, on the other hand, will find a way to influence the majority into following him or her to a preconceived end-state.

There are gradations of leaders. Some are ineffective, some have adequate abilities and some, like General Powell, are widely recognized as great leaders. What makes the excellent leaders stand out is that they recognize that leadership is not a popularity contest. A leader must do what is necessary for the greater good of the organization.

LEADER OR MANAGER?

During any discussion of leaders, leadership, managers or management, questions always arise concerning differences, similarities, choice of terms, etc. Since this is a book for leaders and we are looking at definitions, this is the appropriate time to establish the distinctions between leaders and managers and set the issue aside. To begin this discussion let us go back to the dictionary and see what it says.

> **Manager n. a person who manages; esp. a) one who manages a business, institution, etc. b) one who manages affairs or expenditures, as of a household, a client an athletic team, etc.** 7

For management the dictionary reads:

> **Management n. 1. The act, art, or manner of managing or handling, controlling, directing, etc. 8**

Webster's definitions for leader and management use one common descriptor, "directing." I am satisfied with that word because both leaders and managers do direct activities and operations. But, by way of creating a clearer picture of our leader, let us build some contrasts with a manager.

Imagine an automobile assembly line. The manager watches over the maintenance schedules of the machinery; checks the inventory of parts and their flow onto the assembly line; and monitors the vacation schedules, shifts and peak production periods. This day-to-day routine is undeniably essential and requires a dedicated, intelligent person to make it run smoothly. This person focuses primarily on the here and now and sustains operations which enable personnel to produce automobiles.

In contrast, the leader of an auto assembly plant has a vision that he can automate some manual portions of the assembly process and reduce production costs by ten to fifteen percent. The leader sees the day when they will have to double the size of the plant and has begun formulating a plan to do so. He views sustainment of the status quo as failure, understanding that change and innovation are the engines of success.

The distinction between what managers and leaders do

is not limited to organizations that manufacture things. An infantry platoon of about thirty soldiers trains nearly every day, a trained and ready unit being their product. Someone must manage the training schedule to ensure time, training areas, instructors and required equipment are available. While this is an important function, just managing the availability of resources at the right place and at the right time will not accomplish the mission. Someone must lead the platoon as they consume the resources in order to accomplish a predetermined level of training that represents the desired end-state.

The picture we have painted of the manager is that of an indispensable part of operations; there must be processes in place that keep an organization functioning. The leader's interest in process is from the standpoint of whether or not it will have to be altered as the purpose of the organization is redefined and redirected. Managers focus on an organization's processes while leaders focus on its purposes.

OTHER DEFINITIONS

If we think of leadership as an art and management as a science, we can convert this thinking into the following definition:

Leadership is the art of doing more than the science of management may believe is possible.

There are two points to be taken from this definition. First, since leadership is an art form there is no precise formula for defining it. Second, this definition makes the point that an organization can be taken by skillful leaders where it collectively did not believe it was capable of going. This addresses the concept of synergism, the whole being greater than the sum of its parts.

Harold S. Geneen, retired Chief Executive Officer of International Telephone and Telegraph writes, "Leadership is purely subjective, difficult to define and virtually impossible to measure objectively...." This line of thinking reinforces the point that leadership is an art and not a science. Geneen expected his subordinate leaders to follow "...a philosophy of aggressive anticipation of goals and problems and of effective advanced counteractions to ensure attainment of final objectives." This idea begins to tie together the assertion made at the beginning of this chapter that, what a leader is, is what a leader does. He goes on to make the point that "...leadership is the heart and soul of business management." 9

"Leadership is influencing people by providing purpose, direction and motivation while operating to accomplish the mission and improving the organization." 10

This definition is from the United States Army Field Manual 22-100 and serves to point out the multiple dimensions of leadership:

INFLUENCE. Leadership is getting people to do what you want them to do.

PURPOSE: Leadership is giving people a reason to do something. During WW II General Eisenhower, while praising the troops, observed that American servicemen would do anything they were asked, as long as they were told why it was necessary.

DIRECTION. Leadership is committing to a goal and then communicating the course of action.

MOTIVATION. Leadership is positively challenging subordinates to complete their assigned tasks.

IMPROVEMENT. Leadership is changing organization, operating procedures, or manning levels in order to increase capability and accomplish future missions.

Colin Powell provided another thought when he describes a leader as the "chief disorganizer." His lesson number five reads as follows:

"Never neglect details. When everyone's mind is dulled or distracted the leader must be doubly vigilant.....Good leaders delegate and empower others liberally, but they pay attention to details,

every day.....That is why, even as they pay
attention to details, they continually encourage
people to challenge the process. The job of a
leader is not to be the chief organizer, but the
chief disorganizer."11

In seeking a personal definition of leadership, one can take
from Powell's lesson number five that leadership is vigilance,
leadership is focus on execution, leadership is empowerment.
But his central point is that the devil is in the details and while
leaders need to go there, they have to guard against being
captured and held hostage by the minutia.

DEFINITIONS THROUGH THE AGES

To reinforce the point that folks have been thinking and
writing about leadership for a long time, here is one attributed
to the Athenian General, Chabrias (410-375 BC):

**"An army of deer led by a lion is more to be feared
than an army of lions led by a deer."**

No matter how talented the team members are, their
collective goal will not be achieved without strong leadership.
That astute observation is exceedingly applicable to the
twenty-first century wherein bold, aggressive leadership will be
necessary to deal with the mass of information available and the
pace of operations.

General George S. Patton, Jr. dedicated his professional
life to thinking about leadership and command. He was a
master at finding ways to simplify complex subjects. Patton
wrote, in January 1928:

**"At first blush one would scarcely expect to find the
behavior of a piece of crooked spaghetti an illustration of
successful leadership...it scarcely takes a demonstration to
prove how vastly more easy it is to pull a piece of cooked
spaghetti in a given direction along a major axis than it
is to push it in the same direction. Further, the difficulty**

increases with the size of either the spaghetti or the command."12

Leaders have to get out front and take the organization where it needs to go in order to prosper and survive, otherwise that leader is just working the inbox and pushing the spaghetti in whatever direction it chooses to go.

President Truman gave us many words of wisdom to live by such as "the buck stops here." On the subject of leadership, Truman said:

> "A leader is a man who has the ability to get other people to do what they don't want to do and like it."

People may disagree with their leader's chosen course of action; they may even dislike their leader. In spite of that events can move forward as long as the leader has their respect, trust and confidence. This is summed up in a thoughtful quote by an anonymous author:

> "No man is a leader until his appointment is ratified in the minds and hearts of his men."

WHAT LEADERSHIP IS NOT

In attempting to clearly define leadership it may be instructive to determine what it is not. For example, leadership is not synonymous with power. Being in a position of power does not automatically qualify that person as a leader. The person holding a position of power has decision authority over subordinates, issues and operating procedures. In addition this person must also have the ability to communicate a vision of an end-state throughout the organization, a vision that can eventually be executed. A second example is that leadership is not about getting every detail in line before you launch a program or make a decision. Effective leadership does not require that every detail be thought through before decisions are made or programs launched. Seeking that last bit of information rather than going with your gut can paralyze an organization and in fact increase risk by missing the most opportune time to strike. The challenge is to get the large issues in focus and ensure everyone on the project is working toward the same end-state and then move toward execution.

DON'T BE MYSTERIOUS

Leaders should never pass up an opportunity to define themselves and what leadership means to them. Upon assuming a position of leadership, a person should immediately begin building a case for trust, confidence and understanding among subordinates. A good way to start is to stand up in front of your principle subordinates on day one and tell them who you are, what you believe in, what you like, what you dislike, what you expect from them and what they can expect from you. This is not a touchie-feelie gathering, an expensive three-day off-site to exchange views or a break-the-ice cocktail party; it is straight talk from the boss. For example, these are some of the topics I discussed the day after taking command of Fort Ord and the Seventh Infantry Division, a warfighting organization of about fifteen thousand soldiers. At the time I was an Army Major General (see Military Grades and Military Organizations in the glossary at the end of the book). The audience consisted of my two deputies (Brigadier Generals), my Command Sergeant Major, subordinate commanders of brigades (seven Colonels and their Sergeants Major) and battalion commanders (twenty-eight Lieutenant Colonels and their Sergeants Major). I called it "Covault's Base Line" and my intent was for every senior subordinate leader to walk out of that meeting with a better understanding of how I intended to lead people and lead the organization.

1. *Evaluation reports will not be late.* Every organization should have some system of written evaluations for their leaders. Not doing them on time sends a powerful, negative message.

2. *Every person who rates a subordinate will do a one-on-one review.* Leaders must, on a regular basis, have the courage

of their convictions, look their subordinates in the eye and tell them how they are doing.

3. *Use milestones as a leadership tool.* Telling subordinates to have something specific accomplished by a certain date tends to:
    *   Fix responsibility.
    *   Identify an end-state.
    *   Identify resources.
    *   Force time management.
    *   Identify participants.

4. *Our operating philosophy is maximum centralized planning, maximum decentralized execution.* Plan from the level where there is the broadest perspective, the most information available and the best base of experience. Execute by delegating to subordinates you have trained and who you trust.

5. *Have a top ten list.* An item cannot be added until one gets completed. This forces prioritization, focuses leaders on essential issues and protects subordinates from being overloaded.

6. *Have a plan to leave the organization better than you found it.* No organization is ever as good as it can be. Identify the warts and work to eliminate them during your tenure.

7. *We cannot take risk on environmental issues.* First, doing so may be against the law and secondly the consequences of violating the environment can create such upheaval that an organization gets distracted to the point of loosing its focus.

8. *Have the legal section review your paper.* Obviously this is not always required but it sends the message to subordinate leaders that there can easily be legal issues associated with an action they may be unaware of.

9. *There is a band of excellence associated with what it is we are each charged to do.* Visualize it, define it and strive to attain it.

10. *We do not live in a zero defects environment.* Leaders must

accept honest mistakes, learn from them and move forward.

11. *Directing that a study be conducted is in most instances procrastination.* Most study results are a different version of a previous study or are blinding glimpses of the obvious.

12. *Before expending resources to solve a problem, answer these questions:*
    - Is there really a problem?
    - If so have you defined the problem?
    - If you have problem definition is there an existing program already addressing it?
    - If the problem is already being worked are there milestones leading to a solution?
    - Whatever the status of the problem is there value added in expending effort to find a solution?

13. *Deal with the art of the possible.* Seek excellence but do not needlessly expend time, effort and resources for solutions that are beyond reach.

14. *Be timely and never intentionally late.* Tardiness demonstrates a lack of respect for others.

15. *When providing briefings to me:*
    - Begin each briefing with the words, the purpose of this briefing is...
    - Do not read to me.
    - Do not use a visual aid that cannot be read from the rear of the room.
    - Do not talk when you want me to read.
    - Use short-phrase entries on charts and fill in the details from what you know about the issue.

16. *Meetings should be short.* Good leaders do not have meetings for the sake of the meeting; have an agenda, deal with important issues that can only be worked in a combined environment and presenters must be prepared. Before a meeting is scheduled, convince yourself that there will be value added.

17. *Bring the person who has been or will work the action but not the whole staff.* It may be important to hear from or speak

directly to the action person who is working or will work a project. But leaders must not be expected to subsume the responsibilities of subordinate leaders by briefing the entire subordinate staff.

18. *Establish your own duty day and do not hang around because I'm still at work.* Leaders should not demand that subordinates adjust their life style to that of their leader. Working early and/or late is your prerogative as long as the work gets accomplished on time.

19. *Get away and recharge.* Vacation time is therapeutic and refreshing. Spend quality time with your family, and return with new vigor. Leaders who believe they are indispensable and therefore cannot afford to be away from the job send all the wrong signals to their subordinates.

20. *An eighty-percent solution next week is better than a ninety-five percent solution next quarter.* Leaders get paid to conduct risk assessments, make tough decisions and move forward. Procrastination usually proves to be unhealthy for any organization.

21. *Fifty percent of job-related travel is unnecessary.* Be sure there is value added before going at all, be ruthless in paring down the travel team to the absolute minimum, and spend the least amount of time away.

22. *Travel light.* Get out of the office every day to see your subordinates but do not do so with a large, disruptive entourage.

23. *Take on and defeat bureaucrats who are roadblocks to progress.* Recognize that there are those who are wedded to and completely comfortable with the status quo. Those who resist necessary change must be confronted.

24. *Get a squad within 100 meters and shoot the enemy between the eyes without taking casualties. Does everything we do support this?* Describe succinctly what it is your organization is about and focus everyone on it.

25. *No second chances on breaches of honesty and integrity.* In the heat of everyday operations mistakes will be made, resources wasted, and even some lapses in judgment made

in good faith. These can and will be tolerated but no one for any reason is allowed to compromise their personal honesty and integrity or that of the organization.

There are more, but these twenty-five make the point. While those bits of who I am and what I believe evolved over time, they were all appropriate to that particular audience. The session lasted a total of about two hours including a question and answer period at the end. It got us off to a fast start. Every leader in every type organization as part of defining leadership evolves a list over time of what they believe are the important sub-elements of leadership. My recommendation is to make a set of slides, put three or four talking points on each and talk for an hour. It will save subordinates months of agonizing over minor questions; does he want an executive summary at the front end of every study, does she want a read-ahead the day prior to receiving a briefing, how much detail does he like, does she like desk-side briefings or a cast of dozens? This will begin to get key subordinates immediately in line with your philosophy; they will understand how you work and how you think. This is an important part of being a leader and getting off to a quick start may be the difference between success and failure in today's fast-paced environment. Build your own list over time as your experience level and responsibilities increase. Beware of the person who assumes a leadership position and announces to subordinates that they do not intend to make any changes. That person does not understand the human dimension of the organization; no two leaders are alike and subordinates need to quickly get inside the head of the new leader and understand how he or she intends to lead people and lead the organization

BOTTOM LINE

There are many ways to define leadership. The best definitions place the emphasis on what the leader must do. My favorite comes from an article written by Robert W. Galvin, entitled "Real leaders Create Industries." In it he wrote about the importance of renewal, training to anticipate and certifying leaders. Galvin's definition of a leader:

"A leader is someone who takes us elsewhere." 13

There are many examples of leaders not taking their organizations elsewhere at a point in time when it was essential they do so in order to survive and be successful. Here is a thumbnail sketch of three:

- The fighting doctrine of the United States Army from the 1940s and 1950s was comatose by the 1960s. The outmoded World War II doctrine did not fit with the combat environment in Southeast Asia. Failure to adapt was a significant factor in the United States' collapse in Vietnam.

- General Robert E. Lee, a devout student of Napoleon, failed to either recognize or to accept the impact of new technology on the Civil War battlefield. Rifles that could be effective at several times the previous range and the introduction of repeating rifles replacing muzzle loaded individual weapons significantly changed tactics and techniques of land warfare. While holding fast to Napoleonic thinking and without recognizing the need for change General Lee could not take his army elsewhere.

- At the turn of the twentieth century, there were local companies all across the nation harvesting, storing and distributing block ice. Of all those companies, there is no record of any of them transitioning to refrigeration and thereby surviving.

Leaders take their organization elsewhere or preside over the funeral.

RECAP

1. Every leader should find a definition of leadership they like. In defining what you are, you bring clarity to what it is you are to do.
2. Management has to do with an organization's processes; leadership has to do with its purposes.
3. Leadership is not a passive activity.
4. As a leader in a new position, define yourself and declare

your expectations to your principle subordinates early in the transition. You will be doing everyone a favor, including yourself.

ENDURING LEADERSHIP PRINCIPLES

Great leaders:
Motivate subordinates.
Build consensus.
Seek solutions without compromise.
Act decisively.
Insure subordinates understand how they intend to lead.
Understand that leadership is not about power

CHAPTER THREE

UNDERSTANDING THE LEADERSHIP CONTINUUM

The Leadership Continuum Is The Vehicle Leaders Use To Communicate What Needs To Be Accomplished.

Imagine a company that manufactures, distributes and sells a line of products. For some number of employees on the assembly line there will be a person exercising direct leadership over them. There will be a supervisor with some title overseeing the work of several direct leaders in assembly. Other leaders will be in charge of inventory, maintenance, warehousing, etc. Finally, some individual will have responsibility for overall plant operations. This may be one of several plants with the individual plant leaders reporting to a higher authority at corporate headquarters. Also at the corporate level there are leaders in charge of sales, finance, advertising, etc. all with their lineup of subordinates. All of this can be easily and clearly drawn on a piece of paper to depict what may be referred to as the organization or structure or organizational structure. Whatever it is called is immaterial. What is important to understand is that it is not the lines on the piece of paper connecting the various elements that hold the organization together. What binds the organization together is the relationship among the leaders of the organizational elements. This is called the continuum of leadership from the direct leaders on the assembly line to the corporate Chief Executive Officer.

The purpose of this chapter is to focus on the fact that there is a continuum of leadership in every organization, it is the vehicle for communications and it must be understood if it is to be used to its greatest advantage.

The leadership continuum is an important toolbox in our leadership truck. Understanding its makeup and how to use it is fundamental to every leader's effectiveness. The continuum is a vehicle for performing a number of essential functions in every type organization. But before enumerating those functions, let us look further at structure.

Organizations have three distinct levels of leadership: strategic, operational and direct. For smaller organizations, one person may perform multiple functions; for example in an owner-run operation with a handful of employees there may be only one boss and he or she does the strategic and operational thinking and is also the direct leader. In the next chapter direct, operational and strategic leaders' responsibilities will be described in detail.

While the organizational structure and leadership levels rarely have the clean lines of a perfect triangle, it serves our purposes for depicting different levels of leaders and their span of control.

Note the top to bottom vertical line on the continuum and the fact that it has a directional arrow at both ends. An organization attempting to function with information flowing only from top to bottom will surely fail. Innovation, for example, is a transfusion that gives an organization longevity; innovation more often than not comes from the bottom. If you want to improve the efficiency on an assembly line, talk to the experts, the people who work there every day. Also, the dividing lines between direct/operational and operational/strategic are never as well defined as they appear on the diagram; there are transition zones.

Towards the base of the hierarchy, nearer the point of execution, the leadership continuum is fairly flat as follows:

The top point of this relatively flat triangle represents a direct leader and the horizontal line the subordinate employees. In an organization that is large enough to have a series of leaders at the direct leader level, there will be numerous individual triangles making up the base of the continuum of leadership as follows:

What is described here is a hierarchical organizational structure. The military in general and the United States Army in particular, is the quintessential hierarchical organization; three to five squads in a platoon, three or four platoons in a company, three to five companies in a battalion, three to five battalions in a brigade and so on through divisions and corps (see military organizations in the glossary at the end of the book).

While this extended hierarchy works for military operations, generally speaking organizational triangles should strive to be as flat as possible. Too many layers can cause an organization to become burdensome, expensive, lethargic and bureaucratic. Although it is unlikely that any organization, even one with a small number of employees, will be perfectly flat, fewer layers promote better communications, delegation, empowerment and efficiency. There is even a continuum of leadership in a small fifty-person company. The owner may be the single strategic/operational leader but cannot function with a span of control of fifty and so, by necessity, there will be perhaps three to five subordinates performing direct leadership functions.

Frederick Smith, the founder of Federal Express, in an article, "Creating an Empowering Environment for All Employees," refers to his "flat organizational structure" in which there are just five levels of leaders between the couriers and senior executives.14 Even a relatively new, progressive corporation like Federal Express specifically designed to be flat in order to accommodate a power-down working philosophy is in fact hierarchical in nature. This is so because reducing the number of layers increases span of control and at some point results in diminishing efficiency.

Recently while preparing a proposal to conduct a series of leadership seminars for a financial institution, my colleagues and I asked the company to categorize their leaders. They identified 160 strategic leadership positions, 450 at the operational level and 5000 direct leaders. This corporation had taken a first essential step in defining itself. It is necessary to identify and recognize the different levels because activities such as leader development and leader training must be tailored to the individual based on where he or she is in the continuum.

The leadership continuum is linkage among the leaders of an organization, whatever the structure. Using the continuum, leaders will communicate and do the things that must be accomplished if the organization is to survive. For example, the continuum:

- Facilitates continuous communications between and among structural layers throughout the organization to insure continuity of actions.
- Provides the means to direct. Direction is more than giving orders; it is the act of providing instructions in the context of an organization's defined end-state.
- Provides the means to motivate. As we found in exploring definitions of leadership in chapter two, the essence of leadership is motivating people to work through obstacles and get on with doing what they know how to do.
- Provides the means to instill values. Establishing a value base is a hard, slow, never-ending process. Values must emanate from the top and be clearly discernable all the way to the bottom of the continuum.
- Provides the means to innovate. Innovation is the introduction of new methods; this leads to change. Innovation places greater emphasis on the upward direction of the arrow in the continuum.
- Provides the means to execute. The best plan prepared by the most brilliant leader is not worth the paper it is printed on unless it can get to the direct leader who will

cause something positive to happen. It is not sufficient to create momentum and direction and then take a hands-off approach; leaders must be vigilant and persistent.

- Finally, the continuum provides the means to instill a culture. Every organization has a culture and it is a powerful force that can be either positive or negative. An example of a positive culture is a combination of loyalty, high standards, and caring that permeates the entire workforce resulting in quality products.

Recall a children's party game where eight to ten children line up and the first whispers an instruction in the ear of the second child, who then repeats it to the third child and so on. Finally, the last in line repeats the message aloud. The message is often unintelligible, silly and everyone gets a good laugh. The directive could not have been executed. While this is a good party game, it is a formula for failure if an organization cannot effectively communicate up and down the leadership chain. A functioning, leadership continuum will provide the means to question unintelligible instructions, make timely corrections and move on towards execution.

Every organization should publish a continuum as part of their leader development program. When employees see the organization's structure, they can visualize what their leaders are telling them and it creates a reference point and confidence that information will flow. Visualizing the continuum enhances understanding of the levels of leaders and the role each leader plays.

RECAP

1. A leadership continuum exists in every organization.
2. The leadership continuum is the vehicle that allows an organization to do the things it must do to survive. An organization must have the means to:
    - Direct.
    - Motivate.
    - Instill values.

- Innovate.
- Execute.
- Implant a culture.

3. An organization that attempts to function with information flowing only from top to bottom will surely fail.
4. Every person in an organization should be able to visualize the leadership continuum and where he or she fits into the organization.

ENDURING LEADERSHIP PRINCIPLES

Great leaders:
Use the continuum of leadership to enhance communications up and down the leadership chain.

CHAPTER FOUR

DIRECT, OPERATIONAL AND STRATEGIC LEADERS

Leaders At Different Levels In An Organization Do Not Perform The Same Functions Differently, Leaders At Different Levels Perform Different Functions.

Too often we hear of or observe an effective direct leader promoted to a more senior position (operational level) and fail to achieve his or her expected potential. Too often it is dismissed as the "Peter Principle," and the individual is tolerated for a while, then shuffled laterally to a harmless position, or mercifully forced into early retirement. It is also possible the individual was qualified technically to perform at the higher level; the failure was in leader development. While stepping up that particular rung of the ladder the boss did not help him or her recognize the differences in direct and operational leadership. The person promoted was placed at the operational level, but continued to act like a direct leader. **Use the continuum of leadership to enhance communications up and down the leadership chain.**

While it is important to be aware of the layers of leadership, just understanding the organizational structure falls short of what is actually needed. That is, the layers must also be defined because without definition there is no understanding of what is expected of leaders at the different levels. Equally important is for leaders at each level to have an appreciation for the environment the leaders at the other two levels deal with each day.

The purpose of this chapter is to define direct, operational and strategic leaders and to provide a brief explanation of what they do because they each have a different toolbox and different tools. This is another step in defining the underpinnings necessary for leaders to communicate and interact as they progress from vision to execution.

Let us begin the definition process by making the point that all leadership levels have some elements in common. For example, every leader (direct, operational, strategic) processes information and turns it into knowledge. Also, all leaders are thinkers and analysts; given a certain amount of information they turn it into solutions. They do this by assessing alternatives based on incomplete data and choosing a course of action. This is commonly referred to as decision making. All leaders are decision makers.

Another element all three levels have in common is generating support. There is always more than one course of action to achieve a goal; you, the leader, decide which method the team is going to use. Recall President Truman's definition that put generating support into perspective; that is, motivating people to do something even though they may not want to do it. Influencing people, gaining consensus and generating support is a continuous leader function at every level.

While all leadership levels share some common challenges, they, of course, differ by degree. For example, decisions at the strategic level affect more people than do the direct leader's decisions. A CEO's pronouncement commits more resources in manpower, time and materials and has wider consequences than those of his subordinate leaders.

THE DIRECT LEADER

Direct leaders lead people and execute. This is where

the corporate culture becomes reality. This is where the organization's rubber meets the public road. Direct leadership is face-to-face. Direct leadership takes place in the levels of organizations where subordinates see their leaders all the time, in the shop, on the assembly line, in the warehouse, on the sales floor or during training. Direct leaders' span of influence, over those whose lives they can reach out and touch, allows them to develop subordinates one-on-one. While this chapter will deal with three general categories of leaders—direct, operational, strategic— there is a subcategory within the direct leader level that must be recognized; the first-line leaders. Direct leaders may have a span of control over a number of leaders who are junior to them. These leaders, responsible for the first line of employees, are referred to as first-line leaders, the first level of leadership in an organization's hierarchy.

Compared to operational and strategic leaders, direct leaders and first-line leaders face more certainty on a day-to-day basis in terms of what the outcome will be, given a set of variables. Also issues are more confined in time and space and solutions are more easily defined as right or wrong, black or white, there is less fog of war. Direct leaders and first-line leaders are close enough to the action to quickly see how things work, how things do not work and how best to address problems.

Having asserted that there are three definable leadership levels is not intended to imply that they are completely discrete and separate entities. There is overlap among the three. Direct leadership, for example, exists at all three levels but the degree to which it exists is tied to span of control and the need for direction. For example, a senior executive may have only three or four vice presidents reporting directly to him or her and exercises direct leadership sparingly because the subordinates are knowledgeable, experienced people who need little guidance to accomplish their objectives. As commander of an Army division, a combat unit of about fifteen thousand soldiers, I had direct leadership over two principal subordinate

Brigadier Generals, one in charge of combat operations, and one for support operations. They were experienced, competent professional officers who required very little direct leadership. On the other hand, a first-line leader, on the assembly line, running a branch office, or an infantry squad may have a span of control of ten or twenty subordinates and need to provide constant, detailed direction to his inexperienced team.

Some organizations fail to recognize the criticality of the direct leader level. There is perhaps a tendency to believe that direct leadership is easy or, worse yet, unimportant. One explanation for such an attitude is that some leaders at the operational and strategic levels have never "been there and done that." Most senior leaders in the civilian sector did not begin their careers in the mailroom, moving up to mailroom supervisor and on through the hierarchy. Most senior leaders came out of college and on day one went to work wearing a coat and tie rather than a blue work shirt. Their experience on the assembly line is limited to an occasional walk-through or pep talk to their employees. The fallout from this formula is failure to recognize that the first-line leader has perhaps the most demanding leadership challenge of all. The first-line leader is faced, all day, every day with the most complex element in the entire organization, that is, a group of individuals. Those who the first-line leader is responsible for represent an array of personalities, biases, likes, dislikes, levels of expertise, experience, reliability and strength of character. To mold them into an efficient and effective team, first-line leaders must be part psychologist, parent, enforcer, career counselor and constantly in tune with the direction the organization is moving. This is one area where the military excels. Every senior leader started out with extensive leader training on how to be a first-line leader. Then, upon being commissioned as an officer, they all begin their careers in direct leadership positions and remain there for a number of years.

As commander of an Army division, where I was at the executive level in the hierarchy, I made it clear in both written and verbal guidance that our number one training objective was to ensure we developed the highest levels of expertise at the first-line leader level. Because, in the end, what an organization achieves in total is the result of execution across the foundation of that organization and it is the first-line leader who is there to make things happen. The degree to which operations are executed properly is directly related to the effectiveness of leaders at the lowest organizational levels.

If we expect to hold first-line leaders accountable for having a trained and ready team, it follows that their duties must be specified, preferably in writing. It needs to be a short list, certainly no more than five items, and preferably less. For example, when I made first-line leader training my first priority in the Seventh Infantry Division, it was my responsibility to specify what I expected them to do.

First-line leaders are responsible for their subordinates' personal appearance.

The rule was easily understood – shave, haircut, clean uniform, shined boots. It was a simple daily measure of discipline. It was also a key first-line leader test: can he or she ensure their six, eight, ten subordinates always follow all the rules associated with the "dress code?" Translated to the civilian world, does everyone conform to what is acceptable behavior? Consider the following scenario. A prospective big client is coming in today to receive an important presentation; all those to attend are expected to be in business attire. This also implies a higher level of grooming. You are a little apprehensive about John, one of the key speakers. While a brilliant and reliable worker, his daily routine is to show up for work unshaven, uncombed hair and wearing worn out jeans and sneakers. John shows up in coat and tie, that is, a rumpled jacket, sport shirt with a tie, same faded jeans, sneakers and unshaven, while the other gentlemen in the conference room are in their best dark suits. It is easy in today's dress-down atmosphere to say the dark suit crowd is out of touch. Perhaps so, but that is also irrelevant. The issue is not the specifics of the dress code, but rather the failure to lead at the first-line leader level. John's boss, in his best dark suit, could not motivate his subordinate to meet a prescribed standard specified for the occasion.

First-line leaders' must ensure their subordinates have all their personal gear and that it is clean, dry, properly packed and ready to deploy.

The soldiers spent a great deal of time in the field training, yet when in garrison they had to be prepared to deploy at a moments notice; that is ready to report for duty at any hour, travel to a nearby air force base and be air-lifted to any place in the world where their expertise was needed. During training, often under extreme conditions, personal equipment (rucksack, ammo pouch, canteen, boots, weapons, etc.) would get damaged, wet, muddy or lost. When soldiers came in from a field exercise often the first thing on their minds was to get into civilian clothes and go have fun. This is where the first-line leader laid down the law on procrastination; reminding them they would be released as soon as all their gear was accounted for and properly maintained. This is no different from the construction foreman at the end of the day insisting that all tools be accounted for and ready for use tomorrow morning; or on the assembly line, all machinery cleaned, oiled and ready for the next shift; or in a restaurant after lunch service is completed, all the tables are set, condiments replenished and everything is ready for dinner; or that software and information files get backed up at close of business. It is a simple leader requirement, but if he or she lets the subordinate off the hook just once, overall standards and discipline are on a slippery slope.

My third rule was the heart and soul of first-line leadership. First, let me set the stage by explaining that the U. S. Army trains to tasks; that is, everything everyone does, from the private to the corps commander, has been delineated as a task. Each task must be performed to a prescribed standard given certain conditions (for example, day versus night conditions). Daily Army-wide training revolves around tasks, conditions and standards. There is a list of common tasks for everyone, such as marksmanship proficiency. Additionally, every soldier has a list of individual skill tasks associated with his or her grade and specialty. A communications specialist, for example, must be able to perform a set of tasks that are significantly different from those of an infantry platoon sergeant. And finally, there are collective tasks, those associated with being part of a team. With this well-defined baseline, it was easy to specify that:

First-line leaders are held personally responsible that all of their subordinates can perform all common and individual skill tasks to standard and link those tasks to collective team efforts.

It then became the responsibility of more senior leaders to ensure that resources, (time, training areas, equipment) were available to allow the first-line leaders to succeed.

Every first-line leader in the civilian sector faces the same challenges. Everyone on the framing crew building a house needs to know how to measure an angle and cut a 2 x 4 to fit. Go to a construction site after the framing has been completed and look at the size of the pile of wasted lumber in the dumpster and you will get an indication of how well the crew was trained and thus the effectiveness of the first-line leader.

Up to this point the Seventh Division's first-line leaders could be measured objectively. A soldier either shaved or did not; the equipment was either accounted for or missing; critical tasks either could or could not be performed in three minutes. While those three leader responsibilities could have sufficed, I instituted a fourth, albeit infinitely more difficult to articulate and nearly impossible to measure.

First-line leaders are responsible for the readiness of their soldiers.

If first-line leaders in any organization are performing to the maximum extent possible they know their subordinates' strengths, weaknesses, what motivates them, when they need a helping hand and when they need a kick in the rear end. It is their responsibility, for example, to know when one of their subordinates is partying too hard, drinking too much and not getting enough sleep to consistently perform to his or her potential. Effective first-line leaders are tuned in to their subordinates' lifestyles and step in with firm guidance on what is expected in the way of performance.

Being responsible for readiness is knowing if a subordinate has problems at home, a sick child, debt, or a failing marriage. The first-line leader provides some compassion, some suggestions, or authorizes some time off for the subordinate to get the personal issues worked out. The expectation is that without the personal burdens the subordinate will have his or her mind on the job and perform better.

Being responsible for readiness does not always involve compassion and caring. Sometimes it involves some direction and warning because the first-line leader knows a subordinate's propensity to procrastinate or stretch the rules. A first-line leader might, for example, mention to a subordinate that the safety inspection on his car must get updated on Saturday because there will be no time off next week to do it. The head of the English department knows three of her teachers are ski enthusiasts and next Monday is a holiday. She senses what is coming and makes it known that if they call in "sick" on Friday, they better be home in bed and not enroute to the mountains for an extended ski weekend.

Yes, direct leaders influence fewer people than do the operational or strategic leaders. Yes, they commit fewer resources. But direct leaders are at the heart of all operations because they are at the point of execution. Therefore it is important that they receive training and have their responsibilities clearly defined.

THE OPERATIONAL LEADER

Operational leaders perform a number of functions; the first is as a direct leader. That is, they may have a small personal staff of administrative assistants. While these assistants may be working in the executive headquarters building as opposed to the warehouse, their operational leader is their direct leader whatever other title he or she may have. The operational leader, exercising direct leader responsibilities, must specify a set of standards such as keeping the area presentable to the public, dress code, answer the phone on the first ring, do not use company equipment for personal use, no personal email on company time, no profanity, no smoking, etc.

Second, and this is the transition from leading people to leading organizations, operational leaders ensure subordinates understand what needs to be done. The principal distinction between the direct and operational leaders is in the *how* and the *what*. Direct leaders are part of a team dealing with execution; they are into leading by demonstrating *how* to complete tasks. They lead by direct example using one-on-one skill development. Conversely, operational leaders must concentrate on *what* needs to be accomplished. Hire a bright, energetic team, tell them what your goals are; this is the first step toward achieving them.

When a senior leader is looking inside his organization attempting to determine why a particular operational leader is producing twice that of a, it could be that the lesser productive leader never made the transition from *how* leadership to *what* leadership. A how-leader in a what-leader environment fails because of the larger number of people under his or her direction (span of control), coupled with the breadth and depth of the issues they are confronted with, grinds the organization to a one-issue-at-a-time pace. At the operational level, empowerment of subordinates and delegation are absolutely essential. If it is the boss' intent to make the highest quality widget in the world, the operational leader will set in motion what needs to be done to achieve that end-state. For example, the procurement of the best raw materials, installation of the highest quality-control production equipment and training for a labor force capable of achieving the requisite levels of excellence.

Operational leaders are integrators, constantly seeking synergistic effects. In order for an operational leader to achieve the monthly or quarterly goal, he or she may be responsible for a number of processes that are to work in concert. But if some of the various parts are not functioning properly (excessive machine down-time, new software not installed on schedule, high personnel absenteeism) the sum of the parts, 2 + 2, figuratively may equal only 3. On the other hand, successful operational leaders create a synergistic affect wherein the whole is greater than the sum of the parts, finding a way to make 2 + 2 = 5.

Effective operational level military leaders see the battlespace as a single entity and are able to bring all the warfighting elements together in time and space thereby optimizing their collective impact. The Gulf War provides a classic example of the application of warfare at the operational level. That campaign plan consisted of three principle parts: 1) a thirty-day air campaign to soften the enemy ground forces; 2) a large Marine Amphibious force in the Persian Gulf poised for an amphibious assault (not used but fixated Saddam Hussein); and, 3) land forces executing a huge and powerful left hook that rolled over enemy ground forces from their flank. While that battlespace consisted of thousands of separate direct leader actions, the operational leader, General Norman Schwarzkopf, saw it as a single, integrated, synchronized action.

For operational leaders in any organization there is a battlespace of sorts, where diverse elements have to come together in harmony in order to out-think and out-perform the competition. In industry, the relatively recent concept of just-in-time-logistics is an example of optimizing ordering, shipping and warehousing systems to produce a synergistic affect resulting in the most cost efficient end product.

At the operational level goals are established in the context of what a number of integrated systems can support. If operational leaders were asked to describe in general terms what it is they do every day they might reply that they assess risk and allocate shortages. He or she might go on to explain that in order to achieve goals there are always alternative courses of action and varying degrees of risk. There are never enough resources and it is the responsibility of the operational leader to sort it all out in order to achieve specific goals.

Finally, the operational leader must establish a set of milestones, having identified the end date, end-state and the specific responsibilities for those involved. Some leaders cannot see the parts combined into the whole. Without a vision of the end-state, it is pure luck if the results actually match the original goal. Leaders who stand out at the operational level, can see the end-state, visualize how the parts will come together synergistically, understand the state of the battlespace and can then turn that into a plan of action with specific milestone dates for accomplishing a series of tasks.

Operational leaders perform the duties described above within the context of a broader strategic framework, bringing us to the final category in the leadership continuum.

THE STRATEGIC LEADER

Strategic leaders, as is the case with direct and operational leaders, process information, assess alternatives, make decisions and generate support. While all leadership levels have this common base, the differences between strategic leadership and leadership at the other two levels are enormous. The strategic leader's environment is highly uncertain in nature, the complexity of the issues is magnified many times and there may be numerous outside influences beyond the strategic leader's immediate control.

As the senior military leader in Washington, D.C., during World War II, General of the Army, George C. Marshall remarked:

> "It became clear to me that at the age of 58, I would have to learn new tricks that were not taught in the military manuals or on the battlefield. In this position I am a political soldier and will have to put my training in rapping out orders and making snap decisions on the back burner and have to learn the arts of persuasion and guile. I must become an expert in a whole new set of skills."15

What makes the study of leadership so fascinating is that no one begins his or her career at the strategic level, and most who reach that level have spent decades getting there, only to be faced with a whole new set of circumstances, some of which they may not be prepared to face, just a General Marshall described.

The strategic leader is now on a playing field much larger than his or her organization; it may well be a world stage. The stock market is up and running somewhere in the world nearly all the time and what happened a few minutes ago in the Asian Market may have an impact on your U.S. company in a few hours. Information technology, the pace of play, volume of information and an individual's instant availability makes for a continuous 24/7 playing field. Additionally, the players on the field are not all on the strategic leader's team. By contrast, while coordination or collaboration of a complex issue by a leader at the operational level may also be difficult, time-consuming and complex, it may involve simply walking down the hall to a colleague's office or taking a one-day trip to a satellite office in another city. In either case the operational leader will likely be dealing with familiar people. At the strategic level coordination may be protracted, have a wider impact and be conducted under uncertain conditions with persons previously unknown to you.

The strategic leader must understand where the organization is now and then create a vision for the future. Organizations that remain viable over long periods of time successfully deal with change. Contending with change is not wondering down multiple paths until one seems more right than the alternatives. It is incumbent upon the strategic leadership to describe the future in sufficient detail so that resources can be applied toward achieving that end-state. In order to move forward with a new vision there must be a launch point, which is determined by an in-depth understanding of the organization's current standing. Defining the state of an organization on a moving time line can be incredibly difficult because of the day-to-day influence of factors and forces one has no control over such as the state of the economy, terrorist attacks that alter an entire consumer base, vagaries of the stock market, or political leadership changes. But even with a clear vision of where the strategic leader wants to end up, the path is rarely, if ever, a smooth straight line.

Strategic leaders may find themselves spending an inordinate amount of time building consensus on what needs to be accomplished. At the direct leader level there is a lot of, this is how you do it, now you do it. It is not that simple for the strategic leader who must articulate where the organization is headed and why it is essential that the organization collectively go there. Trial and error or hoping for the best will not get the job done. A Gulf War example was cited above to describe the operational leadership and General Schwarzkopf's vision of the battlespace. Led by President Bush, the National Security Council hammered out the overall strategic framework in which General Schwarzkopf operated. The strategy was to build world-wide consensus against the Iraqi leaders, gain the will of the American people and Congress, establish a coalition of nations willing to take up arms along side the United States and assemble an overwhelming force in the Middle East prior to launching a counter offensive aimed at restoring the leadership and territorial integrity of Kuwait. One can only imagine the uncertainty surrounding the many strategic issues dealt with and resolved in the successful Gulf War campaign.

Strategic leaders must build their own team. The direct leader usually leads those assigned to him or her, having neither responsibility nor authority for forming the team. Employees are hired, assigned to specific positions and then it is the responsibility of their direct leader to mold them into a team to produce the best possible product. Conversely the strategic leader has sufficient authority to hire, move and remove personnel. When it comes to building a senior executive staff or selecting key operational leaders, he or she has the responsibility to select the best and the brightest available. If you see an organization in trouble and begin searching for the cause, what you may find at the strategic level is a leader

who is so insecure he or she purposely surround themselves
with subordinates they consider less bright, less capable and
therefore non-threatening. They have the authority to hire a
strong team but fail to execute this most basic responsibility.
Among the many traits of successful senior leaders is that they
do not care who gets the credit as long as the organization is
best served. Additionally, they have the good sense to stay out
of the way as bright, capable subordinates work their way from
vision to execution.

Complex issues rarely have clear, well-defined edges. The
fog of war is always there, it will not go away, someone has
to deal with it and that someone is the strategic leader. They
must frame the problem; this is part of establishing a vision.
The strategic leader must engage uncertainty and complexity
head on and bring sufficient definition to a problem so that the
organization can work it to a logical, predictable conclusion.
During World War II there was an ample amount of fog for
senior leaders. Prime Minister of Great Britain, Sir Winston
Churchill summed it up best; "True genius resides in the
capacity for evaluation of uncertain, hazardous and conflicting
information."16

RECAP

1. Leaders at different levels perform different functions.
    Therefore, the categories of leaders must be defined in
    detail. In the process of defining what they are, it will
    become clear what they do.
2. There are leader responsibilities common to direct,
    operational and strategic leaders; they process information,
    assess alternatives, make decisions and generate support.
3. The strategic leader finds a way to deal with a myriad of
    external influences and the fog of war. The operational
    leader is the integrator, influencing through policy and
    systems. The direct leader executes.
4. None of the leaders are independent operators; they
    are all part of a continuum of leadership, the vehicle for
    communicating throughout an organization.

ENDURING LEADERSHIP PRINCIPLES

Great leaders:

Recognize that direct, operational and strategic leaders lead differently.

Understand the difference between leading people and leading organizations.

CHAPTER FIVE

SOME LEADERS ARE COMMANDERS

All Leaders Are Held Accountable For The Welfare Of Their People; But Those In Command Have The Added Responsibility Of Being Accountable For The Welfare Of The Organization.

Recall in chapter two we explored definitions of leaders; the first was from the dictionary which referred to a leader as a person directing, *commanding* or guiding. In order to establish a complete set of leadership underpinnings, we need to take the subject beyond basic leadership and briefly discuss command.

The purpose of this chapter is to recognize that some leaders are commanders and to enumerate their extraordinary responsibilities.

Military command, a position defined in the *Uniform Code of Military Justice,* allows some persons to exercise legally recognized authority over others. While rarely titled command positions in civilian organizations, and not having the same defined legal basis as does the military, they do, nonetheless, exist. It is where the buck stops; Chief Executive Officer, Director, Chairman, President are all synonymous with commander.

There is an implied totality of responsibility associated

with command of any organization. It is safe to assert that all leaders are held accountable for the welfare of their people; but those in command have the added responsibility of being accountable for the welfare of the organization. They set the tone for the degree to which their organization is value-based. They are instrumental in establishing and maintaining a desired culture; so much so, that an organization's identity and how it is viewed from outside is in many ways singularly influenced by the commander.

In *At Ease: Stories I Tell My Friends,* President Dwight D. Eisenhower writes:

> **"I have developed almost an obsession as to the certainty with which you can judge a...large unit merely by knowing its commander intimately...I did not realize, until opportunity came for comparison on a large scale, how infallibly the commander and unit are almost one and the same thing."17**

General Mathew B. Ridgway (a senior United States Army commander during World War II and The Korean War) said:

> **".... confidence, spirit, purposefulness, aggressiveness flow down from the top and permeate a whole command. And in the same way do anxiety and lack of resolution on the part of a commander put their indelible stamp upon his men."18**

It is not just the good traits that flow from a commander to inspire the organization; weaknesses can also infect the organization and cause it to be ineffective.

Command also brings with it a moral responsibility. More than any other leader, the commander's personal example must withstand public scrutiny. Remember that old saying about the higher the monkey climbs up the flagpole the more he exposes his backside. Subordinates are watching their commander's backside and emulating what they do and how they go about doing it.

There is a great deal of truth in lesson number eighteen from Colin Powell, which highlights not only the fact that your subordinates will copy your morals and standards, but further implies that being the one setting the ethical code is not a collective effort. He wrote:

> **"You can encourage participative management and bottom-up employee involvement but ultimately the essence of leadership is the willingness to make the tough, unambiguous choices that will have an impact on the fate of the organization....... Even as you create an informal, open, collaborative corporate culture, prepare to be lonely."19**

Command is not about being popular or loved, nor is it about presiding over a democratic organization. It would be easy if all a commander had to do was take a vote of his or her key advisors and go with the majority. But command is not about going with the flow, it is often about going with your gut and sometimes even defying conventional wisdom. Yes, command can be lonely but at the same time it can be the most satisfying position a leader will ever hold. For leaders who thrive on challenge, command is the ultimate professional reward.

Rarely is there only one clear-cut course of action to accomplish a difficult task; move or wait, go right or go left, borrow the money or sell something to raise the cash, go national or try it regionally, keep it secret or go public. There will be strong proponents for both sides and when the decision is finally made you may be faced with an even greater challenge, that of harnessing the talents and energy of the opponents; getting everything and everyone moving in the same direction.

Some persons who are otherwise good leaders may not live up to expectations when placed in positions of commander for two reasons. First, it is human nature to want to be liked.

When you as a commander have to make a tough choice on a highly charged issue, some segment of your organization will inevitably be upset; some long-time colleagues may have some ugly things to say about you; and there may be a public outcry from the community where you have been a highly respected citizen for many years. Some leaders simply cannot handle the criticism, will shrink from their responsibilities and in the future will be unwilling to make the difficult choices.

A second reason for falling short of expectations is that some who have made it to the top have the mistaken idea that the solution to difficult issues can be found in a compromise. A good commander should seriously consider the council of subordinates, but to consciously use some of everyone's ideas, smashing them together in order to keep everyone happy does not demonstrate leadership. That may work for the short term, but ultimately two things will happen. First, a compromised solution rarely carries the strength of a single, clear, well-crafted course of action and the commander will soon be presiding over a flawed program. Second, the best and brightest subordinate leaders will quickly recognize you for what you are, a weak ineffective commander.

The United States Army is in the business of growing potential commanders. By necessity, the institution expends an inordinate amount of time, energy and resources preparing leaders for command. Having done this, special boards are then convened to comb through the files and select a small percentage who will be allowed to command at the battalion level, an organization of 400-700 troops led by a Lieutenant Colonel. In the context of a civilian job description, the requirements are similar to those of a mid-level leader with significant responsibilities for personnel decisions and finding innovative ways to produce the product. The job posting for a battalion commander and its civilian counterpart might look something like this:

Education: Bachelors required, Masters Degree preferred. Fourteen to eighteen years in the

workforce. Eight to ten years experience with high performance ratings while serving in junior leadership positions. Staff experience at senior headquarters desired. Strong leadership skills and people-orientation mandatory. Overall exemplary record of performance.

Subsequently, from that elite group of successful battalion commanders, there will be yet another selection board convened to pick an even smaller number of Colonels to command at the brigade level, an organization consisting of three to five battalions. Irrespective of the years of preparation for command, some fail because the degree of loneliness increases at each successive level. Courses of action are less clear, there are more options, there are more dissenters, there is a greater degree of uncertainty and many find they cannot handle the responsibility. Selecting a commander at any level (direct, operational or strategic) in any type organization is no sure thing.

However, there are commanders who thrive on the daily challenge, who are comfortable in command and typically optimistic. What is it that makes them that way? What should one look for when selecting commanders? Here are some criteria to look for and some that are not as important.

Raw intelligence is clearly not a determining factor in being a successful commander. The best commanders may not necessarily be the brightest among the candidates. Neither is personality a good single measure. The gregarious extrovert who is popular, visible and always seems to have the right thing to say may be a mile wide and a half-inch deep when it comes to the tough issues. Meanwhile the quiet, reserved introvert heretofore making huge contributions from the sidelines may be the diamond in the rough. Look for the consummate team player who epitomizes the philosophy, it doesn't matter who gets the credit, as long as we are collectively successful.

Foremost in selection of commanders is strength of character. Find someone who consistently demonstrates the courage of his or her convictions. A person of principle is likely going to make decisions that, in the long run, are in the best interests of the organization.

A commander is a person who is not afraid to make mistakes. An honest mistake made while being aggressive, innovative and well intentioned that has limited consequences, can be seen as a positive learning experience. But what is even more important is a commander who is willing to encourage subordinates to act in the same manner.

While writing hundreds of fitness reports on subordinate officers during my career, what I diligently looked for were errors in judgment. A person who simply fails to exercise good common sense over time has a high probability of failing as a commander and should not be selected to such a position.

Pay close attention to individuals who are described as having excellent instincts, as they are more likely to know the consequences of a command decision and therefore have tremendous command potential. They tend to understand how subordinates are going to act and react; they seem to know what to say, what not to say, when to say it, what to do and when to do it; and they are out in front at the most opportune point in time influencing people.

The best summation for good commanders is that they are the ones who consistently set a first-rate example. There is nowhere for a commander to hide; even for those who seek to keep a low profile, the spotlight is never completely turned off.

With the above backdrop of desirable and undesirable characteristics for commanders, let us turn to the task of providing a definition. General George S. Patton Jr. spent his entire adult life either in command or preparing himself for the task. He wrote, "A commander will command. What does a commander do? He commands. If he does not do it, he is not a commander."[20] This is not a classic definition by any means, but he does make one good point; you cannot be a commander just by virtue of being in a command position. You have to overtly do things commanders are expected to do before you can be a commander.

In *Patton on leadership, Strategic Lessons for Corporate Warfare* Alan Axelrod retells a wonderful story about General Patton arriving in Indio, California to take command of the United States Army's Desert Training Center. The United States was, at the time, quickly building a multi-million-man Army and learning how to employ large tank formations. Patton was to arrive and take command of the First Armored Corps, an organization of tens of thousands of Army soldiers. One of the elements of the Corps, the Second Armored Division, was in formation for the eleven o'clock ceremony. Imagine Patton arriving on the scene in what was called a command car; no top and a roll bar for support allowing a person to easily ride while standing in the back. He presided over the ceremony as flags were passed; this is normally followed by a speech during which the new commander thanks everyone, says how glad he is to be a part of the organization, look forward to working with you, etc. But there was no speech per se. Upon receiving the colors Patton said, "I assume command of the First Armored Corps! At ease!" For those of you who have not served in the military the term "at ease" serves specific purposes. First when given the order to be at ease, those in formation take a more relaxed stance from that of being at rigid attention, which requires head and eyes focused straight ahead. Second, when told to be at ease, those in the formation are expected to turn their head and eyes toward the person giving the command. Thus, with those two simple words, "at ease", General Patton had everyone in the Second Armored Division focused directly on himself. Then he said:

> **"We are in a long war against a tough enemy. We must train millions of men to be soldiers! We must make them tough in mind and body and they must be trained to kill. As officers we will give leadership in becoming tough physically and mentally. Every man in this command will be able to run a mile in fifteen minutes with a full military pack including a rifle." At that point according**

to the story some overweight senior officer chuckled. "Damn it!" General Patton shouted, "I mean every man of this command! Every officer and enlisted man – staff and command; every man will run a mile! We will start running from this point in exactly thirty minutes! I will lead."21

There are some important points to take away from this scene. After assuming command of the First Armored Corps at precisely eleven o'clock on January 15, 1942, General Patton, in a few seconds, set himself apart. There were perhaps hundreds of men in that formation who were in key leadership positions. But, upon finishing his short dissertation, he made it perfectly clear who was in command of the entire operation with the words, "I will lead." With some pauses for emphasis, those remarks could have consumed only about one minute of time. But in that one minute he articulated his vision of what had to be done; it will take millions of highly trained, physically and mentally tough soldiers to win the war. He characterized the competition for everyone as a tough enemy. Additionally, he set standards for the entire command; not only did he explicitly say everyone had to be physically and mentally tough, he implied a sense of urgency. While some may have been expecting the normal post-ceremony grip-and-grin reception, they were instead instructed to be back in formation with a full military pack and rifle in exactly thirty minutes, not twenty-nine or thirty-one, but exactly thirty. In that one brief sentence standards were set and they did not have to filter down through the ranks as policy papers over a period of days and weeks. Everyone in that formation heard them first hand and those of the First Armored Corps who were not in attendance would understand the standards as the ceremony was retold in the barracks a thousand times that evening.

No one is above the standards set for the lowest ranking member of the organization. Patton makes that point specifically about officers, every officer. He then goes on to clarify that the standards apply not only to those in line units but also to staff. And then the crowning blow, example flows from the commander. Do as I do, not just as I say; I will lead. General Patton was not afraid to act like a commander.

RECAP

1. All leaders are held accountable for the welfare of their people; commanders are additionally held accountable for the welfare of the organization.
2. An organization's culture is in large measure a reflection of its commander.
3. Command portends a moral responsibility.
4. While commanders must prepare to be lonely, they can also look forward to the most richly rewarding experience of their professional lives.
5. A good commander, first and foremost, has great strength of character and provides an example worthy of emulation.

CHAPTER SIX

CRITICALITY OF DELEGATION, EMPOWERMENT AND SPAN OF CONTROL

Leadership Failure Is More Often Than Not Self-Imposed. Furthermore, That Self-Inflicted Wound Is Frequently Caused By Violating Common Sense Rules of Delegation, Empowerment and Span of Control

Span of control, delegation and empowerment represent a cornerstone for the underpinnings of a personal leadership philosophy. These subjects help us understand the factors contributing to a leader's success or failure. Success and failure mean different things to different people and rarely are they objectively measurable. The context in which leadership failure is described in this chapter is one in which efficiency and effectiveness of overall operations are not what they could or should be. That is, subordinates are not provided with a good leadership example; subordinates are not made to feel they are trusted, appreciated for their expertise or relied upon; or, loyalty is not flowing down the continuum of leadership.

As a division commander, one of my principle responsibilities was to continuously assess the leadership climate in twenty-eight battalions. Likewise, a Chief Executive

Officer is doing the same thing for a number of manufacturing plants spread across the country. One does not need a checklist to identify even subtle differences in the subordinate organizations; one can sense it in attitude, timeliness, work ethic, absenteeism, turnover, loyalty, sense of belonging and esprit. Span of control, delegation and empowerment are vital leadership tools that affect all of the factors making up the leadership environment in an organization.

The purpose of this chapter is to discuss how using span of control, delegation and empowerment tools can enhance chances for success; leaving this toolbox unopened is a formula for failure.

Commercial ventures file for bankruptcy every day; obviously there are a variety of reasons and occasionally they are caused by circumstances beyond the control of any person; the economy takes a downturn and demand for high-end durable goods falls off; the 9/11 terrorist attack had a devastating impact on air travel; the development pace of information technology makes long-range market planning extraordinarily difficult. These types of issues contribute to the success and failure of commercial ventures. Notwithstanding all the factors that can cause an organization to falter, failure is more often than not self-imposed. Furthermore, that self-inflicted wound is frequently caused by violating common sense rules of span of control, delegation or empowerment. It is these leadership failures over which we have control that need to be explored.

SPAN OF CONTROL

When in a leadership position there is a natural tendency to want to know as much as possible about what is going on in the leadership layers below, after all you are being held responsible for what they do or fail to do. But, of course, there are limits to what one person can do and the number of subordinates with whom he or she can interact. A good rule of thumb for span of control is that a leader should sustain close contact with what is taking place one echelon down and have a clear understanding of what is happening two levels down. Any leader who violates this rule runs the risk of seeing a dramatic downturn in efficiency and effectiveness.

There are limits on any person's capacity to perform. Being directly involved in day-to-day operational details two levels down in any organization generally leads to any number of problems and the hierarchy of my organization as a division commander provides a good example. Let's look at just one function, that of training and explore the ramifications of span of control. At the first subordinate level of the Seventh Infantry Division there were seven brigade commanders. They each commanded an organization of 2,000-3,000 men and women. Every brigade was involved in some type of daily training regimen. My responsibility was to ensure that training was planned and conducted to a prescribed standard, that time, materials and space were properly resourced and that each brigade's training program fit into my overall training plan for the division. It was part of our mission to be the most highly deployable combat division in the world. That is, able to move the entire combat-ready division, personnel and equipment, by air, faster and further than anyone else. Therefore, training was our number one priority. Keeping tabs on training for seven diverse brigade-size organizations, (Infantry, Artillery, Aviation, Logistics) easily consumed most of the time I had available to devote to training on a daily basis.

Two echelons down in the hierarchy were twenty-eight battalion commanders. Had I attempted to provide the same level of direction and oversight to the battalions as I did the seven brigades, span of control dictated that it would have been impossible unless I devoted all of my time to the training function. For any senior leader to devote 100 percent of their time to any one activity is impossible, other than for short periods during a crisis. My other responsibilities, while not number one priorities, were nonetheless critical and had to be dealt with on a continual basis. They included running a small city (6,500 sets of on-post family housing, hundreds of miles of streets and roads, crime, fire safety, schools, day-care, etc);

budgeting for a $700 million a year operation; morale, welfare and recreational activities for 40,000 military members and their families; community relations; environmental issues; personnel turnover; public affairs, etc. Over-emphasis on any one area, such as training, could have easily led to failure of other functions and the organization would have been far less combat ready.

While I could not provide the same level of oversight to the battalions as I did to the brigades, by necessity I had to have a good understanding of the battalion commanders' training programs. How do leaders sort out their level of involvement, responsibilities and differentiation one and two levels down for any given activity? One way is to set up a review mechanism and ruthlessly enforce its application. An important point to remember is that whatever the mechanism, it must have value added. That is, it cannot be a report for the sake of covering one's backside, it cannot be a meeting held just because it is Monday morning, it cannot be a conference call from the golf course just so a leader can say he discussed an issue with his subordinates. The mechanism must have visible value that is apparent to all subordinate leadership levels involved. Let me illustrate again by using the example from my time as commander of the Seventh Infantry Division. Since training was our number one priority, it followed that the who/what/when/where/why/how could not be left to chance. The mechanism to assist in limiting span of control was a structured quarterly training brief conducted by each of the brigade commanders.

The quarterly training briefings were the number one scheduling priority and it took a major unforeseen event to cause a reschedule; the word cancel never entered into the equation. Each brigade commander had in attendance his respective battalion commanders. This served two purposes; first, I was able to gain an understanding of the issues, problems, assessment and plans two levels down and determine if they were in synch with my overall intent for training. Second, the battalion commanders could hear my guidance first hand, understand why they were or were not getting the priority on training resources; additionally they gained insights into my training intent for the division as a whole. A number of issues were addressed during these briefings. Did we achieve last quarter's training objectives and if not, why? Did unforeseen events (i.e. a battalion was unexpectedly deployed to fight forest fires) throw us off schedule? Does next quarter's training fit properly into the overall annual training plan? The major role I played was in prioritizing resources and looking for answers to the above questions.

The two principle functions performed by a leader of any organization occurred in those quarterly training briefings. As previously pointed out, leaders assess risk and allocate shortages. Leaders, be they military, corporate, service or whatever, never believe they have enough resources. Therefore, they find themselves assessing the risk of doing course of action A as opposed to B and then allocating the shortages for the organization's greater good. In this process someone gets left out, someone is unhappy. That is another one of those times when it gets lonely at the top.

Applying the span of control rule throughout the continuum of leadership provides for consistent but not excessive supervision and oversight. That is, the most senior organizational layer (let's call it layer A) watches carefully over layer B and has an understanding of what is going on in layer C; simultaneously layer B provides scrutiny to C and knows what is happening in D and on down the line. As one moves down the leadership levels to direct leaders, the issues become less complex, require less time to resolve, but yet are vital to overall success of the organization.

The leader of every organization must identify the echelons of the continuum and implement a span of control equation. Failing to do so is taking a serious step toward inefficiency and ineffectiveness as a best-case outcome and total chaos throughout the organization as a real possibility.

DELEGATE OR DIE

Delegate or die. Having asserted how important this subject is in those three words; delegation in and of itself is still insufficient. After delegating responsibilities a leader must take the additional step and transfer the commensurate authority necessary to carry out the prescribed functions. This is called empowerment.

Leaders must realize what they can and cannot delegate. We made a differentiation between some leaders being responsible for the welfare of their people while others have responsibility for the welfare of the organization. The welfare of an organization is closely related to its values. Responsibility for shaping the values of the organization falls on the shoulders of the leader and therefore cannot be delegated.

Operational duties can and should be delegated. There are limits to people's capacity to provide the time and energy necessary to cause some functions to be performed. When these limits are reached, one of two things happens. Either the requisite attention to detail declines with potential disastrous results, or someone is added to the organization to take up the slack and provide an opportunity for success.

Delegation is not simple. Delegation, like leadership, is more art than science. Leaders are always seeking ways to make the whole greater than the sum of its parts; the manner in which we delegate contributes to synergism. You are a leader in the boiler room and part of your responsibility is to ensure the pressure does not build to a level that will cause the boilers to explode. There are two boilers a short distance apart. Your responsibilities have increased to the point that you cannot provide the proper amount of attention to the gauges that measure the pressure. So you hire two individuals, station one at each gauge and tell them to let you know if the pressure reaches a certain level. That is a form of delegation. Someone else is performing a vital function for you. They have been told exactly *what* to do and *how* to do it. Another way to delegate in that same scenario is to hire one person and tell him or her that if the pressure begins to rise, it will do so slowly; keep an eye on both gauges and if either setting gets to a prescribed level let me know immediately. While still having been told exactly what to do, the new employee will study the rate of pressure change, determine how often to check each gauge, move between the two and perhaps realize there is time to also do some sweeping up around the area. Having been instructed *what* to do, this employee is into self-determination on the *how*.

Another way to delegate this task is to hire a boiler assistant. Teach the assistant how the boiler works, the seriousness of the issue if the pressure gets too high, how to regulate the level of pressure and if the pressure does get too high, what to do to remedy the situation on his own. Now we are into empowerment.

EMPOWERMENT

A Major contributing factor to leader failure is the delegation of responsibility without also providing the authority necessary to perform whatever function is to be executed. What if, even after hiring two employees whose specific functions were to monitor the pressure gauges, the boiler explodes anyway? An investigation would ensue and the findings would indicate that the leader could not be located at the critical moment when one of the employees found a gauge to be dangerously high. Had these subordinates been empowered by their leader, the boiler likely would not have exploded.

Empowerment begins with the objective to build expertise in subordinates. In your absence someone has to be available, willing and trained to act on your behalf. This means getting a subordinate comfortable, not only with responsibility, but also with wielding the authority to move forward and make decisions.

Delegation and empowerment also build trust. Trust is a two-way street. Leaders must be able to trust that their subordinates will do well in their absence. Likewise, the subordinates want to be trusted to take their leader's place whenever necessary. In order for this equation to work, trust must be genuine. The boss who, before going on vacation, puts a subordinate in charge and then calls into the office every day to see how things are going is sending a powerful, negative message of no trust, no empowerment, no leader development. The only identifiable outcome is lower morale.

Even worse is the boss who never goes on vacation at all because he or she believes they are indispensable. They drive on relentlessly, never giving subordinates a change of pace; the leader's family life suffers, they become burned out and ineffective and the organization suffers.

Fred Smith, founder of Federal Express, provides empowerment insights in *Creating an Empowering Environment for all Employees*. He makes the point that in the service industry customer satisfaction is paramount. While many companies would be delighted if they achieved a 99.2 success rate, at Federal Express 99.2 success translates into 2.75 million failures per year (1990 figures). Timeliness is a major factor in building customer satisfaction. Empowered employees will make decisions and act, thereby solving the time management problem of employees standing around waiting to be told what to do. Furthermore an obstacle in a corporate culture of empowerment is not the unwillingness of subordinates to accept challenges, but the reluctance of senior leaders to understand that "sharing power means gaining power." Smith ties empowerment into his definition of leadership: "The way I see it, leadership does not begin with power but rather, with a compelling vision or goal of excellence. One becomes a leader when he or she is able to communicate that vision in such a way that others feel empowered to achieve excellence. We must create organizations with a shared vision of excellence." 22

Every organization has at least one boiler, and someone has to watch the pressure gauge. How leaders handle span of control, delegation and empowerment goes a long way toward determining if the boiler is going to power the organization or destroy it.

RECAP

1. Disregarding sound judgment with respect to span of control, delegation and empowerment can be a formula for failure.
2. The formula for span of control is for a leader to pay close attention to details one echelon down and have a general understanding of what is going on two levels down.
3. Delegate not only the responsibility but also the requisite authority.
4. Empowerment and trust go hand in hand. Both must be genuine and both are essential to an organization's success.
5. Organizations should do well whether the leader is in the office or on vacation.

ENDURING LEADERSHIP PRINCIPLES

Great leaders:
Optimize their span of control.
Delegate operational duties.
Empower Subordinates.

CHAPTER SEVEN

DEALING WITH CHANGE

If You Always Do What You Always Did, You Will Always Get What You Always Got.

L ouis Lataif, Dean of the Boston University School of Management, wrote the foreword to *Hope is Not a Method* and in it he makes some key observations about organization and change. He asserts:

> "Much of the way American management works was learned from the World War II practices of the U.S. military. That 'command and control' model of management is structurally hierarchical, top-down driven and precise in its statistical controls. It was taken by American industry from the Pentagon in the late 1940s and early 1950s. So long as U.S. firms competed primarily with one another in the first quarter century following World War II, that management system was effective. The two oil crises of the 1970s altered the competitive playing field for all time. America faced new competition from abroad, particularly from Japan and Germany." 23

Japan and Germany literally rose from the ashes of

military defeat to become major industrial powers. One of
their keys to success was to challenge the American traditional
organization. The important point to take from Lataif's writing
is that in order to remain competitive in a business world that
is becoming ever more global, American corporations have
had to find ways to become more agile and flexible, seeking
out every possible advantage over the competition. They have
had to change. Your company may have spent decades setting
up a world-wide marketing and distribution system only to
find that today the competition is someone with a web site
that can be instantly accessed anywhere in the world, offering
next-day shipping of a similar product direct to the customer's
home. The twenty-first century revolution in terms of pace
of operations and information reach is by no means over and
organizations find themselves having to adapt and change to
new operating environments on the fly.

The purpose of this chapter is to make the point that a
leader is not the steward of the status quo; leaders must sort out
what must change and deal with it proactively.

Since the United States Army was my company for thirty-
two years, I cannot resist including a final thought from Mr.
Lataif. He wrote:

**"It is remarkable, I think, that the American
organization that has arguably reinvented both
its management system and its leadership culture
most dramatically is the United States Army."24**

Let me underscore that point from a personal experience.
While the Cold War raged on unabated in the late 1970s and
1980s and without any particular outside influence, the United
States Army took it upon itself to initiate dramatic changes
in structure and in our warfighting doctrine. Keyed around
four precepts – agility, initiative, depth and synchronization
– the Army conceived, wrote and instituted a whole new
mindset about how we should fight. This, in turn, precipitated
a revolutionary doctrinal shift in how we would train.
Furthermore, we discovered we were not optimally structured

to execute the warfighting doctrine. For two years I led a group of about a dozen staff officers who looked at the structure of virtually every combat and combat support element in the United States Army. We designed new organizations and retooled the old ones to bring structure into alignment with how we were going to fight; that is, with agility, initiative, depth and synchronization. The doctrinal changes took hold, the structural changes were approved and finally completed about the time the Berlin Wall came down and the Cold War ended. Furthermore, the United States Army was precisely organized and trained to a warfighting doctrine appropriate to fight and win the Gulf War in less than one hundred hours of land combat. A long-time friend, General Barry McCaffrey, who upon retirement from the Army held the position of President Clinton's National Drug Czar, put it best at a symposium of Army division commanders after the war when he made the point that we did not win the Gulf War in three days, it took us fifteen years of hard work to be postured to accomplish what we did on the ground in Saudi Arabia, Kuwait and Iraq. The United States Army desperately needed to change; it did and reaped the benefits.

While you may believe your organization could benefit from change do not go into changing the structure, mindset or culture believing it will be an easy task. What can and will happen is not a new phenomenon; political philosopher Nicolo Machiavilli (1469-1527) succinctly summarized change in *The Prince*:

> "....there is nothing more difficult to take in hand, more perilous to conduct, or more uncertain in its success, than to take the lead in the introduction of a new order of things. Because the innovator has for enemies all those who have done well under the old conditions and lukewarm defenders in those who may do well under the new. " 25

When I was working on the redesign of the Army forces, to say I was the most unpopular Colonel in the United

States Army was the understatement of the century. I was constantly knocking heads with the establishment; the two-star commanders of the Army's fiefdoms called Branches which includes Infantry, Armor, Aviation, Field Artillery, Air Defense, Engineers, Military Police, Transportation, Ordinance, Quartermaster and Special Forces. The phone calls I received from some of those senior officers nearly melted the wires. Some openly stated that my career was over; in my own branch, the Field Artillery, I was branded a traitor for even thinking there could be better structural solutions. The Army redesign was officially entitled The Army of Excellence. If you want to know if it was successful ask Saddam Hussein and his military leaders.

Change can be painful for many people in an organization. Once a leader has made the decision to change an essential ingredient in the process is to provide support for those working the details. In the Army reorganization project, I had the top cover from the Chief of Staff; the Army's most senior General. What he had done was to tell the Army commanders in Europe, the Pacific and of all forces in the continental United States, that I would be coming directly to them with new designs as opposed to laboriously working the proposals as staff actions up through their respective staffs. They were to see me personally and comment on the ideas presented. From there I would retool if necessary and take the recommended solutions directly to the Chief of Staff for a final decision. Without that top cover we might still be staffing suggested changes through the branch fiefdoms, getting nowhere and have a structure out of synch with the warfighting doctrine it is supposed to support. A footnote on the Army as a living, breathing, ever changing entity; since the Gulf War it has downsized by about 600,000 personnel, again redefined its warfighting doctrine and is in the throws of another major structural transition in order to remain relevant to the ever-changing world-wide battlespace.

The bottom line in organization is to ensure it works for you and not the other way around. Organization must be the supporting character, never the lead. Fred Smith's FEDEX is a perfect example. He built the company around the idea of empowerment to the men and women who drive the trucks, deliver the products and interact directly with the customers all day, everyday. The structure that developed is, by necessity, relatively flat with only five layers from the delivery people to the boardroom.

Now that you have arrived at the desired operating structure for your company, do not get complacent. A structure right for today may be the first nail in the coffin tomorrow. But knowing when to reorganize is not easy. You will not just come to work one day and find a note on your desk telling you, now is the time. Sometimes it will just feel right and fly in the face of sound logic. It may be one of the times when you just go with your gut. Conversely, there may be times when reorganization is improper in both timing and purpose and perhaps undertaken solely to create an impression that the company is progressing. This is not a new occurrence, Petronius Arbiter, a Roman satirist, wrote in 210 BC:

> **"We trained.... but it seemed that every time we were beginning to form up into teams we would be reorganized. I was to learn later in life that we tend to meet any new situation by reorganizing; a wonderful method it can be for creating the illusion of progress while producing confusion, inefficiency and demoralization."26**

In today's instant gratification environment where businesses are too often gauged on quarterly results rather than on sustained performance there is constant pressure to do something. The decision to act is sometimes translated into restructure and ends up being a self-inflicted wound with no redeeming value.

Throughout the history of humankind, change in operating environments has been continuously redefined from slight alterations over the millennia to what we are experiencing today with information technology. An important point to be made is that in the midst of the current revolution of ever-changing organizational structures, leadership principles are enduring and are as applicable today as they have ever been.

RECAP

1. Organizational change is now, or will at some point, become necessary in order to remain competitive. Watch for the signs and do not get left behind.
2. Change is a high-risk venture and there may be a great deal of opposition. Provide top cover for those employees who are working the action.
3. Leaders who take the organization elsewhere are effectively dealing with change.

ENDURING LEADERSHIP PRINCIPLES

Great leaders:
Recognize that change is inevitable and they must take the organization elsewhere or preside over the funeral.

CHAPTER EIGHT

ORGANIZE FOR ACTION

While It Is True Senior Leaders May Find It Lonely At The Top, That Does Not Mean They Have To Be Alone.

There are two distinct meanings for the word organization. Heretofore, I have used the word organization in reference to the body, the whole, the unified element existing for a specific purpose; it could be a corporation, a small family business, the military, a church, a government agency, etc. Organization in this chapter is going to deal with the issue of getting people best arranged for action. While it is true the boss may find it lonely at the top, a leader who uses personnel to their greatest advantage may create opportunities to dramatically increase overall effectiveness and efficiency.

In this chapter you will find a menu of options or tools from which to choose that can add value to any operation. Most of these fall under the domain of the operational and strategic leaders; they will make personal decisions as to whether or not the individual positions or groups of people will be a part of the organization and, if they are, the role each will play.

The purpose of this chapter is to familiarize you with organizational tools to enhance your operations, particularly during times of change and crisis.

CHIEF OF STAFF

A chief of staff in any sizeable organization can significantly improve overall operational effectiveness. "Chief" of the "staff" clearly describes what the position is and what the person holding the position does. A chief of staff is the alter ego of the boss. The chief of staff is a confidant, sounding board and implicitly trusted to be discreet; therefore, the boss should personally select his or her chief of staff. An effective leader/chief of staff relationship is one in which they will spend considerable time together working informally across a broad range of issues. For example, daily interaction might include a broad range of issues such as: chief do you have a minute, I want to run something by you; take a quick look at this and tell me what you think; chief, we have a problem get the war council together; or chief, give John a call and calm him down, he's gone off the deep end and I cannot deal with him right now.

While a chief of staff will be involved in virtually every action, their primary function is that of integrator. The daily duties performed by assorted staff members vary drastically in content and complexity. While the chief financial officer lives in a different world than the vice president for marketing the various department heads of the staff elements of any large organization cannot be allowed to act as independent operators. Everyone must be working toward a common goal and all share the boss' vision of the end-state. Someone must integrate all of the disparate efforts; someone is responsible for building a synergistic affect. That someone should not be the boss. If the boss assumes integration responsibilities there will be insufficient time remaining for the myriad of other duties for which the boss is personally responsible and that cannot be performed by anyone else. As pointed out in chapter 6, span of control alone will defeat the leader who takes on too many responsibilities. Operational and strategic leaders need a chief of staff.

In any organization there are recurring actions and activities that have to be accommodated; periodic personnel reviews, recurring reports, setting up board meetings, public affairs, etc. An effective chief of staff makes routine things happen routinely. They create a rhythm in an organization so that every issue does not become a crisis. The chief of staff is also an interpreter. Hardly a day goes by in the life of a chief of staff when he or she does not get a call from another senior member of the organization asking for clarification of a statement or direction from the boss. This is where the chief of staff has to assess the relationship with the boss, the unwritten rules between them and the level of assumed authority in speaking for the boss. A skillful chief of staff will have the relationship figured out and even if occasionally oversteps the bounds or misreads the boss, on balance, there will be tremendous value added. The boss and the chief are a two-person team with a special relationship and when it clicks, they can really make an organization excel.

If the leader/chief of staff relationship is a positive one, perhaps the biggest benefit to the organization is that the boss can then feel comfortable being out of the office. I have never seen a successful person lead from behind a desk; I have observed some very poor leaders try to do so. Leaders have to show the flag; see first hand if subordinates are moving in the correct and the same direction. There is always friction in an organization and someone has to sense it, dig out the source and fix it. Someone has to grade the mood of the employees, see the expertise or lack thereof at subordinate leader levels. The devil is in the details and leaders have to frequently get out in the field and get close to the action. I could not have had any understanding of what was happening in twenty-eight battalion commanders' daily training from just having listened to their plans during the quarterly training briefings. Since training was our number one priority, I spent a portion of nearly every day and many nights in the field with them observing their strengths and weaknesses. This was all made possible because my chief of staff was chained to the desk. Someone has to watch over the farm and do the daily chores, but it should not be the operational or strategic leader. If the organization is so fragile it cannot survive the boss being frequently absent; then it will not survive even if the boss is present. The boss who does not get out of the office will be captured by the tyranny of the mundane and runs the risk of losing focus on the larger issues. With today's instant communications the chief of staff can easily stay in touch with the boss on critical, time-sensitive issues.

THE WAR COUNCIL

A war council is a small, select group of action people pulled from throughout the organization for special purposes. There is no formal book definition for a war council but if we can successfully list the criteria for the members, a picture will emerge of what a war council is and does. A functioning war council may not even have a name and in all probability does not have a formal charter. Since its concept flies in the face of tradition, those not included are likely to be less than enamored with the whole idea. War councils do not exist in all organizations and some leaders and chiefs of staff are not inclined to stray from the more formal way of problem solving. Sometimes the war council does not come about as a premeditated act; it just evolves over time based on circumstances and the value they add. More often than not, the war council is born out of crisis. When something has to be done quickly, when the best minds need to be brought together to do some back-of-the-envelope calculations, it is not always the large cumbersome traditional staff that can be relied on for such a task.

The war council should be a low-key operation and used only when necessary. The danger in over-reliance on the war council is that it can undermine normal day-to-day team efforts necessary for long-term goals. Composition of the war council may vary from event to event depending on the subject at hand. It must be recognized that calling up the war council is naturally disruptive and pulls key individuals away from their normally assigned duties for a period of time.

Who are the members of the war council? First and foremost they are individuals in whom the boss and the chief of staff have absolute confidence. Additionally, they can be relied on to be discreet because they are often brought in on the leading edge of a new venture. They are also not shrinking violets and can be counted on to provide an honest opinion even if it flies in the face of where the boss obviously wants to go. They are not yes people.

How might a war council be used? It may be called in for a simple one-hour brain storming session. The boss has an idea and wants some immediate feedback on the potential ramifications. The war council is assembled and everyone lays their best judgment on the table; cost factors, personnel implications, public perception, chances for success, probability of failure and timing. In doing so the boss may get more honest useful feedback in one hour than if he staffed the issue for a month ending up with a six inch stack of paper and some subordinates sitting on the fence not willing to commit themselves at this early point in time for fear of ending up on the wrong side.

The war council may be called together to get a first glance at something a leader has already decided to do but wants to get a sense of how it is going to be received. Who will object the loudest and the most? Who will the natural allies be? It is a tool the boss can use to be proactive and to stomp out small fires before they flare up.

But, as noted earlier, a war council is normally born out of crisis and in my experience its normal function is to deal with crisis. Some years ago I was the chief of staff at the North Atlantic Treaty Organization (NATO) headquarters for Southern European Operations located in Naples, Italy. I had a one thousand person multinational staff consisting of Greeks, Turks, Italians, British and U.S. A United States Navy four-star, Admiral Leighton "Snuffy" Smith, was the commander. We were conducting daily NATO combat air operations over Bosnia, leading a multinational naval task force in the Adriatic Sea carrying out a United Nations imposed maritime embargo on shipping to Serbia and Montenegro and simultaneously building plans for the movement of a large multi-national land force into Bosnia if ordered to do so. So, with those actions, in addition to everything else going on in Southern Europe (multi-national training, exercises, contingency planning) we were, to say the least, fully engaged.

With that background let me set the scene for how and why Admiral Smith and I used a war council. NATO is a political body consisting, at that time, of sixteen nations. It is not a democratic, majority-rule body. Quite the contrary, NATO operates by consensus; all sixteen nations have to agree before anything can happen. Therefore, it should come as no surprise that, given a situation as complex as the one in Bosnia, NATO did not have a consensus among the member nations as to what needed to be done. There is wisdom in the old saying that without knowing where you are going any road will get you there. NATO headquarters sent us down every conceivable road. It was the perfect scenario for the NATO political leaders to constantly ask what-if....?

If you have not been part of a multinational organization you cannot appreciate the multitude of ways nations can stonewall, delay, disrupt and, yes, even sabotage what might otherwise be a relatively easy staff action. On numerous occasions Admiral Smith would get off the phone, walk into my office, lay out what we had to respond to and then we would assemble the war council because we knew that using the whole multi-national-staff would not lead us to a timely, complete, solution that made acceptable military sense. We would articulate what needed to be done, provide the Admiral's intent and give them time to ask a few questions. Then everyone would be tasked. Frequently, we would reassemble briefly to check signals and see if there was a roadblock the commander or I needed to remove. Only in this way were we able to provide clear, concise, timely input to NATO headquarters on a continual basis.

As stated before, the personnel making up a war council will vary according to the issue, but there is always a core element; for Admiral Smith and me, that cast was about ten people. Was there some political sensitivity from using the war council? Certainly there was and sometimes those sensitivities were elevated to a political level and became serious. But leaders will pay that price if, in their judgment, the war council brings value added to the operation and may, in some cases, be the only course of action for success. An eighty percent solution today may be infinitely more beneficial than a ninety-five percent solution a month from now. The war council is not for every leader but can be an invaluable tool if used properly, particularly considering the pace of play in the twenty-first century operating environment where a crisis may be lurking around every corner.

THE KITCHEN CABINET

The *Dictionary* defines kitchen cabinet as, "a group of unofficial advisors on whom a government head relies."[27] The origin of the term comes from the fact that President Andrew Jackson met with his unofficial cabinet in the White House kitchen.

When President Ronald Reagan assumed office in January, l981, he had a kitchen cabinet. The cynics would refer to them as a bunch of cronies from California; the cynics did not get it. A kitchen cabinet can be a valuable tool and is not exclusive to senior politicians; it exists in the business world, in the military and can be helpful in virtually any organization of any size.

A small group, the kitchen cabinet members are normally well known to the person they advise. If you had to capture in a single word what it is they do, that word would be mentor. They are from outside the organization and, therefore, not encumbered by day-to-day operations. They have a wide range of experience and expertise and are usually well connected.

The kitchen cabinet does not get paid and may not even meet as a body; they might be sought out individually by the principal for advice and counsel. While kitchen cabinet members may not have held the same position their benefactor is occupying, they have normally been tested in jobs of great responsibility and can clearly relate to what the incumbent is going through.

What does the kitchen cabinet actually do? They give advice when asked and, when the mechanism is working properly, provide counsel even when it is not sought. The kitchen cabinet members sense the mood of the public and nose around to determine how a particular element will react to a policy on certain issues. Being well connected, members may be asked to make a couple of key phone calls, contact someone to provide off-the-record guidance, or even twist a few arms.

The kitchen cabinet may rarely be tasked to perform specific functions on specific timelines. A tasking to a kitchen cabinet member may be a simple declaration such as; I'm relying on you to let me know how I'm doing. Intelligent leaders at the operational or strategic levels will recognize that sometimes they may be too immersed in details to see the big picture. While concentrating on a serious issue a leader may not perceive that the organization as a whole is drifting off course, has departed from its core competencies and may be in harms way.

A skillful leader will have a vision of where they want to take the organization. Perhaps the most important function kitchen cabinet members perform is as a sounding board. Does it pass the smell test? Does it make common sense? Is this the right time or perhaps exactly the wrong time to launch a new product, marketing campaign, or reorganization? The kitchen cabinet can be an invaluable asset, mentoring a leader on vision and end-state.

THE MOBILE COMMAND POST

Organizations today have offices, production facilities, distribution points, etc spread all over the country and in many cases worldwide. Also, it is not uncommon to find a corporate headquarters with two or more subsidiaries conducting totally unrelated operations.

One of my personal maxims on the role of any headquarters large enough to have a staff has always been, staffs support down. It is not the role of a headquarters to tell subordinates *how* to do their job. Rather they should provide resourcing, systems support, training facilities, market research and keep an eye on the competition all in support of their subordinates.

The staffs-support-down concept is part of an operational or strategic leader's responsibility with respect to the overall issue of organization. The boss must make it clear to everyone in the organization the positions and elements that are in a supporting role and those being supported. Left to its own devices, a senior headquarters staff element, human resources for example, will more often than not assume the lead role over the human resource sections in the subsidiary companies. After all, they all work for the CEO and he resides at the corporate headquarters. In order to not let human nature get in the way of progress, that CEO should prescribe clear written policy concerning the role of the corporate staff and spell out who is supporting and who is supported. This is religion in the military and while we know how vital it is to be clear on this point, it still gets discombobulated all too frequently because we believe it is so obvious everyone will understand. Murphy's Law is always lurking; if something can be misunderstood, it will be.

So, what does all this have to do with a mobile command post? If an operational or strategic leader has put all the right policies in place, has the supporting/supported issue ironed out and sufficiently empowered the leaders of the subordinate companies, there may still be numerous times when a subordinate element needs some temporary help. This could be during a start-up operation, a major expansion, or a physical relocation. A subordinate headquarters may also find itself in an unforeseen crisis and need help.

A wise senior leader has anticipated the potential needs of his subordinates and put together a mobile command post team that can pick up at a moments notice, relocate temporarily and provide some emergency assistance. The CEO may direct each department head in the corporation to have a mobile command post element in place. The mobile command post consists of designated employees who otherwise on a day-to-day basis hold permanent positions within their respective departments but have also been tagged as mobile command post members for specified temporary assignments when called upon. Perhaps the people from marketing get called on to spend ten days with a subsidiary that is expanding into a new region. A couple experts from each department may go collectively to provide general support to a start-up company or to work on the merger of a recently acquired partner.

A more permanent type of mobile command post is a mobile training team. This is a stable fixture and their full-time job is to go from department to department within a headquarters or to outlying company locations to provide recurring services. One example would be to use a mobile training team to conduct an acculturation boot camp for all new personnel, properly indoctrinating them into the organization's culture. A mobile training team could also be used on a temporary basis for the purpose of installing and providing initial training on a new software system or marketing initiative.

The role of the mobile command post is only limited by the imagination of their leader. It can be an invaluable tool; it can also be abused. If the mobile command post is over utilized, there will soon be a loss of confidence up and down the continuum of leadership. Determining when and where to use the mobile command post can be a delicate decision. Generally, those in trouble believe they can deal with their own problem or worse yet, may not believe there is a problem to begin with. The people from higher headquarters usually will not be met with open arms no matter how necessary their presence is. This brings us to the point of selection, training and indoctrination. Staffing of a mobile command post must not be a last minute selection process.

Members of the mobile command post must be especially selected long before deployment. While the most knowledgeable person in marketing may seem like the logical candidate, knowing that he or she has an abrasive personality and generally tends to turn people off should get them red-lined from the team. Additionally do not select a person for the reason that it will be good experience for them. While it is true those on the mobile team will profit from having participated, that is not its purpose. Select experienced, highly respected, people who have good interpersonal relationship skills.

The team membership list is not a secret. It should be a standing published list continuously updated as membership turns over for various reasons. An effective way for the CEO to stay engaged in the process is to occasionally discuss mobile command post operations as an agenda item when the department heads are assembled. The CEO has reviewed the names before hand and says, for example, to the chief financial officer that he does not know a recent addition to the mobile command post team, John Doe, and asks for some background information on him. The CEO responds to the CFO's description by pointing out that his qualifications sound acceptable as long as the chief financial officer is personally comfortable that he is qualified, can be a good team member and will represent the headquarters with dignity. The CEO has made the point clearly to everyone that the mobile command post is important (an agenda item); he or she is personally interested in this issue; members must meet certain criteria; and while selection of members is the department heads' prerogative, the CEO will hold them personally responsible for knowing and training the team members.

How big should the mobile command post be? Small. Unfortunately, at times the size of the team is inversely proportional to the competence and confidence of the leader. It points up the importance of having a strong competent mobile team leader. This has become easier today with the ability to reach back in real time, often by video if necessary and tap into a pool of subject matter experts. The team going forward can be overwhelming to those on the receiving end; the larger the team the more overwhelming it will be. Furthermore travel expenses, accommodations and office space are all factors. Keep it small.

One of my personal experiences as a mobile command post leader occurred while stationed in Hawaii as a one-star Brigadier General. In 1991 a volcano named Mount Pinatubo, erupted in the Philippines. The largest volcanic event of the twentieth century spewed billions of cubic meters of ash over several days, killing 847 people, displacing about one million others, burying everything for miles around, contaminating the air with microscopic dust and sending a dust cloud into the upper atmosphere that circumvented the globe, disrupting world air traffic. Senior officials in Washington directed the four-star commander-in-chief of the Pacific to send help. Both U.S. military bases in the Philippines, Clark Air Force Base and Subic Bay Naval Base, had been devastated by the eruption. Therefore, the assistance needed to come from outside the Philippines. The mission was to get there immediately by any means available (no commercial air traffic was able to get in or out of the Manila area), set up a command post, make an assessment, meet with President Cory Aquino and report back. I was selected to head the team. I vividly recall the first version of the team member list provided to me by the staff had over two hundred people nominated to go. It was what I call the just-in-case mentality; that is just in case you need an expert on every conceivable subject, insure they are included on the team. We departed Hawaii in an air force cargo plane headed toward the western Pacific knowing we could not yet fly into Manila. The team composition was twelve highly competent, carefully selected majors and myself.

The point of the story is that well-intentioned staff leaders will always want to overload the team and you, as the team leader, cannot let that happen. A team of 200 would have overwhelmed our host, as the whole nation was adversely affected by the eruption and we had the communications to reach-back for advice from subject matter experts when needed. We finally landed the large, long range C141 Air Force aircraft on a small island a couple hundred miles south of Manila. From there we commandeered a smaller cargo plane from the Philippine Air National Guard. It was not pretty but the pilot assured us it would fly and he thought he could get into the area. It did fly, a white-knuckle trip all the way, but we got on the ground, established the command post in the U.S. Embassy's small ballroom, set a series of recovery actions in motion and in about ten days successfully accomplished all we could and returned to Hawaii.

Mobile command posts can be an important adjunct to successful operations. But, as is the case with most things successful, it takes foresight, standards, attention to detail, resources and a little luck.

THE SKUNKWORKS

A skunkworks operation is not appropriate for every organization but a skillfully run skunkworks can be an enormous force multiplier, particularly for those who invent things. You may never have heard the term skunkworks. My definition is, a few personnel in a single place going from concept to prototype, good, fast and cheap. Let's break down this definition.

A SINGLE PLACE. By a single place I mean a building, a laboratory, a room. What a skunkworks needs to accomplish will not work effectively or efficiently with its parts and employees spread out across the country, state, city or even the company's campus. A skunkworks operates off of interaction among the participants; even cubicles can be a deterrent. If possible, a skunkworks has everyone in a single room.

A FEW PEOPLE. Are you trying to come up with a new design for a note pad or an aircraft carrier? The project defines the staffing level of the skunkworks. More is rarely better but especially so when it comes to a skunkworks. The primary reason to keep it small is the criticality of interaction; the larger the group the less the interaction. Problems can hide or get lost in a large group, but not when a few members are depending on you to have researched a solution to a particular problem.

CONCEPT TO PROTOTYPE. Some ideas are not good; some are of sufficient quality but ahead of their time; some have utility but will not result in a marketable product. Sorting all this out is both difficult and necessary. Developing a new product can be incredibly expensive if, from day one, it is looked upon as a full-scale production item. The whole company becomes involved, raw materials are purchased, an assembly line is tooled up, marketing plans are set in motion and money is borrowed for expansion. The company may be betting the farm and lose. It is all about risk and prototyping is a way to test a concept before committing to it.

Certainly financing a skunkworks over time is not cost free but it is a way of managing risk. It is also a way of breeding technology breakthroughs. While the work on one prototype never resulted in anything tangible, what the engineers learned from working that project saved time and effort as it was later applied directly to another undertaking.

Innovation has been the lifeblood of America. We have led the world in bringing new concepts to light and then taking the best of them to full-scale production in our free market economy. Some skunkworks have existed because, at the time, it was all there was to the company. An example is Bill Hewlett and David Packard working in their garage in what later became known as Silicon Valley. On the other end of that spectrum is 3M Corporation that has a skunkworks corporate culture. Their engineers are required to spend about fifteen percent of their time working on pet projects. A great success story resulting from this skunkworks mentality involved a 3M employee, Art Fry, who sang in his church choir. He would use small scraps of paper to mark the pages of the various song selections. The problem was that the loose markers would slip down out of sight or fall out. One day at work he was talking to a friend, Dr. Spence Silver, who had invented a non-permanent adhesive for which he could find no use. From that was born what has become an essential element on almost every desk in the world in an array of colors and sizes, the post-it note®.

GOOD, FAST AND CHEAP. A skunkworks is hands-on, in-your-face work. The prototype quality can be controlled every step of the way. There is no subcontractor half a continent away who may be cutting a corner or two and you, as the project manager, may not know it until it is too late. Goodness can be controlled in a skunkworks.

Speed is relative. A skunkworks may work on a complex

project for years but with the interaction and control a skunkworks provides, it may be on a relatively fast track. Then there are the products, like the post-it note®, appearing on the market in a matter of months after conception.

Just as time is relative, so is expense. While a skunkworks is not for every organization, to a senior leader who is constantly struggling with proof of concept and who has perhaps presided over a couple expensive disasters, making the investment in a skunkworks can be beneficial.

Although it applies primarily to turning an idea into something material, a skunkworks can also be conceptual. Many senior leaders in the military, government and corporations, have a small group of perhaps three to five individuals, who act as a brain trust. They may be referred to as a strategy group or long-range planners but what they have in common is no in-box. They are not caught up in day-to-day activities, they have the benefit of sitting back and looking at the big picture, putting some flesh on a new idea to see what it looks like. It is a way to prototype policy before it gets worked by the entire staff and turned into command-wide directives.

An operational or strategic leader would be well advised to look carefully at the merits of investing in a skunkworks for prototyping things or ideas. They will discover a skunkworks formula looks like this:

Small Team + Small Facility + Small Cost = A Potentially Huge Payoff

I have been fortunate over the past five years to be a part of what I consider a quintessential skunkworks operation. Adjunct to John Hopkins University's central academic operation is an organization called the Applied Physics Laboratory (APL). It is a huge physical plant situated in the countryside between Baltimore and Washington, D.C. While there is a requisite administrative, logistics and maintenance overhead, the majority of the approximately 2800 employees are scientists and engineers including several hundred holding doctorate degrees. APL is one of the premier laboratories in the country; over the past five decades they have completed definitive work in communications, radar, missile and satellite technology.

Ed Lee, for whom I have been providing some counsel on joint warfighting, has a couple dozen young, brilliant, engineers and scientists to whom he is fiercely loyal and they all work in a controlled-entry room in the subbasement. Except for cabinetwork, which is constructed elsewhere on the compound to Ed's specifications, everything else associated with prototype development takes place in that one room. There are no meetings, conferences, in-progress reviews or other distractions. Every person on the project is empowered, getting his or her ideas tried, discarded, accepted, integrated through constant personal interaction. While some of Ed's skunkworks engineers have taken prototypes aboard naval ships, none have had any experience in thinking about joint warfighting from a senior military perspective. Ed was presented with a concept for how a theater commander (such as General Norman Schwarzkopf, commander during the Gulf War) would put together an optimum defense against enemy theater ballistic missiles (recall the SCUD missiles fired from Iraq into Israel and Saudi Arabia during the Gulf War) and air strikes from manned aircraft. This was a real world warfighting capability needed by theater commanders that did not yet exist.

First, Ed tailored the joint team by hiring ADM Leighton Smith (Navy), myself (Lieutenant General, Army), Major General Lee Downer (Air Force) as senior mentors to his team on how to plan for and conduct operations in a joint military environment. Valerie Meadows, who had commanded a United States Army Patriot Air Defense unit and is a computer expert in her own right, rounded out the military contingent of Ed's team.

The secret to success for a skunkworks is the leadership. Ed is absolutely uncompromising. He will not allow a short cut or the easy way when it comes to quality; there is no way to know how good something can actually be unless everyone constantly strives for the best. In addition to quality, Ed is also just short of fanatical when it comes to distractions. Outsiders do not have access to his team for any reason; they remain totally focused on the task at hand. He will not compromise on control. Total, absolute control resides in him and gets exercised everyday in "the cellar." He will not let timelines slip because it is convenient to do so; work seven days a week for a period if necessary, but stay on track. Outside forces always try to intervene and interject; Ed ignores them. If I have heard Ed say this once I've heard it a thousand times, "We will keep our head down, ass up and take that hill."

Focus, a small talented team, few distractions and total control are Ed's keys to getting from concept to prototype, good fast and cheap. Following receipt of that theater air defense concept paper, in fourteen months his team had a functioning prototype for theater-wide air defense planning and execution and it was used in an U.S. Joint Forces exercise, providing absolute proof of concept.

The *Dictionary* defines skunkworks as, "A small, loosely structured corporate research and development unit or subsidiary formed to foster innovation."28 By my description it need not be loosely structured or confined to corporate research and development but I do whole-heartedly agree that a skunkworks fosters innovation. The origin of the term is a bit of Americana; it comes from Al Capps' legendary comic strip, *Li'l Abner.* In the strip, Big Barnsmell's operation where he produced his bootleg Kikapoo Joy Juice was called the "skonkworks."

RED TEAM

The red team concept is a little different than the war council and deserves special note as a leader tool. Use of a red team stems from the thesis that an organization is not going to be completely successful until it gets inside the competition's decision cycle. That is, knowing *what* the competition is capable of doing, about *when* they will act and about *where*. Armed with this information any organization's plan is more likely to succeed. So, where does the information on the competition come from? It is unlikely that we are going to be able to call them up and get the answers we need. An alternative is to form a red team. A red team is a small group, very possibly only two or three individuals, specially selected for the task. They will likely operate only for the duration of a specific operation and are most effective during the early planning and execution phases. The red team's task is to understand the competition, how they operate, how they are organized, their culture, their strengths and vulnerabilities.

If we always have to wait until we are well into execution to understand the results of our plan there will all too often be results with which we are not satisfied. The purpose of the red team is to *be* the competition; look at each element of the plan and provide the boss their best estimate as to what the competition will do once you execute action A, then B, C, etc. The whole purpose is to gain an assessment of how successful an operation is likely to be *before the fact.* Where do red team members come from? In the military the most obvious place is from the intelligence community. Intel officers are professionals who spend their lives trying to understand the enemy. In a business hierarchy at least one of the red team members should come from the bottom echelon in the leadership continuum. These are the members of your organization who butt heads with their competitors on a daily basis, on the street, at the point of execution. Do not underestimate the value of what they can bring to the table just because they are on the first rung of the organizational ladder. We must assume the competition is going to react to our stimulus. Knowing what they will do, about when and where before we go there can often mean the difference between success and failure. A red team can provide a potentially huge payoff for a modest investment in a few people's time and energy. For large complex operations, plans are normally executed in phases.

Keeping the red team active for each phase can be beneficial. For example, your organization is a global industry leader but has concentrated on a U.S. and Asian customer base. You have built a multi-phase campaign plan to expand into Europe. Having executed phase one of the plan, the red team should again be assembled to assess how the competition *actually* reacted vs the red team's previous expectations and from that draw conclusions concerning what the competition will likely do in phase two, phase three, etc.

So far the red team's focus has been as that of the competition. However, its uses are only limited by a leader's imagination. Another effective use is to think like the customer. This can provide fast, inexpensive feedback during the planning phase prior to launching a new product or to determine what the impact will likely be if a current product is changed. Every leader is looking for an edge over the competition; a red team can be an inexpensive yet effective tool to achieve that advantage and can be invaluable when it comes time to build a strategy.

COACH

One final thought on organizing for action. Remember all you are attempting to do is find a way to optimize the organization you have and make it most effective and efficient. Sometimes all you need is a little coaching from a subject matter expert. They are out there on every subject, you just have to find them and tap into their minds.

I have a business partner, Rusty Petrea, who is a master at finding and using coaches. Two ventures he is currently involved with are building a wine import business and constructing a personal golf course. On day one of both projects his personal level of expertise was near zero. For the wine business he and his wife cast out a wide net and came up with at least a half dozen experts on issues ranging from how to find the right wines, to how to get the required government permits, to shipping, handling, storing and marketing quality Italian wines. What the coaching has allowed them to do is to get smart quickly, work many of the issues simultaneously and take the business from a vision to execution in less than eighteen months.

Simultaneously, Rusty has been working his vision to build a personal 18-hole, three-green golf course. Again, the first thing he did was to line up a group of subject matter experts to coach him on dirt, grading, drainage, grass, greens architecture, irrigation, etc. With this assistance he will get from vision to the inaugural golf tournament in a little over a year. Using coaches is low cost with the potential for enormous value added and is applicable to every leader at every level.

CO-CAPTAINS

There is no intent to end this chapter on a negative note, but on the subject of organizing for action something needs to be said about co-leadership. The appointment of co-captains is an acceptable concept for a high school football team, one from the offense and one from the defense. They have few, if any, substantive responsibilities and little, if any, authority. Appointing co-captains is a way to recognize players for their hard work, the example they bring and perhaps for being a leader on the playing field. Being a co-captain of the football team or cheerleading squad is more ceremony than substance, as it should be. But when we see grown, responsible individuals from large important corporations merging their companies and announcing they will be co-CEOs, watch out. While we recognize leadership is an art and not a science, there are some physical laws that apply. One of those laws is that two people cannot sit comfortably in the same chair. One result of having co-captains will be two blurred leadership continuums superimposed over each other with no clarity for either. Loyalties, up and down the continuum, will be divided. In the real world, where leaders have to actually lead and make tough choices, "co" is a four-letter word and a perfect formula for failure.

RECAP

1. Leaders must put the right pieces in the right places at the right time for all the right reasons with a goal of tailoring the organization to create synergism.
2. A chief of staff is a force multiplier. Every large organization should have one.
3. Normally born out of crisis, the war council may be a senior leader's only vehicle to arrive at viable solutions on a tight time-line.
4. A kitchen cabinet can be an invaluable informal group mentoring an operational or strategic leader on vision and direction.
5. The role of a mobile command post is only limited by the imagination of senior leaders, but keep it small.
6. The skunkworks formula: small team + small facility + small cost = a potentially huge payoff.
7. Co-captains are fine for the high school football team, but in the real world co-leaders is a formula for failure.

ENDURING LEADERSHIP PRINCIPLES

Great leaders:
Optimize the talent in their organization.

CHAPTER NINE

MOLDING THE CORPORATE CULTURE

A Culture Exists In Every Organization; It Is A Powerful And Pervasive Force.

A culture exists within every organization; it is a powerful force that must be understood and continuously nurtured. An organization can have either a singular or multi-faceted culture which can have a positive or negative overall impact. An existing culture could be the result of a long-term deliberate internal campaign or it could have haphazardly developed over time and be difficult to define. Those inside the organization may be so close to the issue they cannot realize the impact a negative culture is having. It may, therefore, fall to the kitchen cabinet members to inform an operational or strategic leader what is really going on with respect to the organization's culture. The tools in this toolbox are more subjective, but nonetheless important.

The purpose of this chapter is to discuss and provide examples of what a corporate culture is.

The word corporate is simply used here as a synonym for any large organization. Culture, a factor in every organization's day-to-day activities, is not confined to the corporate business world but is also applicable to virtually any organization: the military, church, political parties, government agencies, charitable organizations, etc.

Among the multiple types of cultures found in organizations, one of the most important is associated with character. It is an issue of goodness. Do the policies of an organization demonstrate that the leadership genuinely cares for its people? Is there a written or unwritten code of ethics? Are policies of caring executed vigorously or just in the policies and procedures manual for show? Can the people of this organization be believed? Are honesty and integrity hallmarks of the organization or is its character such that how its leaders will react from event to event is unknown? Are decisions rendered in a compassionate manner? The character of an organization can no more be camouflaged than can that of an individual. Character is easily recognizable because it resonates from every action and decision. Leaders at every level establish the character for their organization by their personal example. Character is fragile and must be constantly nurtured and checked.

There is a story in American business that demonstrates a culture of caring. William Procter and his brother-in-law, James Gamble, formed Procter & Gamble in 1837. Initially they manufactured candles and soap. Ivory Soap® became a success when too much steam was accidentally introduced into a batch of soap and it made the bar float. The public loved it. While still successful, by the mid-1880s the company was in internal turmoil, suffering fourteen strikes and 50 percent turnover within a two-year span. Procter knew the company had to make a cultural shift; his employees needed to be heard and issues resolved.

The founding Procter's grandson, William Procter, wrote an article in 1919 entitled *How We Divide With Our Men* chronicling a generation of work to shift the corporate culture to one of caring and sharing. Procter & Gamble undertook a whole series of positive employee actions in the late 1880s. They were the first company to engage in profit sharing with employees. Other innovations included giving Saturday afternoons off with pay, providing insurance benefits and setting up a stock ownership program. They established an employee committee to ensure communications were open between leaders and subordinates at every level.

During World War I Procter & Gamble employees consistently worked overtime and were paid time and a half. The company knew that when the war was over they would have to cut back to a normal eight-hour day, which would mean considerably less pay for most employees. William Procter asked the workers to meet and recommend a new pay scale. The committee report speaks volumes about the corporate culture that had been put in place over the previous thirty years. The employees' reported that they wanted the eight-hour workday but decided unanimously not to specify what the wage should be. They acknowledged that Procter & Gamble leaders had always treated them fairly and were confident they would continue to do so. Soon thereafter corporate leaders announced a new eight-hour wage scale that would provide employees as much compensation as they had previously received for ten hours work. At Procter & Gamble every employee suggestion was considered and implemented, unless it was deemed impractical. William Procter said of this, "I always feel that if I talk with our men and cannot convince them that they are wrong, the chances are they are right."

Procter wrote in 1919, "The chief problem of 'big business' today is to shape its policies so that each worker, whether in office or factory, will feel he is a vital part of his company."29 The problem Procter defined was not confined to his generation. Although it is true that there are generational shifts in attitudes, beliefs and strength of character, building employee loyalty is as important today as it was in 1919 or one thousand years ago regardless of the type organization. Procter understood the importance and power of a corporate culture based on genuine caring and sharing.

A corporate culture can also flow from policies and procedures; rules that everyone in the organization is expected to follow. There is a military example that illustrates this point perfectly. The United States Army has operated the disciplinary barracks at Fort Leavenworth, Kansas since 1875. The disciplinary barracks is the only long-term maximum-security confinement facility in the Defense Department, incarcerating about 500 armed forces personnel convicted of serious offenses. Regardless of the crime, every new prisoner is first housed on the sixth floor of the prison. Those convicted of the most heinous crimes such as murder never leave the sixth floor. But, for example, a nineteen-year-old soldier convicted of possession of a few grams of marijuana is not a thief, not a serious threat to society but is a convicted felon with a three-year sentence. He is given a strict, totally uncompromising set of rules to live by on the sixth floor. After a set period of time and if his conduct has been perfect, he is moved to the fifth floor where there are some perks, such as television privileges, as well as a new set of somewhat less strict rules. And the process continues floor by floor until he could be outside the prison all day working on the prison farm where they grow most of their own food, the cabinet shop building furniture, the flower shop, etc. He may even live in an unguarded barracks outside the prison walls. However, just one breach of the rules and he is not backed up one level or two levels, he is back on the sixth floor. It is a powerful corporate culture based on a code of how one is to conduct one's self and it works.

Operational considerations can also define a corporate culture. An example of an operational culture in retail is Nordstrom department store. In 1901, John W. Nordstrom used his stake from the Alaska gold rush to open a small shoe store in Seattle. The Nordstrom family of employees built a thriving business on the principles of quality, value, selection and service. As stated in their web site, nordstrom.com, "As we celebrate our 100th Anniversary and a century of service, we remain committed to the simple idea our company was founded on, earning the trust of our customers, one at a time."30 Nordstrom deliberately built a reputation around the concept of uncompromising customer service, no matter how obnoxious or ungrateful that customer might be. This operating culture is not without risk. It is easy for Nordstrom's strategic leadership to espouse the policy and advertise it, but in the final analysis the culture is at the mercy of the most recently hired sales associate. Nordstrom's operating culture is put to the test thousands of times a day, not in the corporate headquarters offices but at the point of execution on the sales floor of every store. The Nordstrom commitment to a culture goes far beyond corporate policy. What is the criteria for hiring new employees, how are they trained, how are they evaluated on their job performance, what happens to those who do not work out? Defining and executing a corporate culture for operational considerations requires a commitment of both time and resources.

But, even with a pledge from the strategic leaders, dedication to an operational culture does not always work and sometimes the reason it does not is because it is just simply a bad idea. As a junior officer in the United States Army, I and about a million of my fellow soldiers, was subjected to a new operating theme called "zero defects." It had a nice ring to it and was easy to comprehend what was desired. Leaders at all levels are accountable for how things are going for their team or group; ultimately every first-line leader in the United States Army, under this new operating policy, was held responsible for having zero defects. The policy was successful in that it quickly imposed a corporate culture. That was the good news. The bad news was that the culture caused most people to operate from inside your comfort zone because if they went outside the "box" they were likely to get into unfamiliar territory, make a mistake and have a "defect." Not achieving zero defects became synonymous with failure. If the leader was labeled a failure he or she concluded it had to have been because the subordinates let them down. The unspoken leader directions to subordinates was to stay in the box and just do the things we have always done and not been criticized for. Innovation, which habitually flows from the bottom up, stopped and therefore the Army stagnated. It was awful and the timing could not have been worse. The Army leadership was still searching for new doctrine and structure twenty years after the end of World War II. Zero defects came along at a time when innovation and change were desperately needed; we were at the front end of what would be a long war in Vietnam. There were a host of political and military reasons for our failures in Vietnam and the zero defects culture certainly was a contributing factor.

Failing to learn from the zero defects debacle, the Army did it again in the early 1970s. The United States had rescinded the draft and the military services were struggling with the transition to an all-volunteer force. This was also a time of general societal unrest brought on by anti-Vietnam demonstrations, anti-authority attitudes, the civil rights movement and the drug culture.

The Army needed a slogan to get the all-volunteer force movement energized. The recruiting catchphrase to America's young adults was, "The Army Wants to Join You." Translation, bring your lifestyle, your haircut, your racial biases, your drug culture, your anti-authority attitude, even your criminal record and we will become a team. As an organization, the United States Army barely survived that period because without discipline and respect for authority it was a pathetic warfighting machine. Particularly at the direct level, leaders were greatly hampered because the "employees" had been told by the "board of directors" to dictate the corporate culture. It took a vision and years of hard work to turn all that around. One of the many factors in turning the corner was a new recruiting slogan, "Be All You Can Be", one of the most successful lines in the history of advertising.

Conversely, one of the great success stories in establishing a corporate culture also comes from the United States Army. The purpose of relating this series of events is to emphasize the necessity for commitment in time, energy, personnel and dollars to correct a bad situation such as the one described above in the 1970's Army.

Creating a new positive corporate culture, takes a senior visionary leader within the organization to not only change the culture but also get the changes institutionalized.

First, a little background to set the scene as to why the Army needed to change. For generations each unit in the Army underwent an evaluation called an annual training test (ATT). This would be the focus of several months of effort, working on basic tactics, techniques and procedures, moving on to more complex operations, all of this culminating in the ATT conducted by the tested unit's next higher command. Some unit evaluations were easy, some hard, some fair, some impossible, depending in large measure on the personality and professionalism of the testing commander. The results were pass or fail and if you failed the unit would normally be retested within a couple of months. If you passed, there was a big sigh of relief, a few weeks spent basking in the glory and then the unit started all over again moving toward the next annual test. This system of peaking annually for a single performance could not sustain combat readiness for the Army as a whole. Furthermore, there was no Army-wide standard applied to the tests and therefore no way of knowing if a unit that just failed based on standard prescribed by a specific testing commander was perhaps more combat ready than an identical unit at another installation that passed under less demanding criteria. . There was a pass/fail mentality, there was cronyism involved and there was no way to measure Army-wide readiness. The result was a situation wherein the integrity of the institution was constantly in question.

While most senior leaders in the Army ultimately became involved in the transition to a new culture, the single senior visionary who drove the culture shift was General Carl Vuono who capped his distinguished career in the Army's most senior position, Army Chief of Staff. As a Major General and division commander in Germany, Vuono had the vision for change and drafted the training doctrine to make it happen. He not only experimented with new training procedures in his division, he influenced a generation of officers who were assigned to his command. During the succeeding years two things occurred that had a significant impact on the success of the culture shift. First, following division command, Vuono held three key positions at the three and four-star levels where he was able to advance his doctrine and begin to bring the whole Army aboard. The day he became Chief of Staff of the Army his first order of business was to change the status of the new training doctrine from "draft" to "approved." Then he set about institutionalizing it during his four-year tenure. Secondly, two colonels in Vuono's division, Gordon Sullivan and Dennis Reimer would follow Vuono as Chief of Staff of the Army thereby providing twelve consecutive years of consistent policy from the highest position in the organization.

The new training and readiness culture General Vuono brought about began with the concept that everything an officer and enlisted person is expected to do can be identified as a "task." There is a set of common tasks for everyone, individual skill tasks for different grades and specialties and collective tasks for leaders of all organizations, squad through corps. Entire organizations had to be formed to sort out the tasks and put them in writing. It was an enormous undertaking. Then, for every task, a condition had to be stated and for those conditions, a standard was dictated. Task, condition and standard became a whole new way of thinking about how to go about preparing and sustaining combat ready organizations.

For every task and condition there is a standard, a single Army-wide standard for every task for every soldier. With this concept came consistency in Army training; a soldier transferring from Germany to Fort Sill, Oklahoma would find his or her new unit training the same tasks to the same standards as the unit they departed from. As a result, the impact of inevitable turnover was drastically reduced.

While all proficiency is perishable, expertise for different tasks dissipates over varying time intervals. It is analogous to watching pre-season football games. Generally the team's timing is off, they commit too many penalties and the offense finds it difficult to sustain long drives and score points. With this new system the Army could determine, for example, that if an infantry platoon had not been in the field training to its collective tasks for the past sixty days, their proficiency had likely fallen below combat ready status; just as the football team that had not been on the playing field for several months is not ready for the season's opening game. This provided a way to constantly measure readiness at all levels at all times consistently throughout the Army. The integrity of the readiness system had been restored.

Most people are competitive by nature. Putting a standard in front of a soldier or a leader is like waving a red flag in front of a bull. The task/condition/standard concept took root in soldier basic training. Each drill sergeant was to bring a recruit along to the point where he or she could perform, let's say for example, one hundred individual tasks to standard by graduation day. Drill sergeant Jones had trained 110 tasks to standard during the last cycle; so drill sergeant Smith, not to be outdone, pushed just a little bit harder during the next cycle and trained 115 tasks to standard. Then there is the question of the standard itself. While the Army standard is to be able to perform a particular task in sixty seconds, one soldier believes he can do it consistently in fifty seconds; competitive juices began to flow and fellow soldiers followed suit. In complex collective tasks all across the Army the bar kept being raised. The institution was in competition with itself, being all it could be.

It then became incumbent on operational and strategic leaders to capitalize on the momentum of the culture shift. Raising the bar on the training environment was one way to do so. Recall as a youngster playing cops and robbers or war games; "Bang, bang, you're dead," "No I'm not, you missed me." We had to get beyond that in the Army. Therefore, for training purposes, every weapon in the United States Army today is equipped with a small attachment that fires a directional beam of energy along with blank ammunition. Every soldier, officer and enlisted, in training is also required to wear a small receiver on their helmet. If the receiver activates, you have been "shot" and become a casualty. The soldier then pulls a sealed card out of his pocket and it tells his buddy or his leader the severity of the wound, dead, sucking chest wound, broken leg, etc.; it has to be dealt with. It may be 2 a.m., zero illumination, cold, raining, muddy and there is a soldier (not a doctor, not a nurse, not a medic) inserting a real IV into his or her buddy's arm while their squad leader is bringing a med-evac helicopter into an unimproved landing zone. Realism had been brought to daily training. You would have had to be there in the 1970s to see how pathetic the United States Army had become to fully appreciate taking a million-person organization and completely changing its culture down to the last soldier. It has to be one of the great success stories in America.

What can direct, operational or strategic leaders take away from this story about the Army's cultural transition and put into their day-to-day functioning leadership toolboxes?

- Senior leaders need to frequently spend some quality time assessing the culture of their organization. They need to be pragmatic and recognize that they may be too close to the organization to accurately assess the culture. If they come to that conclusion, they need to seek outside help, perhaps from the kitchen cabinet, in making the evaluation.

- Having concluded that there needs to be a change in the organization's culture, the senior leader needs to have a vision of the end-state while recognizing in the early stages of change that all of the details will not be immediately comprehensible.

- Leaders must recognize it may take years or even a generation for changes to take hold. Leadership progression becomes very important because if succeeding leaders hesitate in the transition to a new culture the momentum can be lost and the organization can be left in turmoil with a half-baked solution.

- Establishing a desired corporate culture will take resources, lots of resources, perhaps resources not envisioned during the early stages of cultural transition. The simple yet enormous undertaking to define every task for every soldier in every grade in every specialty in the

United States Army was not one of General Vuono's initial resourcing objectives.

- There is nothing more potentially traumatic for an organization's personnel than to change its culture and it cannot be accomplished with a simple decree or in a short period of time. Leaders have to stay tuned in as the corporate culture transitions, sense where it is going well, dig out the naysayers, deal with them and seize the moment when it is time to move to the next level. The process is very subjective and it takes a courageous, sensitive, well-trained leader to pull it all together.

Because creating a culture is one of the most important and difficult tasks they undertake, leaders must use every resource at their disposal. For example, the war council can help brainstorm courses of action and determine the means required. For a large organization, changing the culture may necessitate the creation of a mobile training team to teach all leaders how to properly conduct an after action review. A senior leader in the midst of a corporate culture shift may need to hear periodically from his kitchen cabinet members who can give the leader a confidence boost that the culture is taking hold in spite of the grumbling from the timid souls whose comfort zone is being invaded. No leader should attempt to create or change a corporate culture unless totally committed, properly resourced, prepared to work it for years and ready to do battle against those who oppose it. And rest assured there will be subordinates who are not in favor of change. They can be grouped into several categories:

- Opponents: Some are so adamantly opposed they become roadblocks and have to be removed.
- The here-and-nowers: Those who live in the present and simply cannot grasp the vision; recognize them and bring them along, educating them, one concept at a time.
- Fence sitters: Those who are not openly opposed, but also not very supportive. They want to be able to jump to either side, depending which would benefit them the most. Drive

on toward success and eventually they will fall in line, but recognize them for what they are, self-serving individuals who should not be advanced in the organization.

- Supporters: Among them may be those honest souls who initially voiced an opposing view but once the decision was made, got on board and became active proponents. Use them as spokespersons; move them to key positions even to the extent of removing a vocal naysayer and replacing them with an ally. Such an action will send a powerful message or even a shock wave throughout the organization.

There is an old saying, "For every complex problem there is a simple solution and it is usually wrong." That is especially true when it comes to changing or shifting an organization's culture. It will always be an extraordinarily complex undertaking because what are being changed are peoples' beliefs and attitudes for which there is no quick, simple solution. It cannot be done with a memo, email, phone call, off-site, or a directive; it is every leader's ultimate challenge.

THE AFTER ACTION REVIEW

There is one final point to be made concerning the Army's transition. Perhaps the most significant culture shift came about as the result of institutionalizing the after action review, the AAR. In the United States Army the AAR is religion; for every training event, no matter how small, there *will be* an AAR. It is an integral part of the training. Time is allocated for the AAR when the training is planned. The after action review *is* training and that is the culture shift. Every leader is schooled in how to conduct an AAR, but the AAR is not designed just for the military alone, on the contrary, it is applicable to any organization, at any level, engaged in any activity. It can be a powerful tool for every leader if used properly and frequently enough to become part of the organization's makeup, standard operating procedure and culture.

In order to gain a better understanding of the after action review, it is necessary to dissect it by looking at the who/what/where/why and how, beginning with why. The details presented here are for the most part contained in a United States Army publication, *Training Circular 25-20.31*

WHY CONDUCT AN AFTER ACTION REVIEW? Leaders at every level must use every opportunity to improve employee, subordinate leader and organizational performance. To do so they must find a way to determine what happened and what did not happen during critical events. The after action review is the best tool available to identify deficiencies, how to correct them, how to sustain strengths and focus on high performance.

WHAT IS AN AFTER ACTION REVIEW? An after action review is a professional discussion of an event, focused on performance standards, that enables leaders and employees to discover for themselves what happened, what did not happen and why it happened. It is a tool leaders and organizations use to get maximum benefit from every task and event. The AAR provides candid insights into specific employee leader and organizational strengths and weaknesses from various perspectives; feedback and insight critical to ongoing operations; and details often lacking in an after action report compiled by an individual.

Feedback compares the *actual output* of a process with the *intended outcome*. By focusing on the standards that were expected and by describing specific observations, leaders and subordinates together decide how to improve their performances. Because leaders participating in the AAR actively discover what happened and why, they learn more than they would from a critique alone. A critique only gives one viewpoint and frequently provides little opportunity for discussion of events by participants. The after action review has several distinct advantages over a critique:

- It is not the objective of an AAR to judge either success or failure.
- The AAR specifically focuses on what was to have been accomplished, while the climate of the critique keys on what went wrong, thereby preventing candid discussion of events and stifling learning and team building.

- Generally more people participate in an AAR which automatically enhances the chances of leaning from the strengths and weaknesses.
- The basic fabric of the AAR is to discover why things did or did not happen.

All after action reviews follow the same general format, involving the exchange of ideas and observations and focusing on improving proficiency. After action reviews are conducted during and/or immediately after the event; focus on intended objectives; focus on individual, team and leader performance; involve all or nearly all participants in the discussion; use open-ended questions; are related to a set of expectations or standards; determine strengths and weaknesses; and link performance to subsequent operations.

WHO SHOULD ATTEND THE AFTER ACTION REVIEW? As many of the participants as possible should attend the AAR. At the direct leader level, it should routinely be possible for every subordinate to not only attend but also be an active participant. For operational and strategic leaders it may be impossible to have every person who touched the project attend the AAR, but as many of the key persons as possible must be there. At the strategic level for example, assume the President of the United States directs an after action review surrounding events and actions that occurred during the six months following the 9/11 terrorist attacks. There were tens of thousands of federal employees involved and they could not all attend a single AAR. The President's AAR might include only the Cabinet Secretaries, key White House personnel and the leaders in the House and Senate from both political parties. This AAR would review what did, did not, should, should not have happened at the most senior levels, focusing on policy, information flow and inter-governmental actions. But this should not be the only AAR concerning 9/11 actions. Inside each federal department and agency, AARs should take place to review what did and did not happen at those levels. Furthermore, AARs would be conducted within the various sub elements of the departments. So, just within the federal government, on the issue 9/11 alone there could have been, should have been, hundreds of after action reviews. Now think about the impact 9/11 had across the nation and the applicability of after action reviews for every state and local government, corporate America, schools, literally every organization affected in some way by the actual events of that day or the potential impact of additional terrorist attacks. The bottom line on who should attend the AAR is the maximum number of people possible.

WHERE IS THE AFTER ACTION REVIEW CONDUCTED? By far the best place to conduct an after action review is on site. If the objective was to build a bridge, go to the bridge. If the project was a crises planning action where everyone worked in one large room and interacted over long hours and days, have the AAR there where the action was and where everyone can better relate to what happened and did not happen.

HOW IS THE AFTER ACTION REVIEW CONDUCTED? After action reviews can be formal or informal. Formal AARs should be planned from the outset as part of the project or event. There should be a pre-designated place, a known list of attendees, an AAR leader and a specified time. Informal AARs are on-the-spot coaching tools conducted in the middle of an on-going event for the purpose of providing immediate feedback and discovering what changes can be immediately implemented. For example, there may be a designated production rate on an assembly line. The leader knows the goal is achievable but the team is not performing to standard. The leader should stop the line and conduct an informal AAR. Get the employees to think about and discuss what is going right, what is going wrong and determine what needs to be done in order to meet their quota.

The key to the actual conduct of an after action review is the spirit in which it is carried out. The environment and climate surrounding an AAR must be one in which the employees and subordinate leaders openly and honestly discuss what actually transpired in sufficient detail and clarity that not only will everyone understand what did and did not occur and why, they will, more importantly have a strong desire to seek the opportunity to do it better the next time. The following techniques will help create an atmosphere conducive to maximum participation: the AAR leader should enter the discussion only when necessary to move the process along or get it back on track; reinforce the fact that it is permissible and encouraged to disagree; focus on learning and encourage participants to have the courage of their convictions and express opinions; and use open-ended and leading questions to guide the discussion.

These are steps that can be followed in conducting an AAR:

- Open the discussion by reviewing its purpose and sequence to ensure that everyone understands what an AAR is and how it works. For example, you can point out that the after action review is a dynamic, candid, professional discussion that focuses on performance against a standard. Everyone's' insights and observations will help the organization identify and correct deficiencies or maintain strengths. The AAR is not a critique. No one, regardless of rank, position, or strength of personality, has all of the information or answers. The AAR will not grade success or failure.

- Review the mission and intent of the project for which the AAR is being conducted. That is, *what was supposed to happen*. Use maps, operational graphics, posters, or other visual aides to highlight what needs to be discussed. Ask subordinate leaders to restate what they believed their mission was.

- Summarize events. That is, *what actually happened*. The AAR leader should guide the review using a logical sequence of events to describe and discuss what happened. Avoid asking yes or no questions. Rather open-ended questions have no specific answer and allow people to reply based on what was significant to them.

Open-ended questions are also less likely to put people on the defensive. For example, consider the case of an organization that just concluded the deployment of their crisis action team and is beginning the AAR. This is a standing team of on-call members, one of whom is on duty at all times after normal operating hours for the purpose of initiating crisis team actions. The AAR leader begins by asking the duty officer if she used the recall roster.

Response: "Yes."

Leader: "Was it OK?"

Response: "Ya, it was all right."

Leader: "No problems?"

Response: "Nothing major."

This obviously is going nowhere fast. The reason why is that the AAR leader is using questions that generally can be answered with a "yes" or "no". Open-ended questions are much more effective and are also less likely to put people on the defensive.

The use of open-ended questions that have no specific answer will allow people to reply based on what was significant to them and will tend to emphasize accountability. Let's start the AAR over.

Leader: "What did you do first when the call came in concerning the crisis?"

Response: "I began the recall of team members."

Leader: "And?"

Response: "I reached nearly everyone."

Leader: "Who was not reached?"

About now John recognizes he is going to have to take responsibility for his actions so he raises his hand and admits, "She couldn't reach me because I was on vacation and had failed to put my assistant on the roster." Then the chief of staff interjects, "Boss, I'll take this for action and insure we are three deep on the recall roster.

Leader: "Good, let's move on. What was the most significant factor during the first hour?"

Response (from several members): "The press. The word leaked out and we were swamped by press queries."

Leader (to the public affairs officer): "What about it, Jim?"

Jim: "I'm not on the team and didn't know about the press problem for several hours. No one called me."

Chief of staff: "Boss, we need a top to bottom review of the team composition, I have it for action."

The questioning technique can have an enormous impact on the success and usefulness of an AAR. What was emerging from the crisis team AAR was what actually happened vs what was supposed to have happened and accountability by the participants.

The AAR is not a critique or lecture; the leader does not tell the participants what was good or bad. However, the AAR leader must ensure specific issues are revealed, both positive and negative in nature. Skillful guidance of the discussion will make certain the AAR does not gloss over mistakes or organizational weaknesses.

One of the strengths of the AAR is the flexibility of its format. There are several techniques that can be used to guide the discussion. The most obvious is the chronological order of events; this technique is logical, structured and easy for everyone to follow. An alternative approach is to focus on separate operating functions such as marketing, finance, research or production. However, leaders using this method must be careful not to become engaged in a long discussion of a specific operating element and lose sight of the big picture. Another method is to sort out key events and discuss them one by one. This may be particularly effective when time is limited and it is essential that participants not get sidetracked.

On the use of statistics during an AAR, recognize they can be a double-edged sword. While statistics provide facts to reinforce strengths and weaknesses, the danger lies in statistics for statistics' sake. Chart after chart of ratios, bar graphs and tables quickly lends itself to a grading of performance. This stifles discussion and degrades the AAR's value. Statistics and statistics-based charts should be used only to identify critical trends or issues and to reinforce teaching points.

The after action review is an activity wherein leaders are willing to stand up in front of peers and subordinates and publicly take responsibility for their actions. When, for the first time, subordinates hear their leader state that he or she understands the reason the organization did not succeed was because insufficient resources were allocated or decided on too late, this may be a culture shift of major proportions. It may not be easy to institutionalize the after action review, but having done so the honesty, integrity, trust and loyalty that flows from its use will strengthen an organization beyond measure.

Establishing, molding and maintaining a corporate culture is both a challenge and a never-ending responsibility for every leader. Those who fail to recognize the power and importance of a corporate culture or are unwilling to actively work the issue must be content to lead in an environment that is not of their choosing.

RECAP

1. A corporate culture exists within every organization. It is a dominant and omnipresent force. It may be either helping or hurting the organization.

2. An organization's character is by far its most important cultural trait. Without trust, honesty, integrity and a genuine caring attitude emanating from the leadership, an organization will struggle every day.

3. To build a new culture or attempt to alter an existing one, the starting point must be a clear vision of the end-state.

4. Leaders must steadfastly resolve to stay on course and resource the transition. It may take many years for a new or altered culture to become institutionalized and a part of the organization's fabric.

5. Every leader should anticipate active opposition to change.

6. The after action review, if properly used by every leader

in the organization, can have a greater positive impact than any other daily activity and become the basis for an operating culture in any organization.

ENDURING LEADERSHIP PRINCIPLES

Great leaders:

Establish and cultivate a positive culture.

CHAPTER TEN

THREE PILLARS OF LEADER DEVELOPMENT

Leader Development Is The Second Most Important Responsibility Of Leaders At All Levels. It Is Called Building A Bench.

You are the CEO of a thriving corporation, the business is entering into a critical period and all systems will be at full throttle. Your chief of staff, your right hand man, suddenly becomes critically ill and is indefinitely, perhaps permanently, unavailable. Simultaneously a couple of key leaders announce their abrupt departure to a competitor. You need help, fast. Is this the time to spend weeks conducting an external talent search for replacements? After finding the right personnel, can they get up to speed in time to help you through this operation? There are leaders who believe turnover is inevitable, are constantly going to the headhunters for replacements, spend too much time interviewing applicants and yet cannot understand why their organization seems unsettled.

On every leader's short list of things to do, right up there next to setting a positive example and establishing a value-based corporate culture, must be leader development. Because leadership is an art, there is a skill set associated with being an effective leader that cannot be assimilated all at once or even over a short period. Becoming a good leader is an iterative process of learning and practicing at each step of the way. A leader development program must be in place and functioning in order to orchestrate this learning and practicing process.

The purpose of this chapter is to provide architecture for an organization-wide leader development program.

Recall the comments in the introduction concerning Helmuth von Moltke, the prolific author and brilliant military strategist. One of Moltke's greatest, lasting contributions is in his writings on leaders and leadership. During his thirty-year reign as Chief of the Prussian and German General Staff, Moltke completely changed the training for military leaders because he recognized that technology (railroads) had changed the battlefield into a vast battlespace supplied by rail. Larger battlespace necessitated decentralized operations and therefore decentralized decision-making. Success was measured by how well subordinate commanders could make timely decisions on their own and work from an understanding of their senior leader's intent. Moltke came to the conclusion that, one cannot rely on natural genius for the development of senior leaders. From that assertion he set about changing the entire culture of his officer corps. Leaders are not appointed; leaders develop over long periods of time, through hard work, planning, resourcing and mentoring. That one cannot rely on natural genius for the development of senior leaders is a powerful statement sending a compelling message about the importance of leader development and the overall culture of an organization.

Leader development is a leadership commitment; it is never ending and it is multifaceted. Leader development is expensive in time and resources and simultaneously one of the most cost-effective programs an organization can have. Leaders have to unwaveringly commit to a formal program and be an active participant. While it takes a truckload of toolboxes to build a house there is one special toolbox for the electrician. In it are the tools necessary to eventually make the electrical system function. Using this analogy, the leadership truck has arrived; let's find the toolbox for leader development and describe some of the tools available to every leader.

Leader development is all about building a bench and keeping it filled with good people. Recall the CEO above who is having a personnel crisis. The leaders who come through these situations in good shape are the ones who can look to the bench and pull up a leader in training to fill the void. Is that person from the bench equal to the person you unexpectedly lost? Perhaps not, but you have the advantage of knowing their strengths and weaknesses, and can therefore know when you may have to step in to help them along. Those from the bench are ready now, eager and are already part of the team. Being on the team is more than mere presence; it is knowing others' capabilities, the operating procedures and the corporate culture. Occasionally, to everyone's great surprise and pleasure, a rookie brought up to fill a critical void turns out to be a diamond in the rough.

Early in the 1999 National Football League season, the St. Louis Rams' starting quarterback went down with an injury. Coach Dick Vermeil could have quickly looked around the country for a proven, recently retired quarterback and offered him five million dollars to come back and play. But instead, he turned to the bench to Kurt Warner, a virtual unknown to both league insiders and fans. What even coach Vermeil did not know was the strength, resolve, skill and leadership that would surface virtually overnight. Warner demonstrated instant leadership and incredible technical skill, leading his team from their habitual low standing in the league to a Super Bowl victory. He knew the operating procedures (the play book), the weekly game preparation routine, what his bosses expected and the strengths and weaknesses of his teammates. Coach Vermeil recognized the importance of these positives in the midst of a crisis (the crisis being a game coming up on Sunday that could not be postponed) and went to the bench rather than to the market place.

As with anything that is beneficial and worthwhile, building a bench is hard work. But the payoff is enormous. The two most significant long-term benefits are loyalty and stability.

STABILITY

The old adage about the grass always being greener on the other side of the fence is a human failing with which many leaders are confronted. People are always looking for something better, whether it is better pay, a better office, a better retirement plan, a better commute, better perks or a better boss. A leader's challenge is to convince each individual in the organization that better is right here and a key tool in doing so is leader development. Demonstrating leader development fosters long-term stability. If employees can see that they are being looked at, looked after and groomed for advancement they are much less likely to be looking over the fence for greener pastures.

Many of you, from your leadership studies, are familiar with the famous experiment conducted by Harvard Business School professor, Elton Mayo between 1927 and 1932 on the shop floors of the Western Electric Hawthorne Works in Chicago. Working conditions were improved for a select group of women on the assembly line and production increased dramatically. The initial conclusion was that better working conditions equals better output. Then the conditions were returned to their original norm and production went up even more.32 The reality is that people need to believe someone cares about them and recognizes they are critical members of the organization. A leader development program is an essential weapon in a leader's arsenal as he fights for stability in the work force. A corporate culture of caring reinforced by a leader development program that clearly demonstrates a promote-from-within policy, contributes to a more stable and consistent work force at all levels.

LOYALTY

The second benefit of a good leader development program is loyalty. During the past generation of professional sports (football, basketball, hockey and baseball) in the United States there has been a dramatic shift away from player loyalty to their respective organizations. Pay scales, disproportionate to the value an individual brings to the game, along with the concept of free agency, have placed loyalty a distant second to the almighty dollar. Sadly, we are experiencing the same shift in the business world. Enormous signing bonuses, stock options and gross annual income in the tens and even hundreds of millions of dollars have caused a drastic increase in turnover among senior leaders in corporate America. According to the Web Site *Best of Biz,* "CEO tenure is becoming shorter and less secure in each individual appointment....in the first 5 months of 2001 there were 473 departures, a 22 percent increase over the same period the previous year. A recent Drake survey of 476 companies in 25 countries shows: 50 percent have CEOs who have been in that post for less than 3 years and 66 percent have appointed at least one CEO in the past 5 years."[33] Loyalty to a company is under attack by personnel placement agencies that are dangling extraordinarily tempting job offers in the faces of employees at every level.

The information technology boom in the Silicon Valley in California at the turn of this century provides another example of loyalty or the lack thereof. With intense rivalry for qualified people in a fast-paced, highly competitive industry, employees found they could post their resumes online and receive nearly instantaneous feedback and offers that may include a signing bonus and salary increase. The alternative was to stay where they were and wait for the next review period, months away, when a raise would be considered. When loyalty is under attack it is important to have a strategy to retaliate.

In a study of employee turnover at the University of Wisconsin Center for Community Economic Development, it was determined that, "The number one issue facing business is finding and keeping good employees. Nationally, the average annual employee turnover rate for all companies is 12 percent. In our 1996 Wisconsin study, we found that 75 percent of the demand for new employees is simply to replace workers who have left the company. Replacement costs include the cost of attracting applicants, entrance interviews, testing, travel/moving expenses, pre-employment administrative expenses, medical exams."34 In this type of environment it may seem easier to look at turnover as an inevitable part of doing business and absorb the constant dollar drain. But that is the shortsighted view. The strong, steady leaders who understand the value of loyalty and stability will intensify their efforts, build and sustain programs that will persuade employees to stay put.

A leader development program is not rocket science but it does need to have some definition, some recognizable parts, elements that can be looked at, discussed and resourced. The military is in the business of recruiting and training leaders and I am convinced, beyond any reasonable doubt, that the United States Army has the best end-to-end leader development doctrine of any organization in the world. It uses a simple three-pronged approach to leader development that can be effectively adapted to any organization. Institutional development, assignments and self-development are the three pillars. Defining what these pillars are and how they work in any organization will characterize the leader development program for leaders at every level.

INSTITUTIONAL DEVELOPMENT

Institutional development in the United States Army is a well-financed machine that tracks individuals throughout their careers. There are separate tracks for officers and enlisted men and women. While I am not suggesting any civilian organization should put together and maintain an institutional program that encompasses all that the United States Army does, many of the pieces and concepts have universal application.

Let's begin by describing the U. S. Army's institutional development pillar of the overall leader development program for officers and then look at its applicability to any organization. Generally colleges and universities are the recruiting source for all organizations. The military has the added advantage of turning out young leaders each year from the services' military academies, the Army's U.S. Military Academy at West Point, the U.S. Naval Academy, the U.S. Air Force Academy and the U.S. Coast Guard Academy. The academy graduates are extraordinary young men and women who not only volunteered for the military regimen but also were hand selected from a large pool of high school applicants as well as men and women serving in the U.S. armed services. The U.S. Military Academy at West Point, for example, annually selects only about one out of ten applicants for admission. While it is true that corporate America can turn to business schools for its entry level leaders, what is also true is that most have had little if any leadership training as part of their college education. However, officers entering the military from the Military Academies or the Reserve Officer Training Corps (ROTC) programs on campuses across the country have undergone extensive leader training prior to graduation. In these programs young men and women are taught basic leadership principles and provided extensive opportunities to participate in practical exercises where their performance is reviewed and graded. Equally important, leader training during college years is an acculturation process; call it an acculturation boot camp. First and foremost a young leader must understand the value set, the operational imperatives, the totality of the culture of the organization they are about to become a part of. While in college ROTC students attend a summer camp where the emphasis is on leader development. The camp provides an opportunity to gather all cadets on one level playing field for the purposes of making an early assessment, as accurately and as professionally as possible, of that person's leadership potential.

Acculturation is an area where the military excels. Call it new employee orientation, call it whatever you want, but it is an enormously important essential first step in leader development and is far too often overlooked by most organizations. The military is value-based; honesty and integrity override all other considerations. Taking care of people is the military's first leadership lesson. To assume newly hired young corporate employees will understand these basic considerations is a mistake. Recruiting the best and brightest from America's universities is a major commitment of resources, but to assume they will automatically get off on the right step is generally a false premise.

It is not my intent to condemn any single generation, but there are some disturbing statistics that indicate cheating has become commonplace on many campuses over the past two decades. What is even more disturbing is that the majority of the students do not see anything wrong with these practices. That alone suggests an underlying value set, which should make any organization uncomfortable. In his book, *How Good People Make Tough Choices,* Rushworth M. Kidder cites some chilling statistics. A Louis Harris survey of high school students conducted in 1989 found that 65 percent said they would try to cheat on an exam for which they felt ill prepared. Sixty percent admitted to having cheated on tests in high school. A public relations organization, The Pinnacle Group, found in a 1989 survey that 66 percent of students said they would be willing to lie in the future to get ahead in business. A Rutgers professor's survey of over 6000 college students in 1990-91 discovered confessed cheaters in the following intended specialties: law school 63 percent, arts programs 64 percent, public service and government programs 66 percent, medical school 68 percent, engineering 71 percent and graduate schools of business 76 percent.35 An organization can choose to ignore the problem and hope it will go away or be proactive with an acculturation boot camp program.

If your organization's continuum of leadership has an active, pervasive leader development program, newly hired leaders will soon see that what they were told during the acculturation process is the normal operating environment. The individuals you want to keep will see it, comprehend it and quickly fall in line. While the military has the advantage in this area by working acculturation prior to graduation from college, it is possible for any organization to catch up by having a good program in place for their young leaders from day one.

In the United States Army, acculturation is only the first step in a series of actions that fall under institutional leader development. After commissioning, all new Army officers attend a six to nine-week basic course studying the skills required of their branch, be it infantry, artillery or logistics. Leader training is a part of the basic course followed by an assignment to their first leadership position as a platoon commander. After four or five years, those officers who remain in the United States Army return to school for about nine months to an advanced branch course in preparation for the next leadership level at company command. While not in command, officers are assigned to staff positions at various headquarters levels from battalion through department of the Army. To this point, an officer has been focused at the direct leader level, accumulating tools essential for the leadership toolbox required at the operational level. At about the ten-year point, selected officers (about sixty percent of each year group) go to Ft. Leavenworth, Kansas, for a year to study command and staff at the operational level. At about the fifteen years of service point, a formal board is convened to select top performing Lieutenant Colonels to command battalions. Successful battalion commanders are almost assured selection for a year of study at the United States Army War College, Carlisle, Pennsylvania, where they will be exposed to the development of national strategy and leadership at the strategic level. From the small list of war college graduates (about 125 per year) another formal board selects a few Colonels to command at the brigade level. From those who succeed at brigade command about thirty to thirty-five per year will be selected to become the United States Army's Generals and from that group a small number will command the Army's ten divisions and four corps.

I took you through the United States Army's institutional leader development program to make a couple of points. First, leader development is a principle business for the United States

Army; that accounts for the effort and resources put into it. With a rigid hierarchical structure and succeeding levels of command, each infinitely more complex than the preceding command, this institutionalized leader preparation is essential. One of the keys to a formal process such as the one the United States Army has is its integrity. Those officers being considered for battalion or brigade command must have confidence in the integrity of the formal board selection process. It was not always that way. Before the Army wrote an all-encompassing training and leader development doctrine, selection for senior command was by the good old boy network. When a large organization places itself in a position where its integrity can be questioned, it surely will be. In order to survive, that organization must have a value base sufficient to answer those who will question its integrity.

While leader development may not be the principle business for civilian organizations, as it is for the military, neither can it be ignored. Civilian organizations normally do not send their officers to yearlong leader development schools as they transition from level to level up the leadership continuum. Even if they could afford to do so, the schools simply are not available. Therefore, it falls to the leadership of an organization to build its own program. While there is no precise formula for success, there are some fundamental elements that should be considered.

The first essential element is to have a recognizable program. Periodically sending out a memo to all concerned announcing a lecture on leadership is not a program. The program should be written down; it should have a stated purpose; it should contain steps and milestones, making it clear to every leader in the continuum where he or she is in the process.

The first rung in the leader development ladder should be the acculturation boot camp, setting a foundation of values. Company employees must be made to understand that they will be treated with respect; leaders will genuinely care about subordinates and treat them with compassion. The company must have a reputation for honesty and integrity in dealings with its suppliers and customers. Following on the heels of the acculturation boot camp should be a one-day session wherein operational or strategic leaders point out and put into perspective the three or four duties of first-line leaders. Do not underestimate the value and payoff from young leaders who have a clear and common picture of what is expected of them especially when they hear it from one of the organization's senior leaders.

The next formal event is a specially crafted two or three day off-site for those leaders who are making the transition from direct to operational or operational to strategic leadership positions. It is not the intent of a promotion to set a person up for failure, yet many newly promoted leaders do not live up to expectations. One of the principle reasons is they continue to try to be a direct leader in an operational environment or an operational leader in a strategic job; an environment so different they soon become overwhelmed by span of control or by focusing on the wrong problem areas. They need to be helped through the transformation, shown and taught how to use the tools in the new toolbox required for their expanded responsibilities. A functioning institutional leader development program will assist with the process.

When United States Army officers are selected for promotion from Colonel to Brigadier General, that group of 30-35 officers assembles in Washington, D.C., for a weeklong session commonly referred to as charm school. While there is nothing particularly charming about the course, it does serve to indoctrinate those in attendance to the suggestion that being a General is a monumental professional progression. Personal scrutiny will increase exponentially. The breadth of responsibilities may be enormous involving budgets in the hundreds of millions of dollars whereas heretofore budgeting was taken care of by higher headquarters. Now you are the higher headquarters. There is a direct parallel to officers in civilian organizations. They are often referred to as officers of the corporation, executive level or senior management. Irrespective of the title, the transition to that level is no less significant than selection to be a General in the military and they need help with the move to new and different levels of responsibility. Promotion to the levels discussed here is a huge professional shift and the leader development program must do whatever it can to set this select group up for success.

A footnote to the Army's charm school is that spouses are participants in this and other selected leader development sessions. Many leaders rely heavily on their spouses to play a key role in their success and the achievements of their organizations. Including them in institutional leader development programs will add value to the organization, have a positive impact on stability, be another factor contributing to loyalty and will be important to the value base of the organization in terms of caring and sharing. While commander of the Seventh Infantry Division and Fort Ord, for example, my wife Deborah worked every day on quality of life issues for soldiers and their families. There was a network of spouses, serving on committees and working tirelessly without pay as part of the culture of caring and sharing. Her leadership and the network of hundreds of volunteers she put in place played an important role in the overall success of the organization. Never underestimate the value of building teams and ambassadors of good will within the organization.

Another part of the overall program should be a company policy that every time there is an off-site, whatever its purpose, there must be an agenda item for discussion of leadership. One way to do that is for a selected operational or strategic leader to make the leadership presentation. In that way, the organization's leadership doctrine gets explained, emphasis is placed on the subject and it is relevant to whatever the purpose of the off-site conference may be. In large companies, perhaps spanning the globe, the leader development program may have a mobile training team available to work at off-site conferences and other gatherings. This could be an internal team or a contract group of practitioners who have tailored a program to the company. When using a mobile training team to teach and mentor leaders, there is one overriding consideration for every member of the team and that is they must be *credible*. They must have an experience base at least equal to and preferably greater than those they are teaching and mentoring. A bright young articulate person who looks and sounds good on the stage may have a wonderful message but age tells a more profound story; they may be able to talk the talk but have not walked the walk. Do not make the mistake of using a speaker or instructor who has not "been there and done that" at the direct, operational and strategic leadership levels. Even the best message from a dynamite presentation gets lost if delivered by someone who is not credible.

A second point on credibility has to do with the choice between a theorist and a practitioner. The theorist may have all the degrees, may be a best selling author and may provide a riveting presentation, but yet has never been in a leadership position. They do fine until it comes time for the discussion period, then their answers and illustrations are limited to case studies because they have not been in the trenches, lived the moment, had the adrenaline rush of success, been a party to a gut-wrenching failed program, served as a trusted member of a war council, been mentored by a master craftsman, or been lonely at the top. Those who have walked that walk can talk about leaders and leadership from the heart; they have credibility.

An additional part of an organization's institutional leader development program might be to send every person promoted to a certain level to an accredited leadership school. There are some good established programs around the country varying from a couple days to a week or more in length. A company could, for example, have a policy that everyone who makes it to the tenth floor at corporate headquarters immediately goes off to the Acme Leadership Institute. This is a way of using an external entity to provide a common base for an organization's entire leadership level.

Another valuable tool for the institutional leader development program is mentoring. It may be the most powerful tool of all because it is constant and pervasive. A mentor is an advisor, a teacher and a coach. Mentoring is sometimes misunderstood to mean that some select few individuals will receive preferential treatment. If used in that context, it is not mentoring and is unhealthy for the organization. Mentoring cannot be delegated; the only way to pass on *your* beliefs, *your* knowledge and *your* understanding of the organization from *your* position is to do it *yourself.*

Mentoring can be passive, active or both. Even if there is no mentoring program per se, even if the word is not used, mentoring is an on-going activity. Passive mentoring is what leaders at every level do on a daily basis. How they act and react to routine actions or to crisis actions; what character traits they routinely exhibit all have either a positive or negative influence on subordinates.

Active mentoring encourages leaders at every level to spend some quality time at one-on-one counseling. Counseling includes the entire spectrum from a verbal reprimand for exercising poor judgment, to praise for good work, to general discussions about how things are going, to teaching new methods and techniques. Providing young leaders with a broader perspective is a way of pushing them towards creativity and innovation. For example, a promising young subordinate had done some excellent work researching background information for a presentation you have to make to the executive council. Although it is a closed session, you make a special request for this rising star to get a seat in the back of the room. By experiencing the interaction among the participants, that young person may learn more in one hour than they would by reading ten books on leadership. Mentoring opportunities such as this become routine in an organization if there is a stated policy on mentoring and leaders know it is not only acceptable, but they are encouraged to expose young leaders to events in the board room. It can also serve as a test. Perhaps a question gets thrown to the young observer in the back row. Does he choke on his tongue or stand up, look the CEO in the eye and provide an informed brief answer? Can a young prospect be trusted to be discrete or was he holding court at the water cooler the remainder of the day providing a vivid description of what took place behind closed doors?

Mentoring can also play a key role in the process of sorting out personnel for promotion or new assignments. For example the boss seeks your advice on moving young Jones to a more senior position. You respond that you have been working with him, given him a number of opportunities to be a star, even put him on the crisis action team, but he has not yet provided an indication he is up to the task. Mentoring is a way of getting to know subordinates, in depth.

The effectiveness of a mentoring program is in large measure tied to the corporate culture. For example, chapter nine contained a discussion of the after action review as a major corporate culture statement. The after action review is also the purest form of public mentoring. An AAR bares the soul of the organization and each individual and sends a powerful message that good leaders are open, honest and not afraid to admit imperfections or even failure.

The institutional leader development program is the central pillar of the three. It can and should be multifaceted. The institutional leader development program must be formal, written down and frequently discussed. The senior leaders select the tools that are right for their particular organization and work continuously on implementation. Nothing worthwhile or as important as leader development is easy; it must be worked every day. It is all about building a bench.

ASSIGNMENTS

The second pillar of a leader development program is assignments. Again, this is not terribly difficult but it should be the result of deliberate policy developed within the organization and someone needs to watch over it. For example, the policy will spell out the details associated with assignments to selected positions. The idea is that positions at every level in an organization vary according to their degree of difficulty, visibility and potential to test an individual's capabilities. A number of the most demanding positions can be specifically identified for their professional development value and used to not only educate and train the incumbents, but also to sort out those who can cut it from those who do not appear to be up to the challenge.

The second part of the policy on assignments is that at a point in each person's career, be it after a period of time, for example every year, or after two or three fitness reports, or whatever the criteria, they will be subject to some type of review process. The purpose for reviews is to allow all levels of leadership to begin sorting out those who have demonstrated the greatest potential to be assigned to the most demanding positions and put them on a different track.

After about ten years in the United States Army I received orders to the Army's personnel headquarters to serve as an assignments officer for my contemporaries, a group of about 2000 Field Artillerymen in the rank of Major. Upon arriving I discovered that about ten percent of the files had a cover sheet on them that simply read, "TRACK." Officers with a TRACK file were consistently tested in the most demanding assignments. Many were selected to return to universities for graduate studies. A little known fact is that the vast majority of senior officers in the United States Army have a Masters or Doctorate Degree. These tracked officers were watched carefully. As an assignment officer I was empowered to send officers anywhere on my own initiative with one exception, my boss would initial off on the assignment of every TRACK file.

Whatever system is put in place, there must be a periodic review process associated with it. A person who appeared to be a fast burner and led the pack at level one and level two, may have hit the wall when moved to level three. It happens all too frequently and it is important to figure out why. Perhaps there was a crisis at home, now resolved, causing the hiccup in performance and another chance is justified. Perhaps he or she folds up under the pressures associated with a higher-level job. Perhaps, put in a position of having to lead others, you find their interpersonal skills do not measure up to the requirement. When some individuals are put under pressure, you detect a character flaw such as unjustly blaming others, lacking integrity, not genuinely caring, or unethically using subordinates. Or, on the positive side, you find a person so talented and so quick they need to be moved ahead of their contemporaries.

Another benefit of a periodic review process is to identify the late bloomer. You hire someone who, on the surface, gave little or no indication during the interview process or on paper that they had strong or hidden leadership potential. Perhaps you saw a mediocre college grade point average or nothing in the first or second assignments caught anyone's attention. It is possible that previous leaders did not know how to surface this person's strong points and then, for whatever reason, you begin to notice that everything this person touches turns to gold. While he or she may currently be behind contemporaries, put them on a TRACK and see if they continue to out-perform those around them.

The United States Army has a formal review process. Boards of officers, sworn to be impartial, convene to select those who will be promoted to grades Captain, Major, Lieutenant Colonel, Colonel, Brigadier General and Major General. Additionally, formal boards select those who will attend year-long schools and those who will command at the battalion and brigade levels. It is resource intensive, but a necessary process. I am not suggesting every organization should mirror the United States Army's process but neither should it be haphazard, totally unstructured, or give the impression that it lacks integrity. Whatever the system, it should be written down as part of the leader development doctrine or policy and it has to be resourced. It is all part of the process of cultivating good people who know the corporate culture, who have bought in to the organization's values and who are loyal. It is all part of the process of having the right people identified and available on the bench to fill inevitable vacancies. Hiring from within does not go unnoticed and breeds loyalty and stability throughout the continuum of leadership. Leaders at every level see what is happening and feel a sense of belonging, a sense of personal worth to the organization.

Not everyone will get promoted, not everyone should and only a small percentage deserves accelerated promotions. Every organization should consider a program that selects a few individuals each year for promotion well ahead of their contemporaries. Those selected early for promotion will also be included in an accelerated assignment process, moving from key position to key position quickly as part of leader development. They will be continuously scrutinized in the most demanding jobs.

Understandably there needs to be some mechanism, some historical personnel record, for use in the personnel sorting process. Whatever reporting vehicle is used, it is essential that leaders at the operational and strategic leadership levels devote their personal attention to the details of the reporting system and the resourcing required to make it all work efficiently, effectively and with integrity. Personnel evaluations, fitness reports, efficiency reports, whatever you call them, are the most difficult and contentious part of the entire leader development program. Virtually every leader rating a subordinate will evaluate somewhat differently against a given set of standards; some are generous by nature, always giving the benefit of the doubt while others are hard nosed and believe in dishing out hard lessons. Some raters simply do not have the personal fortitude to look subordinates in the eye and tell them they did not measure up, resulting in reports that are more favorable than they should be and, therefore, false.

There are some axioms that apply to personnel rating systems. Here are four:

- There is no perfect system.
- There is no single system that everyone is going to be completely comfortable with.

- Doing right by the system consumes a great deal of a leader's time.
- Whatever the system, over time the ratings will become inflated.

   So, what to do? Remember that any system is better than not having one at all. Keep the process simple and on a single piece of paper, front and back. Key on three critical issues:

- How did this person perform in the job relative to the standards set for the position?
- What is this person's potential to succeed in positions of greater responsibility?
- Finally there must be a section on character. If a person has a tendency to be less than honest, lacks integrity, cannot be trusted, or will knock down subordinates to get to the head of the line, this must be known early. There can be no second chances when it comes to character deficiencies and an organization's leaders have to be apprised of this as soon as it is uncovered.

Any system that includes numerical ratings will become inflated over time. There are two methods for dealing with inflation. One is for those reviewing the performance reports to recognize the leaders who consistently rate high or low and to take that into account when assessing an individual's record. Secondly, even if the rating system is basically numeric, require a short written paragraph describing the rated person's performance and potential. These written documents will facilitate sorting out the TRACK personnel from those less qualified.

The assignment pillar in the leader development program is more than moving folks from job to job. To have an assignments policy that makes sense, it must involve moving the *right people* at the *right time* for all the *right reasons*. It begins with a rating system designed to define capability, potential and character. The personal ratings, in turn, provide the basis for a selection process that, at every level, sorts out those most promising for assignments to positions of greater responsibility. The assignment pillar must have a foundation in leader development doctrine and policy. Additionally, the program must be properly resourced; it is going to eat up a great deal of every leader's time and energy. Finally the program must have an underpinning of integrity, an ad-hoc, good-old-boy based system will eventually crumble. All of this taken together is part of the process of building a bench.

SELF-DEVELOPMENT

The intent of the third pillar in the leadership development program is to provide employees with amply resourced opportunities to demonstrate their desire and commitment to improving themselves both professionally and personally. One challenge is to ensure every leader knows that self-development is part of the leader development program. This is an ideal topic for the acculturation boot camp, ensuring everyone knows this pillar is based on self-initiative and what the organization will do to assist. Explaining the program to new recruits and young leaders also reinforces that learning how to lead is a never-ending process.

Proper resourcing will put the self-development pillar on a firm foundation and enhance the program by providing opportunities for those who demonstrate an interest in improving themselves. Resourcing might be as simple as stocking a library with books and articles available for all to use. Everyone in the organization should be encouraged to contribute materials they believe are good sources of information on leadership. Making leadership a topic of conversation at the water cooler and in the cafeteria fosters team building and a sense of belonging.

Leaders at all levels should schedule time during the workday for professional development sessions. This provides an opportunity for subordinates to interact with bosses and provides time to think about leadership and what avenues to pursue to improve themselves. Once a month shut down the office for a long lunch, or for the last couple hours on a

Friday afternoon, gather subordinates and explore professional development subjects. For example:

- The company's personnel evaluation system.
- Counseling techniques.
- Leadership formulas used by famous leaders in history.
- Review a new book from the company's self-development library.
- An open question and answer session.

During these sessions avoid talking shop. If you make that mistake, the session becomes just another routine meeting and will have nothing to do with leader development. Most people lead busy lives; long working hours, long commute, and family demands. When it seems there are not enough hours in the day, even your most energetic employee will need a nudge now and then to keep him or her thinking about continuing to hone their leadership skills. Leave a good article or book on their desk and some time later ask what they thought about its message.

Continuing education is a huge factor in the self-development pillar and can be worked into an organization's fabric in numerous ways. For example, a bachelors or graduate degree could account for some number of promotion points in a system that requires employees to meet a minimum point value in order to be considered for promotion. Another method is to provide full-time, fully funded education for a few individuals selected from a list of applicants. A third idea is to authorize a few hours per week away from the job to be part-time students. Instructors for graduate courses could be on site in the evenings for those who want to take advantage of the opportunity. The company may have a program to pay all or part of the tuition for continuing education.

The combined effect of the three pillars of a leader development program should all point toward building a bench. Late in 2000 Jack Welch, the legend-in-his-own-time CEO of General Electric, selected Jeffrey Immelt as the CEO-designate. This announcement was headline news and written about extensively in newspapers and magazines all across the country.

An article written by Gary Strauss for *USA Today* provided insights into the depth and vitality of GE's leader development program. When Jack Welch reached "down" and selected a forty-four year old as heir apparent, what caught everyone's attention was the number of GE officials, senior to the CEO-designate, who might become top candidates to lead other companies. In his article Strauss quotes Jeff Christian of headhunter Christian & Timbers, "GE is the best school for CEOs. They pick and groom great potential CEOs early. They top everyone's list in technology, electronics and manufacturing." Strauss goes on to say, "Arguably the best company at identifying and developing managers, GE has a deep talent pool." Looking into the future the article points out, "Should GE and 44-year old Immelt remain healthy, Immelt could run the show for sixteen years or more. Ambitious GE executives in their forties and fifties longing to run their own shop will look elsewhere. Given Immelt's promotion, it is the guys in their thirties who will have a shot at being the next CEO and there are fifty of those guys on a fast track."36

In just a couple short paragraphs from the article one gets a clear picture of a company with leaders committed to a strong leader development program. Jack Welch is one of the best-known and most highly respected business leaders of our time; when he departed GE he left behind a great legacy, the bench he built.

RECAP

1. Without a bench an organization can find itself up the preverbal creek without a paddle, just at a time when it needs talented people the most.
2. Defining, resourcing and institutionalizing a multi-faceted leader development program is a serious commitment for leaders at the operational and strategic leadership levels.
3. An effective leader development program will be cost-effective, pervasive and positive because it fosters employee loyalty and stability.
4. There is a tool kit for leader development – pillars,

libraries, personnel rating system, accelerated promotions, assignments policy, internal and external training courses, college studies, etc. The size, complexity and interaction of its parts are only limited by the imagination of the organization's leadership.

5. Remember, Moltke warned us over one hundred years ago that one couldn't rely on natural genius for the development of senior leaders. Leader development is the responsibility of every leader at every level.

ENDURING LEADERSHIP PRINCIPLES

Great leaders:
Continue to study the art of leadership.
Know their subordinates.
Mentor subordinates.
Build a bench.

CHAPTER ELEVEN

CHARACTER

Honesty And Integrity Of An Organization's Individual leaders Will Be a Key Determinate of Success Or Failure.

So far part one has described what it is that constitutes a foundation for leadership at every level, termed *the underpinnings*. It follows that the final chapter of part one should be on the subject of character because no matter how positive an organization's culture, no matter how diverse and well founded the leader development program, no matter how prepared the organization is for action, if it is not sitting atop an immovable foundation of uncompromising character traits then the organization will ultimately fail. The ingredients for what we envision when we think of a traditional foundation are simple: sand, cement and water formed into concrete. The elements necessary for a foundation of character are more numerous:

- Honesty
- Sincerity
- Truthfulness
- Ethical Behavior
- Moral Fiber
- Candor
- Honorable
- Uprightness

- Openness
- Just
- Values
- Goodness
- Decency
- Principled
- Reliability
- Integrity

But while more numerous, the properties are no more difficult to recognize. It is just as easy to identify an honest person as it is to distinguish water. It is as easy to recognize an organization that subscribes to strong ethical principles as it is to identify sand or cement.

The purpose of this chapter is to articulate the premise that there can be no second chances when it comes to the issue of character.

If one is honest they do not lie, cheat or steal. A person with integrity lives by a code of ethics consisting of sound moral principles. In order to capture all the relevant qualities of character necessary for a leader or an organization to be successful, let's say the foundation needs to consist of the dynamic duo of *honesty and integrity*. Honesty and integrity are the underpinnings for the underpinnings of leadership. This chapter is about the character of leaders and the character of the organization.

Wouldn't it be wonderful if our entire society were populated with people who all subscribe to a lifestyle based on honesty and integrity? Obviously it would be, but do not hold your breath; it is not going to be that way. Fortunately, in most cases leaders emerge who create an environment wherein honesty and integrity prevail over those who are less principled and some acceptable disciplined operational direction emerges. When this formula fails on a large scale, tyrants such as Adolf Hitler, Joseph Stalin and Saddam Hussein emerge and have a profound impact not only on their own people, but the whole world. When the formula fails within an organization the consequences are more confined but still devastating for those associated with that group.

Creating a culture based on honesty and integrity is the responsibility of every leader at every level, direct, operational and strategic. Strategic leaders have a dual responsibility for their own strength of character as well as responsibility for the character of the institution. Without creating a pervasive culture, without the power of example, honesty and integrity will not be present throughout an organization. And, if honesty and integrity are not understood and practiced on a daily basis at every level by every leader, the reputation of the organization will soon be in jeopardy.

A particular direct leader on the assembly line wants to turn out more items than his fellow direct leaders are producing, thereby hoping this will lead to recognition, reward and promotion. He instructs his subordinates to cut some corners and in doing so create more but lesser quality items. The completed products from different assembly groups are merged, boxed and shipped. Eventually the inferior products from the one assembly group fail, product complaints increase, consumer loyalty shifts, retailers switch brands and sales plummet. This is cause and effect. This is the reality of breaches of ethical behavior. This is why the character of an organization must be strong throughout the continuum of leadership.

But breaches of honesty and integrity will not be confined to a slow lumbering assembly line with repercussions months later. In today's fast-paced environment serious actions can take place with the stroke of a key or the click of a mouse and have potentially catastrophic consequences. Imagine the number of opportunities there are today for employees to forward information via email outside their company. This can include confidential policy data, status of special projects, secret leading-edge technology or patent pending competitive advantage projects. Adherence to a common set of values must reach and be understood by everyone in the organization.

It is not enough for leaders to simply create a principled

environment; it must be actively and aggressively enforced. More than one person knew about cutting corners on the assembly line. Creating a culture of honesty and integrity means creating an atmosphere wherein someone is willing to raise their hand and say, "This is not right," or "Do not send that email." And, just as important, if there is a culture consisting of strong values, the person who is willing to stand up for what is right must be comfortable that there will be no personal repercussions for having had the courage of their convictions.

Creating such an environment begins with the clear understanding that breaches of honesty and integrity will not be tolerated. This is not an area where three strikes and you're out is operable. It must be a commonly understood rule that there are no second chances when it comes to compromising the reputation of the organization. Consider the statement of a leader who relates to his boss that he knows one of the assistants can not always be trusted but he is a key subordinate leader on the project and the company cannot afford to lose him at this time. This is a dangerous statement and coming from a project leader speaks volumes about his moral underpinnings. Furthermore, senior leaders who accept that argument are no better because the issue is no longer about the invaluable subordinate leader on the project, but the integrity of the institution.

It is rare for someone to be forced into a position of leadership; being a leader is usually a personal choice. One aspect of leadership that is always present and all-powerful is example. Everything a leader says and does is an example, be it good or bad, to those observing or working for that person. There is wisdom in the observation that the higher up the flagpole, the more one's backside is exposed and this is precisely why senior leaders, and remember they *chose* to be leaders, cannot separate their private and public lives. One cannot have a code of ethics for their personal life and another for the workplace. The reason is simple: as a CEO, a politician or a senior military leader, many aspects of your private life become public. The public is interested in who you are, your family life and what you do during your leisure time. A leader who is observed espousing a policy of honesty and integrity at work but living a different code of ethics at home is correctly tagged as a hypocrite and no longer an effective leader. Genuine ethical behavior is internalized and if it is not it will never be legitimately externalized.

When President Clinton, despite previous public denials, was found to have been having an affair with a young White House intern, it was both shocking and disappointing to observe that about one half of all Americans believed it is performance that counts in the oval office and that as long as Clinton was doing an acceptable job as President, what he did in his private life is unimportant. Well, it is important when that person is in a position to have an adverse impact on the moral compass of the nation. There is now a young generation who have not only observed the national debate and the impeachment defense, but many have heard their own parents declare that "it" is acceptable as long as you do not get caught. We should all shudder to think of the leader development challenges ahead as some individuals in the next generation enter the workplace with this warped set of ethical values. It is an issue of chipping away at the goodness of America. There is a wonderful adage (author unknown, often erroneously attributed to Alexis De Tocquevelle in his book, *Democracy in America*) that professes America is great because she is good and when she ceases to be good she will cease to be great. Leaders at every level must see as one of their principle duties, the providing of goodness to their organization.

It has been said that an ethical signpost points in many directions. But if the collective moral compass of an organization's leaders is pointing in the proper direction, finding the right solution will not be that difficult. From time to time there will be an opportunity lost because it conflicts with the values of the organization. There may even be some less-principled leaders who will argue the company cannot survive if they stay on the sidelines while the competition moves forward. But those who clearly understand the value of operating with a foundation of honesty and integrity will recognize the consequences of compromise for short-term gain. Once the integrity of an organization is bargained away, it will soon find itself on a slippery slope. Value-based organizations are in business for the long haul and will not only endure but will prosper, not *in spite* of passing on the short term unethical deal, *but because* they passed up the opportunity to becoming engaged in an operation not in tune with their values. Is it unethical to even consider options that fly in the face of an organization's values? Absolutely not and doing so can be a method of establishing and reinforcing a corporate culture. There is rarely a problem or issue with only one clear-cut solution. Most leaders prefer to have their staff lay out two or three courses of action. When a solution is presented that is otherwise attractive and potentially profitable but is inconsistent with the company's ethical standards, the boss has a perfect instructional vehicle to use in reinforcing the operating code.

We live in a competitive environment where there is constant pressure in our professional lives to get ahead, make more money, receive more promotions and be more successful. As a result, leaders in every type of organization have a responsibility to themselves, their organization and society to press the issues of honesty and integrity. An organization's commitment to ethical conduct cannot be lip service, a one-time shot, or a once-a-year comment in the annual report. Leaders must use all the tools available to them. For example:

- Upon taking the helm of a new job gather key subordinates together and lay out your operating dos and don'ts. Make it clear that a breech of honesty and integrity is grounds for termination.
- Do some research to gain an understanding of the people in the organization. Find answers to questions like: What motivates them, what is important to them, how do they feel about the organization's direction, what is their ethical baseline?

- Determine what it is that will make the entire organization successful and focus on those issues.
- Publish a code of ethics in a clear, concise statement. It will inform employees what the organization collectively believes and how business is to be conducted.
- Make ethics and strength of character the central focus of your leader development program. In spite of your efforts, be prepared for someone to cross the ethical line. Investigate the issue in detail and if it is necessary to fire the individual, do so promptly and then explain why.
- Whenever considering courses of action, openly debate the moral pros and cons of going a certain direction. Only through frequent dialogue on the importance of doing what is right will senior leaders begin to hear their words coming back to them, evidence that their message has worked its way through the continuum of leadership.
- Include ethics training in organization-wide new employee orientations, acculturation boot camp, off-sites, training sessions and senior executive seminars.
- Other tools include open-door policies, confidential email addresses, the after action review process, or a specific contact in the Human Resources department. A tool frequently used by organizations is called a hot line. This can be a special phone number or a drop box for anonymous messages available for use by anyone in the organization. Once established, this places a special burden on the senior leadership to deal with the correspondence. On the positive side, everyone in the organization knows the boss is not afraid to get bad news and the corporate culture will support bringing breaches of honesty and integrity to light quickly.

People want to tell the truth, the organization's policies must provide them the tools and opportunities to do so.

When leaders identify all the tools they want to have in their ethics toolbox, what is it they want to accomplish? Those who clearly understand their responsibility want to establish and sustain a value-based organization. Enduring organizations (corporations, nations, professional, private, educational, political, religious) are compassionate, caring, honest and have a solid moral conviction. In other words, they have character. Frequently you will hear the United States described as a nation of laws, usually coming from a lawyer-politician. While it is true that laws are a part of the foundation of this great nation, the United States is first and foremost value-based. There are a variety of polls that report sixty to seventy-five percent of Americans believe we are in a "serious state of moral decay."37 Many also believe the terrorist events of September 11, 2001 provided a wake-up call and will serve to shift our nation's moral compass back to a more favorable heading. Time will tell.

I was fortunate to spend my professional life as a member of a long-standing value-based organization, the U.S. military. For many Americans the fact that the U.S. military is value-based comes as a surprise because their vision of what the military is and does is as a result of viewing Hollywood's depiction of service members, in particular its leaders. Hollywood takes great care to generally characterize senior leaders as power-hungry, self-centered, uncaring, unprincipled, buffoons standing around giving meaningless orders to junior enlisted members. Nothing could be further from the truth; with few exceptions U.S. military leaders subscribe in word and deed to the values of the organization.

One lesson from my thirty-two years in uniform is that as a leader you can never become complacent about honesty and integrity. The U.S. military is a product of society and constantly infused with young people who bring their individual biases and prejudices. For many there is a huge transformation required in order for them to fit into the long-standing value set. Some cannot conform and are weeded out early. Some attain senior rank and for whatever reason yield to temptation and cross the ethical line; and, when that happens, it is usually headline news. Some of you will recall media reports in 1999 that an Army two-star General had made a pass at a female General officer. She reported the incident when she became aware that he was slated to be assigned as the Army's Deputy Inspector General. What can we take away from this story? First is that in a value-based organization its senior leaders are held to a high standard of personal conduct, both in and out of their offices. Ask yourself, had this happened between two vice presidents in your organization, would it have been national news on every major network? The second observation from the incident is that the General's career was over. No second chances, particularly for senior leaders in a truly value-based institution.

When an organization is serious about protecting its values, safeguards are put in place to ensure continued oversight. The mechanism used by the U.S. military, since its inception, has been the Office of the Inspector General. It is an established fact that every person in uniform, regardless of rank, can at any time request to see the Inspector General associated with their particular unit or post. Back to the two-star General to make an additional point; considering that nothing else was uncovered during the investigation, we can give the General in question the benefit of the doubt and conclude that his pass at the senior female colleague was an isolated act of indiscretion. Since it happened in the privacy of her office, she could have just kept it to herself. But, when the General's pending assignment as Deputy Inspector General of the entire United States Army was announced, the integrity of the institution was at stake and she came forward. The third point to take away from the incident is that in the end, as a senior leader herself, she understood that a value-based organization's foundation must be protected.

And then there is the Enron Corporation, the multi-billion dollar energy company that declared bankruptcy in late 2001. It was a defining event in the business world and captured headlines for months. One reason it was daily news is the pervasiveness of the "badness." The board of directors looked bad, the last two CEOs looked bad, several of the top executives looked bad, the Wall Street analysts looked bad and the outside accounting firm looked bad. The Enron mess smelled from one end to the other. Many of the hundreds of articles and news shows concerning the Enron meltdown concluded that it came about as a result of a bad business plan, others said it was dreadful accounting practices and still others blamed it on the 2001 recession. But when one looks inside that operation and sees the overt actions that deceived stock holders, analysts and accountants; when one looks at the timing of pronouncements from senior executives concerning the good health of the company within weeks of its collapse; when one looks at the application (or lack thereof) of its own code of ethics; when one looks at the hundreds of millions of dollars worth of bonuses and stock options paid to senior officials as the company was coming unraveled; and when one sees the disparity in profits and losses from stock between senior executives and those employees with Enron stock in the 401K program; when all those factors are brought to light the reason why Enron collapsed is simple, it collapsed because there was no goodness. The elements of character listed at the beginning of this chapter (honesty, integrity, reliability, sincerity, candor, uprightness, openness, truthfulness, honor, moral fiber, ethical behavior, decency, principled leaders) were absent from Enron. Had these character traits existed in the hearts and minds of the individual leaders throughout the Enron continuum of leadership, if the leaders had believed in accountability and had those values permeated the day-to-day operations of the company, it is highly unlikely they would have folded and so many thousands of loyal, innocent Enron employees would not have lost their jobs and fortunes.

Rushworth M. Kidder, in his previously referenced book, *How Good People Make Tough Choices,* writes in the preface about the results of interviews he had with some world leaders and prominent citizens in a variety of vocations. He writes, ".....six issues stood out as central to our future agenda. Five were not surprising: 1) the nuclear threat, 2) environmental degradation, 3) the population explosion, 4) the North-South economic gap between the developed and the developing worlds and 5) the need for education reform. The sixth, surfacing in interview after interview, caught me by surprise: the breakdown of morality. It was as though these interviewees were saying, 'Look, if we don't get a handle on the ethical collapses going on around us, we will be as surely doomed as we would be by a nuclear disaster or an environmental catastrophe.' Ethics, they were saying, was no mere luxury: it was central to our survival."38 Those prominent interviewees were sending a powerful message.

With all this as background, the question is, how does one go about creating a value based organization? Like so many things in life, the best way is to use the building block approach. The three bricks in the foundation are ethics, morality and integrity. Ethics is something we learn; learning our duty and the reasons for it. Ethics is all about knowing what I ought to do. Hopefully this is learned in the formative stages of life but leaders must be constantly vigilant for subordinates who bring a warped sense of ethics to the workplace and be prepared to deal with the issue quickly.

The second building block is morality. This is how humans treat other humans. Ethics is knowing the right thing to do, morality is doing the right thing. When these two, ethics and morality, come together as positives we have a person of integrity.

Integrity is the quality of being of sound moral principle, upright sincere, faithful and trustworthy. Character is not something you have but is what you are and can be observed every day in what you do. Every one of us makes a conscious choice with respect to our character. The building blocks of character are ethics, morality and integrity. A person of character who is leading an organization now has an opportunity to begin to build a value based organization.

Example is everything; leaders who do not demonstrate strength of character in both their private and public lives will not be successful in establishing a value based organization. Having established a value base, leadership remains a hands-on activity. That is, subordinates will deviate from the path you have set and every transgression must be dealt with promptly and firmly.

I believe there is a continuum of behavior in the workplace that can be helpful to leaders in dealing with subordinates who get off track. On the left of the continuum are honest mistakes. Having instilled a culture of empowerment and change, subordinates will feel free to innovate and in so doing will make honest mistakes that can and should be tolerated and forgiven. Of course an employee who does so continuously probably needs some firm mentoring.

Moving to the right on the continuum of behavior a leader will encounter errors in judgment. This is more serious than honest mistakes and must be dealt with promptly. However, before dropping the hammer on someone, the leader must first ask themselves if, through training and mentoring, the subordinate knew better than to take the action. Take for example the case of a subordinate leader who invites a client out for dinner, which is acceptable company policy to include ordering wine with dinner. The wine however cost $100 a bottle and the two of them consumed a bottle each. Have you set the standards for this type activity and have you insured all of your subordinates understand the rules? If so, and this is a first offense, the subordinate must understand that his or her actions were a serious error in judgment and will not be tolerated in the future. That subordinate is on notice, but errors in judgment probably do not fall in the category of one strike and you are out.

Moving to the right side of the continuum of behavior we encounter breaches of honesty and integrity. This is serious and cannot be tolerated if the organization is to endure. Is your policy one strike and you are out, or two, or three? The answer is what you have defined as the standard for your organization. Once established, the standard must be upheld. This is where the value base of the organization becomes so important. If that senior leader who has to deal with breaches of honesty and integrity is not a person of character, he or she will be seen as a hypocrite and rightfully so. That organization cannot endure.

During your many sessions with subordinates when you discuss ethics, morality, integrity, honesty, character and values, draw the continuum of behavior on a chart and talk about it; it can assist you in bringing clarity to this important subject.

Successfully establishing and enforcing a set of ethics for any organization is challenging, never-ending work, time consuming and expensive. Is there a payoff? If so, how do we define it, how do we measure it? Measuring is the difficult part because we are dealing with subjective values. But defining the payoff is easy. The fallout from exercising honesty and integrity at every leadership level is *trust and confidence*. If subordinates cannot trust their leaders because the leaders have not proven themselves to be honest, the leader/led equation is unsolvable. If leaders at every level fail to demonstrate integrity in all their actions, they cannot possibly expect to gain the confidence of their subordinates. Looking at the equation from a positive aspect, anything is possible when throughout the continuum of leadership, as every employee looks up, there is a special trust and confidence in the next leader. If this special relationship begins with the lowest ranking employee looking to their first-line leader and continues to the executive vice president's view of the CEO, everything else the organization attempts will be made immeasurably easier and their chances of success are very high.

RECAP

1.   Honesty and integrity are the ultimate underpinnings for any successful organization.
2.   Strategic leaders have a dual responsibility; responsibility for their own character as well as that of the institution.
3.   Breaches of honesty and integrity cannot be tolerated at any level by any leader; there can be no second chances.
4.   Never underestimate the power of example. The more senior the leader, the more powerful the example becomes.
5.   Leaders cannot hypercritically have one set of values for their private lives and another for the workplace; and the more senior the leader, the greater the consequences.

6. Compromising integrity for short-term gain puts an organization on a slippery slope.
7. Senior leaders must identify a set of tools for establishing and maintaining a value-based culture and apply them often.
8. The payoff from honesty and integrity is trust and confidence. With those four elements in place, anything is possible.

ENDURING LEADERSHIP PRINCIPLES

Great leaders:
Are accountable for their actions.
Set a proper example in their private and public lives.

PART TWO

A FRAMEWORK FOR ACTION

CHAPTER TWELVE

LEADERS ARE PLANNERS

Leaders Who Are Taking The Organization Elsewhere Are In A Constant State Of Planning.

P lanning is what leaders do. In any sizeable organization, when the boss has a problem, an issue, an idea or a project that has to get worked out, there will usually be a number of persons involved in finding a solution. Therein lies the problem. How does the leader communicate the problem to all those involved? Once communicated, how can the boss be sure those working the issue received the correct message? Are they all marching down the same path, or are a couple of key players out of synch with the others? Is everyone who should be involved actually in the game and on schedule?

Answering these kinds of questions is what campaign planning is all about. Campaign planning is not about creating a bureaucracy or a layered approach to problem solving; it is about taking the organizational structure that exists and applying a framework for action to problem solving that uses the continuum of leadership to link the strategic, operational and direct leaders in a common purpose. Without a framework as a reference there is the risk of confusion, conflicting priorities, misunderstanding, delays, inaction and lack of coordination. As we transition to the twenty-first century with 24/7 global operations and an accelerated pace of play, leaders must seize every advantage if they are to survive and prosper. There are a number of toolboxes yet to be opened which, if used properly and consistently, will enhance any leader's ability to get from vision to execution quickly, easily and efficiently.

The purpose of this chapter is to define planning and the leader's role from vision to execution.

Recall in chapter seven the point concerning the importance of change, change or die. An organization satisfied with the status quo is an organization that is standing still and is therefore being passed up by the competition. An organization keeps moving forward through the implementation of plans. Some plans are simple, involve only a few people, are not resource intensive and are executed at the direct leader level. Some plans may not even be on paper or may literally get sketched out on a napkin during a coffee break, but they are nonetheless plans. At the other end of the spectrum is the strategic leadership laying out a grand scheme that will eventually spawn dozens or even hundreds of supporting plans at the operational and direct leadership levels. These large, multifaceted plans are often referred to as campaigns involving numerous teams or groups within an organization, if not the organization in its entirety. A campaign is a series of organized actions aimed at accomplishing a stated purpose and typically focused on a path toward an identifiable end-state such as corporate imaging, re-branding, new product line, a political campaign or combined air/land/maritime actions in wartime. Regardless of the magnitude of the problem at hand, leaders are the ones who make it happen.

A LEADER'S ROLE

LEADERS INITIATE THE PLANNING PROCESS. Innovation often comes from those at the point of execution. A plan has been formulated as a result of molding together a number of ideas that bubbled up through the continuum of leadership from workers on the assembly line. Nonetheless, it takes someone with authority to build the plans or authorize the planning process and set things in motion.

LEADERS RESOURCE THE PLANNING PROCESS. A project, no matter how small, is going to cost something. Cost may be one person's time or the expertise of hundreds. Cost may be workspace, materials, travel expenses, or consultants' fees. Some leader will have to resource the plan.

LEADERS GUIDE THE PLANNING PROCESS. Rarely is a plan so cut and dried that in the first instance every aspect of the project is crystal clear. Someone has to grab it by the back of the neck and guide it down an uncertain path.

LEADERS SORT OUT THE ALTERNATIVE PLANS. How many times have you been involved with a project and discovered there is only one possible solution? I suspect almost never. There will be multiple courses of action with differing costs, timelines and levels of involvement. This is where leaders earn their pay. Each course of action may likely have proponents, even zealots, who are adamant that their solution is the best. Assessment, course of action comparison, sorting out, whatever name you prefer, a leader has to step forward, make the tough calls and then act. Compromise is rarely the best solution. Taking what appears to be the best parts from differing solutions in order to form a plan that pleases everyone, in the end pleases no one and may not pass the make sense test.

LEADERS DIRECT IMPLEMENTATION OF THE PLAN. Having gone through the planning process, resourcing, guiding, sorting out and finally selecting the best course does not mean the project will actually be launched. Even small organizations may have plans for multiple projects thought out, ready to go and their proponents are pressing for a green light. Again, it falls to the leader to prioritize and direct implementation of one plan while another goes on the back burner for the time being. But just giving a project the green light is not enough; leaders must remain engaged throughout implementation; the remaining chapters will describe the framework to do that.

Now that we have established the relevance of planning to every organization's operations, let's attempt to define planning, break it into parts and describe what it is and what it is not.

PLANNING IS PROACTIVE THINKING AT ANOTHER LEVEL. A leader cannot be expected to have all the best ideas. Skillful leaders are good listeners and pay close attention to suggestions from their subordinates. Additionally, effective leaders find appropriate incentives to promote proactive verses reactive behavior. Leaders should always seek to build a team wherein everyone is an active player, empowered in the planning process and thinking beyond their own level. The direct leader may be able to see all aspects of a problem, formulate a plan of action and lead subordinates through the execution. The more senior the leader, the greater the complexities of the issues they face and the broader are the range of problems to be solved. Therefore, operational and strategic leaders need help and the assistance comes from their subordinates; it follows then that the subordinates find themselves in a situation where they are thinking *for* their leader and *like* their leader, in other words at a higher level. Many people are reluctant to leave their comfort zone where there is routine, what they know best and where life is relatively risk free. This is where leaders at every level earn their pay. Those who do not think about going elsewhere do not want to go elsewhere and are comfortable with the status quo, must be taught and encouraged to think proactively at another level. It falls to the existing leadership to create a corporate culture in which innovative thinking is not only encouraged but also rewarded with good fitness reports, promotions, bonuses, or stock options.

PLANNING IS A JOURNEY NOT A DESTINATION. Imagine you are going to drive from Washington, D.C. to Nashville, Tennessee using only state and county roads. You cannot visualize a clear straight line at the outset. There may be some dead-end roads along the way. Although you saw the dead end sign, you pressed on, resulting in wasted time and effort. But the next time you see the same sign you immediately go into damage control and find an alternate route. There will be unexpected detours, roadwork that slows you down, causing milestones to be missed. There will be some days with extra hours behind the steering wheel in order to make up for lost time. About half way there you experience engine failure causing a major reassessment of resources available to continue the mission. But you repair the car and move on only to find yourself hopelessly lost. A catastrophic accident is even a possibility, canceling the project altogether. It is simple to visualize the parallel examples in the business world such as positive or negative product acceptance; advertising schedules out of synch; market research that missed the mark; an unanticipated employee strike; increased fuel costs; an economic downturn; or a "9/11" event that impacts an entire industry. Planning is a journey and an uncertain one at that; but it does not have to be a guessing game. The remaining chapters identify a set of tools for developing a framework for action.

PLANNING IS IMPERFECT. Of course, we all strive for the perfect plan; we want to produce this magnificent document that gets rave reviews from the boss, set it on automatic pilot on day one and let it fly. Unfortunately that usually does not happen. In spite of our diligence, Murphy's Law will be lurking at every juncture: if something can go wrong, it probably will. Leader guidance and decisions will be required throughout the implementation and execution of any plan.

In the military, an integral part of the planning process is an attempt to be ready for the unexpected. In combat situations there is no choice because the unanticipated can lead to needless loss of life. While not as catastrophic in non-military activities, the military model can nonetheless be useful to any organization's planners. It is called building branches and sequels.

BRANCHES. You have an approved plan and hope that everything has been accounted for, but knowing that hope is not a process you direct the staff to build some branches. Building branches is nothing more than going through a "what-if" progression. This may be a time when the boss assembles the war council and conducts a brainstorming session to surface the unexpected. Using our Washington, D.C. to Nashville analogy, *what if* we have a mechanical failure? Join a roadside assistance service. *What if* there is a snowstorm in the mountains? Take along a registry of all hotels along the route. Branches are contingencies off the approved plan in the event things do not unfold as expected. They may not take much time or effort to produce, but the devil is in the details and not being surprised by the unexpected can make life a lot more comfortable. But you should also realize that the what-ifs might not be trivial. In my last job in the military as chief of staff of the NATO headquarters in Naples, Italy, we were planning for multi-national ground force operations in Bosnia. Considering the delicate political, religious and ethnic issues involved, a serious what-if was whether or not certain countries would participate when it came time to deploy forces. If not, who would take up the slack and provide the forces required?

You have a plan to market a new product. The advertising campaign has been initiated, the sales force has been trained, production and distribution schedules have been set and you hear via the industry grapevine that there may be some labor unrest at a plant that is to provide the necessary raw materials. Is warehouse space available to stockpile materials now? If you rented space for additional materials, what is the impact on cash flow? This is what building a branch is about, answering the what-if questions. You have a brilliant plan, it is about to be executed and you have worked every branch imaginable. What now? Build a sequel.

SEQUELS. Sequels are subsequent operations based on alternative outcomes of the base plan. You have a military mission to take control of a town. The plan of attack is based on intelligence that concludes the enemy will fight at every approach to the town, falling back to set up a strong defense in the town itself. The plan involves air support, artillery and engineer support, a combined infantry and armor assault, air defense, overhead surveillance, attack helicopters, air assault helicopter operations, all the complexities of modern warfare. The assault begins, resistance is light and for reasons unknown the enemy abandoned the town and what was planned to be a two or three-day fight is over in a few hours. What now? You can sit there while a new plan is formulated and run the risk of losing momentum or proceed with the sequel, which is based on the premise of a quick victory. In this example, the principle element of the sequel is how to accelerate the logistics flow in order that the force does not outrun its support while continuing to attack and maintaining pressure on the enemy.

Sequels are necessary for outcomes that are potentially positive or negative. It seems that each year in late fall a particular toy emerges as the favorite and as Christmas draws near parents are scrambling to find that particular item. As inventories dwindle, toy manufacturers who have worked a sequel are prepared to focus production and distribution of a particular sold-out product in order to meet the pre-Christmas demand. On the other hand that same company may have developed a sequel to shut down production lines for toys that are not moving. Planning for sequels is mostly common sense, but a leader has to take the initiative to make it happen.

PLANS ARE NEVER FINAL. The last element of the definition of planning is that there is no such thing as a final plan. This may be a bit of an overstatement because it is possible to lock down a plan and declare that no one is allowed to tinker with it. But reality says a plan will continue to get worked on right up to the point of execution. The reasons vary but the primary one is that new information continues to emerge and the closer we get to a previously designated future point in time the more we are likely to know. This leads us to the question of what to do if we do not have all the information we would like to have at the point in time when the plan goes into affect.

The plan for a complex action must contain a list of assumptions. It is not possible to have 100 percent of the information one would like to have at the outset. The assumptions list is significant and needs to be completed early to ensure the planning is not proceeding based on a false premise. Using our trip from Washington, D.C. to Nashville, the planners will not be able to predict the weather with absolute certainty and may discover they are assuming that if they encounter snow and ice in the mountains the trip will be cancelled. You declare that to be a false assumption, square away their thinking and move on with the planning. Dealing with assumptions is a critical element in the framework for action.

There is another reason the plan will rarely be final and it is an unfortunate one but, nonetheless, all too prevalent. It revolves around indecisiveness on the part of some leaders. There is an old cynical saying, "Indecision is the key to flexibility." There are some leaders who will not take an eighty percent solution, go with their gut and move forward into execution. Their fear of failure causes them to procrastinate and seek out the last drop of information before approving a course of action. They are the leaders who seem to be constantly tasking subordinates for one more study on various aspects of the problem. Recall back in chapter eight, when discussing the time and place for a leader to engage the war council, I described the organizational climate and structure of the NATO Headquarter in Naples Italy where I was the chief of staff. We were engaged in planning for NATO ground operations in Bosnia. This situation provides an excellent example of what can result if any level of leadership, especially at the strategic level, lacks a clear vision of the end-state. The centuries old, deep-seated ethnic hatred (principally a Christian/ Muslim religious confrontation) existing in the Balkans provided NATO with a very complex problem. From 1993 to 1995 my staff was planning for NATO ground operations in Bosnia. The governing body of NATO functions by consensus, therefore our hard work on an operational plan was at the mercy of every political leader at NATO who thought they had a new and novel approach to the problem. Just when we thought we could see closure on the latest plan, we would be sent off on another tangent. The governing NATO body did not want the plan presented to them because they did not want to have to take a position and make a decision. So they just kept us working on what-if scenarios.

A situation like that can be terribly frustrating and it takes strong leadership skills to keep a staff mentally sharp, engaged and willing to continue to give their best efforts. One way to deal with indecisive senior leadership is to concentrate on the core issues, continuing to refine the plan as new and better data becomes available, all the while satisfying the what-ifs from above as marginal issues. To illustrate how complex the core elements of some plans can be, the Bosnia ground plan, dealing with issues such as available ports, airfields and road networks, logistics, intelligence, medical, communications, civil affairs actions and the composition of the ground forces, was approximately ten thousand pages. The amount of work to be done associated with the core issues kept the staff focused on the central problems.

Planning is proactive thinking at another level. Planning is a journey not a destination and there is no such thing as a perfect or final plan. It is vitally important that leaders think of planning as a process, not merely an act. Understanding the process is another set of tools for leaders at every level.

THE PLANNING PROCESS DEFINES THE PROBLEM. Or perhaps, better stated, the process forces us to define the problem. It is important to get this right because remember, the subordinates who will actually build the courses of action are being asked to think proactively at another level. In building campaign plans, subordinates are going to be thinking *for* the CEO or *for* the presidential candidate or *for* the military joint task force commander. Likewise, at the direct leader level, employees are going to be encouraged to think a level or two above their positions and reveal innovative means to improve operations. As their leader, at every level, you are going to expect and encourage innovative thinking by subordinates. Therefore it is vital that everyone not only understand the problem but also see it in the same context with an identifiable end-state.

THE PLANNING PROCESS EXPOSES STRENGTHS AND WEAKNESSES. We discover in planning for the road trip from Washington, D.C. to Nashville that none of the participants are experienced at reading a map. Having identified this vulnerability, the plan will be altered to include some instruction on map reading prior to departure. You also discover that everyone making the trip is an accomplished camper. Knowing this strength, one course of action will be to stay at campsites, thereby saving on hotel costs. Uncovering strengths and weaknesses also applies to the competition. While a competitor has a product of equal quality, their advertising campaign is weak. Perhaps if our plan includes a dynamite advertising campaign we can grab the market share necessary to be successful.

THE PLANNING PROCESS ALLOWS US TO GET INSIDE THE COMPETITION'S DECISION CYCLE. Planning frequently involves preparations to do something bigger, better, faster and sooner than the competition. When this is the case, getting inside the competition's decision cycle means knowing first of all *what* they are going to do. This is the most basic piece of information about your competitor and without it you will be flying blind. Once you have determined what they will do, the second step is to estimate about *when* and about *where* it will happen. Let's say you have a good product, dominate the market and you know your chief competitor is planning an advertising blitz to capture some additional market share. Will they offer rebates, lower prices, or free credit? What form of advertising will they use? When will the ad campaign begin? Where will they concentrate their efforts? Figuring out what the competition will do and about when and about where is called situational awareness. The ultimate goal is to also understand *why* they are going to do it. If you understand why you will have transitioned from situational awareness to situational understanding and that should be the goal. Planning is a continuous process. While you may be comfortable with your market share at this time, you are constantly in a state of planning to either sustain that share or increase sales. Getting inside the competition's decision cycle is a vital part of that process.

THE PLANNING PROCESS PROVIDES AN OPPORTUNITY TO GET THE BOSS' ATTENTION. Recall from chapter three, the point was made concerning the importance of the vertical line in the leadership continuum, allowing communications to flow in both directions. An organization that attempts to function with information flowing only from top to bottom will surely fail. Innovation is the lifeblood for most organizations and ideas frequently bubble up from the lower ranks. Many times innovation begins in the form of a problem statement and more likely than not the best solutions come from those closest to the action. If you want to get the boss' attention do not simply throw a problem at him or her but build a plan and simultaneously present a solution. Better yet, go through the planning process and develop two or three courses of action with advantages and disadvantages for each. The boss is the resourcer, the decision-maker and is constantly besieged with problems. Presenting a plan of action rather than just another problem tells the boss that you have thought about the issue from other perspectives. It is advantageous to look at the matter from the bottom up and the top down and having done so, you will have a much better likelihood of getting the boss' attention.

THE PLANNING PROCESS FOCUSES INFORMATION GATHERING. In chapter one we discussed information overload as one of an organization's greatest challenges as we transition into the twenty-first century. A leader's goal has always been to turn information into knowledge but with more and more information available, the sorting process becomes increasingly more difficult and time consuming.

The U.S. federal government spends tens of billions of dollars every year in support of the intelligence community consisting primarily of the Central Intelligence Agency, the Defense Intelligence Agency and the National Security Agency.

Additionally, within the military hierarchy of the Army, Navy and Air Force there are top-to-bottom intelligence staff elements. The challenge is turning information into knowledge a leader can use to gain an advantage. Intelligence is so vital to the success of military operations, our government maintains the entire apparatus in place and functioning during peacetime in order to ensure the intelligence community is trained and ready to support operational commanders when a conflict arises. Another reason it is important to sustain intelligence functions on a continuous bases is that putting together a coherent picture of a situation is a process of identifying bits and pieces of information over time and fitting them together. Think of an artist setting about to paint a picture of a landscape. Initially all you may see is the shape of the hills, a few tree trunks and outlines of buildings. As the artist refines the work (finds more bits and pieces of information) there will be snow and rock formations on the hills, branches and leaves on the trees, and varieties of trees and shrubs. Over time what it is we are looking at and looking for becomes increasingly clear.

While no private organization can ever be expected to match the magnitude of the U.S. government's intelligence effort, many may choose to allocate a portion of their operating budget to the information gathering function. Call it market research or industrial espionage, the planning process focuses intelligence gathering. Increasing globalization over the last few decades has changed existing organizational environments and created data gathering and analysis challenges. Planning for operations in another country or region of the world, forces senior leaders to make educated decisions on that area's demographics, infrastructure, import regulations and most importantly, the cultural demands. Without a functioning intelligence force and effort in place, leaders will find themselves running into roadblock after roadblock based on either the absence of information or misinformation.

THE PLANNING PROCESS PROVIDES AN APPRECIATION FOR SCARCE RESOURCES. There is never enough stuff; that is, time, people, workspace and capital.

In the final analysis, every plan simply has to make sense. As leaders guide their subordinates through the planning process they consider various courses of action. There is always the question of how much quality is enough to be successful in the market place. The automobile industry provides an example. No one is going to knowingly buy a car that is likely to break down frequently, regardless of how low the price is. On the other hand, there are automobiles of such quality they cost hundreds of thousands of dollars. Manufacturers seeking a sustained market share are constantly planning how to apply scarce resources to take quality to an acceptable level at an affordable price.

THE PLANNING PROCESS CHALLENGES ESTABLISHED RULES AND PROCEDURES. The planning process is similar to turning over rocks; one never knows for sure what may be lurking underneath. As we uncover more information and turn it into knowledge, we may find that what appeared to be sound guidance is, in reality, a deterrent to progress. For example, a company leader provides guidance during the initial phase of planning to maintain the existing information technology system because the next programmed upgrade is not scheduled to be purchased for another three years. But as the staff continues to turn over rocks, they determine the cost benefit of the new project hinges on a faster more capable area network. It became necessary to challenge the initial guidance.

In any organization rigid, established procedures can be mind numbing and begin to foster a bureaucracy biased toward the status quo. The planning process will expose these weaknesses and provide an opportunity to challenge long-standing procedures that are no longer appropriate or applicable to the current environment.

THE PLANNING PROCESS ASSESSES RISK. Moving the organization forward is rarely risk free. It is human nature to fear the unknown and some timid souls in positions of leadership will not go there. For leaders who understand the necessity of change, the planning process provides the mechanisms for conducting an analysis of alternative courses of action and the relative risks associated with each. In today's high tech environment the success of a plan of action may hinge on the recruitment of a number of specialists. A risk analysis determines they are in short supply, in high demand and hiring them will require signing bonuses and salary levels that will stretch limited capital to the point of jeopardizing the entire operation. Determining this information sooner (during the planning process) rather than later (during the early stages of execution) can be the difference between success and failure.

The following chapters are going to lay out the framework for action elements. First a leader must *chart a course*. That course is based on a vision of where the organization or project is going and a strategy to get there. With that in hand a leader must then enlist the efforts of all those who will be involved. To do so he or she must move to the second element of the framework and *declare expectations* by providing a mission statement, intent and guidance for planning and operating. Leadership is not a passive activity; having declared expectations, leaders cannot expect the road to success to be smooth and without obstructions. Leaders must proactively weigh in and vigorously pursue the third element of the framework by *creating conditions for success*.

RECAP

1. Leaders who are taking the organization elsewhere are in a constant state of planning.
2. Leaders:
- Initiate the planning process.
- Resource the planning process.
- Guide the planning process.
- Sort out alternative plans.
- Direct implementation.
3. Leaders must find a way to get staff members to think innovatively and outside their comfort zones.
4. Planning is a process that allows us to:
- Define the problem.

- Expose strengths and weaknesses.
- Get inside the competition's decision cycle.
- Get the boss' attention.
- Focus intelligence gathering.
- Gain an appreciation for scarce resources.
- Challenge established rules and procedures.
- Assess risk.

5. There is no such thing as a perfect or final plan.
6. The plan for any complex operation must contain a list of assumptions.
7. Planning is a journey, not a destination.
8. Planning is proactive thinking at another level.
9. The framework for action elements include:

CHARTING A COURSE
- Vision
- Strategy

DECLARING EXPECTATIONS
- Mission
- Intent
- Boss' Guidance

CREATE CONDITIONS FOR SUCCESS
- Leader Backbrief
- Centers of Gravity
- Critical Information Requirements
- Shaping the Battlespace

ENDURING LEADERSHIP PRINCIPLES

Great leaders:
Know how to plan.
Use a framework for action.
Communicate with clarity and brevity.
Act with agility.

CHAPTER THIRTEEN

VISION: THE FIRST STEP

Bits And Pieces Of Information Coalesce Into A Vision Of Where The Organization Can Go, Or In Some Cases Where It Must Go In Order To Survive.

There are three distinct pieces to the framework for action. First a leader must chart a course, then declare what it is he or she expects subordinates to do and finally create conditions that will provide opportunities for success. There are sub elements to each which will all be explained and illustrated in detail throughout the following chapters. Within charting a course there are two issues to deal with, vision and strategy.

A framework for action that is understood and utilized throughout an organization provides direct, operational and strategic leaders the toolbox they need to take an idea and see it through to completion. But where does the idea come from? Anyone can come up with an idea, but it falls to a leader to take it and see where it can go, what its potential can be and how all the pieces will coalesce into something useful. There must be a vision of an end-state. Recall the point was made in chapter nine that one of the requirements for molding a corporate culture is that there be a visionary who can see the organization as it will be after institutionalizing a new and different culture. The first step in using the framework is to decide where it is you want to go, that is, a vision of the end-state.

The purpose of this chapter is to provide some historical examples of visionaries and to describe how to determine if a vision is viable.

Advances over the past 150 years in how we communicate provide wonderful examples of individuals who had a vision and were able to see it through to an end-state that has had a profound impact on our lives. Thomas Edison, more than any other single person, was responsible for the foundation upon which has been built the technological revolution of the electronic world. His approximately 1100 patents are testimony to his work. From his laboratories came the phonograph, the carbon-button transmitter for the telephone, the incandescent lamp, a commercial light and power system, elements of the motion picture technology, etc. Edison published an article in 1926 entitled *Machine and Progress* in which he reveals his vision of what mankind needs to do to realize its potential. Edison wrote, "We must substitute motors for muscles in a thousand ways. A human brain is greatly hampered in its usefulness if it has only two hands of a man to do its bidding. There are machines each of which can do the work of a multitude of hands, when directed by one brain."39 He envisioned a society wherein tasks drudgingly performed by humans for centuries would be freed up by machines. Thomas Edison was a visionary.

In 1900 at the age of nine David Sarnoff immigrated to the United States from Russia with his family and became one of this country's foremost visionaries. Upon arriving in New York, he immediately went to work selling newspapers on the street. Sarnoff was full of entrepreneurial spirit and by the time he was thirteen had saved enough money to buy his own newsstand. His introduction to the electronics world occurred at the age of fifteen when he bought a telegraph key and taught himself morse code. Armed with this new skill, he sought a job with the Marconi Wireless Telegraph Company of America and was hired as an office boy. He became a telegraph operator in 1908 and his drive and ambition earned him rapid promotions at Marconi. In 1915 he sent forward an idea for a radio music box. At the time, radio was being used primarily for communications by ships at sea. But Sarnoff believed radio would ultimately become a necessity in every home. "The idea is to bring music into the house by wireless," he wrote in a memo. His superiors at Marconi resoundingly rejected the idea. But a twist of fate gave him new hope and a new opportunity; the Radio Corporation of America (RCA) was formed in 1919 and absorbed the Marconi Company, including Sarnoff. In the early 1920s Jack Dempsey, a prizefighter, was an enormously popular sports figure. On the second of July 1921 Sarnoff had arranged the live broadcast of a Dempsey fight and sales of radios took off. His vision of bringing entertainment into everyone's home had been fulfilled. As General Manager of RCA in 1926 he formed the National Broadcasting Company which would be central for his next vision. Vladimir Zworykin had patented a prototype television in 1923. Even while radio was in its infancy, Sarnoff envisioned television as the next grand step in mass communications and by 1928 had set up an NBC station for experimentation. Before it was even accepted as a viable communications medium, Sarnoff foresaw black and white television as only a stepping-stone to full color broadcasts. While leading RCA for forty years, he succeeded in making television available to every household in America, changing our lives forever. Sarnoff was a true visionary.40

Gordon Moore envisioned the processing power of microchip technology doubling every eighteen months while the cost fell by fifty percent. That was in 1965. In 1968 he was a cofounder of Intel Corporation and serves today as Chairman Emeritus. This is one of the grand visions of our time and has become known simply as "Moore's Law."41 Gordon Moore defined a revolutionary movement that would forever change the lives of people throughout the world and the way all organizations operate. It is this kind of keen foresight and power of imagination that has made the United States a superpower in every sense of the word.

Notwithstanding their greatness, visions in our practical day-to-day world are not normally on the scale of those of Edison, Sarnoff, or Moore. We could fill the remainder of this book with vignettes of countless visionaries who impacted humanity, but instead let us turn to the practical matter of what to do with a vision. Most visions are simply ideas for where to take an organization; this can be at any level of leadership. The direct leader in the Army, for example, may simply envision everyone under his control earning a maximum score on the physical fitness test and undertake a workout regime over several months to achieve the objective. The direct leader on an assembly line sees an end-state where, with a few time and motion changes in the way his subordinates work, they will be turning out significantly more product with no loss in quality and perhaps at less cost. The operational leader in a warfighting scenario can envision the combined effects of air power, psychological operations, naval support, deception operations and all the elements of land combat. He directs the production of a campaign plan to achieve the envisioned end-state. The strategic leader of a corporation engaged in manufacturing a product sees the interaction of worldwide economics, promotional campaigns, labor supply, and raw materials and brings them all to bear in a plan of action.

In day-to-day operations, the toolbox for vision can be closely aligned with innovation and change. Perhaps a series of suggestions have emerged over time, moving through the leadership continuum. As ideas flowed up through the leadership continuum they were perhaps commented on, enhanced and put into an operational perspective. All of the bits and pieces then begin to coalesce at the strategic level into a vision of where the organization can go; or in some cases where it must go to survive. But the need to innovate or change is rarely crystal clear. A vision is most often shrouded in fog, which can create tremendous anxiety for strategic leaders because they have the added responsibility for the welfare of the institution as well as tens of thousands of employees, not to mention responsibilities to the board of directors and stockholders.

With all of the uncertainty surrounding the first glimpse of a vision, it is instructive to investigate the ideas before launching a program; give them a good airing, see if you can dissolve some of the fog. A helpful tool for doing so is to look at the end, ways and means.

The *end* is obvious if the vision has been transformed into a clear, concise statement of how the situation will look once executed. Granted there will be elements that are unclear, but on the whole the end-state must be described in sufficient detail that others can adequately ascertain where it is the organization will be going.

The *ways* lays out a concept of operations to get from the present to the future state. At the direct leader level the ways may simply be a demonstration by the leader as to how the new process will work. At the strategic level the concept will have to describe how a number of processes will synergistically come into play and because of their complexity, some of the elements may be described in more general terms due to the absence of detail at this early juncture. If a strategic leader's vision is ultimately set in motion, the details will be unearthed and worked during the planning process.

The *means* has to do with resources. What will it take in terms of time, money, materials, manufacturing space and manpower to get the organization to where the leaders envision taking it? This may only be a back-of-the-envelope estimate at this time but it should be sufficient to clarify the vision and shed light on the risk involved in moving forward.

Some of the best lessons on leadership come from a study of a remarkable period in U.S. history, that of the Civil War. General Winfield Scott, a leader in the U. S. Army from the War of 1812 to the Civil War, seventy-five years old and having commanded the U.S. military forces for almost twenty years at the outset of the Civil War, was highly regarded and considered by many to be a brilliant strategist. By the beginning of the war, the Union Army had shrunk to about 700 officers and 14,000 enlisted soldiers. President Lincoln conferred with General Scott directly and frequently. Lincoln's vision was to preserve the Union; that is maintaining territorial and political unity was what he foresaw as the *end*-state. The *means* to achieve that end, according to General Scott, would be a Union Army rebuilt over time to tens of thousands in strength. And finally, the *way* to achieve President Lincoln's desired end would be to defeat the collective will of the confederate states. To do so, the Union Forces would need to secure the Mississippi River with 60,000 soldiers and gunboats deployed from Illinois to the Gulf of Mexico, impose a blockade of all southern ports sealing off the south and prepare to defeat the Confederate Army on the ground. All of this, he concluded, would take three to four years.42

Thinking through the end, ways and means is an excellent tool for sorting out the viability of a vision. Perhaps a leader will want to confer with the kitchen cabinet or at least call in the war council to do a quick assessment. Is it feasible? Is this the time? Who will object and why? Armed with data and confronted with the realities of the ways and means, some leaders will conclude, for a variety of reasons, some good, some fallacious, that the risk is too high and another course of action must be sought to achieve the end. Some leaders may lack the courage of their convictions and abandon the idea altogether even though they know in their heart it is the right thing to do.

While we can surmise that President Lincoln had a clear vision of the desired end-state during those conversations with General Scott, we can only speculate on whether or not he believed General Scott's prediction of a protracted war necessitating expansion of the Union Army by many times its present size. What is clear, however, is that President Lincoln concluded the ways and means were not politically feasible at that time. Therefore, President Lincoln's initial reaction was to authorize a call up of 75,000 volunteers to serve for a period of only ninety days. During that short period of time the Union Army did not engage in a single military action and those

75,000 troops had little if any impact on the outcome of the war. The postscript here is that the Civil War ended four years later after building the manpower strength of the Union Army to the levels proposed by General Scott.

In order to illustrate how a corporate CEO could use the tools available for transiting from vision to execution, we must develop a fictional company that can be carried through the remainder of the book as we explore all the elements of the framework for action. The Acme Corporation is a relatively small public company operating in two regions, the northeast and southeast sections of the United States. It has been a successful enterprise with a stable product line for the last couple decades. The CEO of Acme Corporation has for the past few years envisioned marketing the Acme line of products worldwide, but has never felt comfortable enough to move forward with the idea. Recently, however, the research department developed a technological improvement for their products that will provide, at least temporarily, a significant advantage over the competition and the Acme Corporation CEO sees an opportunity to capture greater market share. He calls together his kitchen cabinet and lays out his vision of an end-state in which the Acme Corporation is operating on a worldwide scale within the next few months. After an analysis of the ways and means there is general consensus that worldwide distribution is unachievable at this time. But if they move quickly, expansion throughout the continental United States is feasible. Having vetted the vision, the CEO now has a clear and realistic idea of where he wants to take the company. He also realizes it is only a matter of time until the competition catches up with Acme's improved product, so timing is of the essence. The CEO will initiate a team effort, build consensus and ensure every subordinate leader shares the vision and sees a common end-state. He must create and use a framework for action to get from vision to execution.

Many of us have been involved in a project where the so-called leader declared that we will just get started and see where this takes us; the details will eventually sort themselves out. Perhaps they will, but it is also unlikely the project will move efficiently and effectively. Trial and error is a process of sorts, but, as they say, not a good way to run a railroad. There is no framework associated with a let's-just-get –started methodology. That is why vision is such an important first step in the framework and why our Acme Corporation CEO has charted a clear path for his subordinate leaders.

Vision is a simple statement of WHERE the leader intends to take the organization

Using a framework is not bureaucracy; it is not layering or hierarchical; it is not a time-consuming sequential set of actions. The framework provides the means to work dynamically, to set the entire continuum of leadership in motion. Motion and action, in and of themselves, are not necessarily helpful unless some force has caused the organization's energy to be aligned toward a common end-state. The CEO is the engineer of this train, moving on a specific track; he is responsible for initiating the next move by providing the answer to the question: what is our strategy to get to the end-state?

RECAP

1. Vision is the first step in taking the organization elsewhere.
2. Is the vision viable? Look at the end, ways and means to sort out the road ahead.
3. Hope is not a process. Senior leaders must articulate a framework for action and vision is the essential start point.
4. Vision is a simple statement of WHERE the leader intends to take the organization

FRAMEWORK FOR ACTION

CHARTING A COURSE
Vision
Next is strategy

CHAPTER FOURTEEN

THREE RULES FOR DEVELOPING STRATEGY

Strategy Is The Alignment Of Assets To Their Greatest Advantage.

Solutions to complex problems usually require serious thought and a great deal of work. What are the major issues? Who will be the major players? What resources will have to be committed? These and many other questions will be solved during the planning process. But before people are thrust into the project's details there needs to be a general game plan that charts a course for everyone to follow. Flowing from that game plan will be the remainder of the framework for action elements. That game plan is called a strategy. As was discussed in the previous chapter, articulation of a vision provides everyone a picture in their minds' eye of WHERE the leader is taking the organization. Vision is the first element of charting a course, the second element is strategy. Strategy will tell key players and subordinate leaders HOW, in general terms, they will collectively go about getting to that end state.

The purpose of this chapter is to describe the three rules for developing and executing a strategy and illustrate how they fit into the framework for action; they are not complicated rules, yet absolutely essential to the success of any complex operation.

The first rule is to have a strategy. Every organization has strengths, weaknesses and core competencies established over time. Experience has demonstrated that certain combinations of persons or teams tend to compliment each other and create a synergistic affect. These factors need to be taken into consideration before launching the planning process. If not thought through, too much may be left to chance and the leaders may fail to leverage that which has been successful in the past. There is always some risk associated with venturing into new or uncharted territory but the successful organizations are the ones which recognize how to minimize risk, which in turn maximizes their chances for success. They do this by beginning with a strategy. This discussion of the first rule for strategy leads to a logical definition. *Strategy is the alignment of assets to their greatest advantage.* That is, not every endeavor is going to have the first team working it full time; the individual resources to be dedicated to a project may simply be the best combination of what can be made available at the time and must be used to their greatest advantage.

When Saddam Hussein invaded Kuwait in 1990 and President Bush decided to counter that action by deploying U.S. armed forces to the Middle East, this was not a knee-jerk reaction that took place within a few days. Bush's National Security Council assisted him in laying out a strategy to first build consensus among world leaders that Saddam Hussein must be stopped. Then a coalition of nations was formed, all of them outspoken critics of Iraq's aggression. Finally, the U.S. deployed an overwhelming force of half a million men and women to the Middle East. The coalition, timing and combination of U.S. air, maritime and land forces was the alignment of assets to their greatest advantage. The strategy was successful and when finally launched in a counter offensive, the coalition force defeated Iraq's most elite units in approximately two and one half days of land combat.

Working a project without first thinking through a strategy usually results in incrementalism; that is, beginning with some combination of assets, realizing they are insufficient, adding more, still not right, add more, etc. This methodology is time consuming, inefficient, frustrating to those working the issues and usually unsuccessful. The Vietnam War was fought that way, beginning with advisors to the South Vietnamese Army, committing U.S. ground forces, bringing in air and maritime power one element at a time, then adding army divisions and support units incrementally over a period of years until the total joint force numbered about half a million U. S. personnel. And then after ten frustrating years of combat we packed up and went home.

If we are to follow the first rule of strategy and HAVE ONE, where does it come from? The answer is you create it. There are three parts to strategic planning. First, is an over-arching view of the operating environment called an external analysis. Secondly, you must conduct a brutally honest evaluation of the organization's underpinnings called an internal analysis. Finally, you will develop and assess alternative courses of action to achieve the vision; this is called conducting an analysis of alternatives.

EXTERNAL ANALYSIS (step one of strategic planning)

The thesis here is that a business person in daily competition can be likened to protagonists in a battlespace. Using this analogy, you must develop information which assures a thorough understanding of the battlespace. Battlespace understanding incorporates several elements; two of these are attracting new customers (the market) and creating competitive advantages. In order to have clear battlespace understanding you must know what the competition will do, about when they will be capable of doing it and about where it will occur.

THE CUSTOMER: Assume for purposes of illustration that a company is going into Russia seeking customers for a variety of insurance products, personal as well as commercial lines. Questions that must be answered concerning the customer include, but certainly are not limited to: will we target small business, the medium market, high end, combinations of small/medium, medium/high or all of them? Where will we look; gradually moving from west to east, a reasonable radius around Moscow or the entire country simultaneously? Where are the customers now? Where will they be near-term, in five years, ten years, by region, by commercial category? How will they react to our product? What will attract and motivate the potential customers? What is the impact of their culture on our operations? Of course this list can go on and on and should until you are satisfied that you have posed all the right questions, the answers to which will provide you viable strategic alternatives.

THE COMPETITION: Who are they? Where are they? What is their market share, by region, by category? How will they react to our initiatives? Is their business flat or growing; how much, where?

The Red Team can be a key to developing battlespace understanding. Recall the function of the team is to "be" the customer and/or the competition. Get them on board early in the strategic planning process, resource them, give them time to research, develop and mature.

Battlespace understanding results from the accumulation of pertinent facts and assumptions about the external factors. Make yourself a cautionary note at this point in the strategic planning process. It is vitally important at this juncture to distinguish between fact and assumption. Moving forward believing an important research element is ground truth when in reality it is an assumption can be very dangerous.

Building battlespace understanding of the external environment is the first step of your campaign; yes, you are building a campaign. Before proceeding with the strategic planning explanation, a few points need to be made about your campaign. First, what is it? A campaign is a series of organized actions aimed at accomplishing a stated purpose and typically focused on a path toward an identifiable end-state. At the front end of your campaign, where we are now with the external analysis, you will find yourself facing three problems. One is you don't know what you don't know. The planning process is all about discovery and as time goes on you will sort it all out. But at the outset it is important to recognize that you don't know what you don't know. Secondly, early in the campaign plan you will be making some number of assumptions. The assertion here is that in any complex undertaking you will never have all the facts you need and will make some assumptions. As time goes on all of them must be addressed and a determination made as to their validity. Finally, there is fog. While your vision clearly tells you where you want to take the organization, at the far end of the campaign plan your vision is blurred. What will the economy be doing here and globally, will we be at war, what will the price of oil be, etc? All these are valid questions but at this point they are shrouded in fog. As you move through the campaign the end-state will become much clearer. This brief discussion of campaigns was inserted to emphasize the point that you must distinguish between fact and assumption.

Moving forward with strategic planning, from this extensive base of knowledge you need to look at strengths and vulnerabilities. In doing so you must be brutally honest or risk hanging a strategy on a weak element. Build a chart with four columns; in the first column list your organization's strengths (capital, global reach, experience, wide product range, lower cost structure, etc). The second column contains your organization's vulnerabilities (near-term focus, planning expertise, unknown in the region, etc). Then list the competition's strengths (known in the region, trusted, current market leader, etc). Finally, determine from your external analysis the competition's vulnerabilities (slow to change, cost structure, slow legacy systems, etc). The results of this analysis will become the basis for answering "why" you are or are not pursuing a particular strategy.

A game plan is beginning to emerge, but you must constrain your urge to approve a strategy and jump into operational planning. You are not finished; in order to complete the strategic plan you must answer the tough question, "Is this within the art of the possible?" To find this answer you must look internally.

INTERNAL ANALYSIS (step two of strategic planning)

Now we get to the point of the entire Part One of this

book, Underpinnings. The internal analysis which is an essential part of strategic planning involves looking at your organization's underpinnings and honestly answering a series of tough questions that should include but are not necessarily limited to the following:

VOLUME OF INFORMATION AND PACE OF OPERATIONS: Are you so bogged down with these two elements that you can not go elsewhere or have you mastered information management and can effectively move on?

A "GO ELSEWHERE" ORGANIZATION: Do you and your subordinate leaders deal with change easily and routinely or will you have to improve in this area before executing a new strategy?

SPAN OF CONTROL: What will this new strategic initiative do to span of control? Will it become too great to deal with? Do you have a "vehicle" to assist in being deeply involved one level down, understanding what is happening two levels down and then seeing all levels occasionally?

DELEGATION: Do you routinely delegate effectively enough to take the organization where it needs to go?

EMPOWERMENT: Will your subordinates feel empowered to deal with the inevitable dilemmas subordinates will face each day as you get into execution?

ORGANIZING FOR ACTION: Do you have a "go-to" person such as a Chief of Staff whose availability (chained to the desk) will allow you the flexibility to travel as needed? Will he or she take care of the routine business routinely? Do you have a War Council to help with strategic planning? Do you need to consult with your Kitchen Cabinet to help you "see" the forest for the trees? Do you need a Coach who knows the new region and its culture? Is your Red Team available, activated, up to the task?

EXTERNAL ORGANIZATION: Are the collaborative tools in place to effectively deal with an unconventional organizational structure? If not, what must be done to overcome anticipated shortcomings?

CULTURE: Have you defined the organization's culture?

If so, will it support emerging strategies? If not, what changes are required? Must you personally lead the change? Will subordinates follow? How long will it take to change the culture? Can you execute the strategy and change the culture simultaneously? If not, what then?

LEADER DEVELOPMENT: Do you have a bench of trained subordinates who can think strategically and translate their thoughts into a campaign of their own for their part of the plan? If not, are they capable of learning and changing? Can you coach and mentor them through this framework for action or must some of them be replaced? Is there time to get key individuals through required corporate training? Will some pending assignments need to be accelerated or put on hold?

OPERATIONAL ENVIRONMENT: do you need to change the way your organization operates? Are communications down the continuum of leadership working? Do all of your subordinate leaders understand and use some framework for action? Do you and your subordinate leaders effectively deal with ideas coming up the continuum of leadership from the point of execution, capturing innovative ideas and templating them to other leaders? Do you lead by walking about or are you routinely tied to your headquarters? Is maximum centralized planning, maximum decentralized execution the best way to operate? If not, what then should it be?

ENHANCED OPERATIONS: Do you have a vehicle in place such as the After Action Review to provide low cost value added?

A brutal and honest assessment of the state of your organization will provide confidence that the underpinnings are sound and will accommodate moving to the third and final step in strategic planning. Likewise, if there are shortcomings, and it is likely there will be some, are you postured to work through the deficiencies while aligning assets to their greatest advantage and launching the project?

ANALYSIS OF ALTERNATIVES (step three of strategic planning)

By now you have developed an in-depth understanding of the battlespace and identified the strengths and vulnerabilities of your organization and that of the competition. The final step in strategic planning is to assimilate all the facts, data and assumptions and then develop options for the way ahead that make sense.

Recall our ACME CEO has a vision to expand operations across the continental United States. His in-depth review of external and internal factors has given him the confidence to move forward with an analysis of alternatives. He is considering two overall strategies; both involve establishing new regional operations that mirror their ongoing successful northeast and southeast regions. Alternative one is to move incrementally east to west across the U.S. establishing regional headquarters over the next two years. The second is to establish all the regional headquarters simultaneously.

A good method for assessing the advantages and disadvantages of each is to build another matrix with course of action one and two on the vertical axis. Then across the top of the matrix list all the factors bearing on the courses of action; for example, time required, cost, market share, manpower, training, risk, etc. this can be as complex and detailed as you want it to be in order to get to the point where you can draw some logical conclusions and make a decision. As you analyze the options keep cycling back and asking yourself, am I aligning assets to their greatest advantage?

While the red team was invaluable in developing the external analysis, now, during the analysis of alternatives, is an opportune time to call in the war council. These are a few bright individuals in whom you have the utmost trust and confidence. They can assist in sorting through the facts, grading the assumptions, drawing conclusions and can be counted on to provide an honest opinion of the emerging game plan. Once the boss has reached a tentative decision, he or she may want to run it by the kitchen cabinet or a coach for a final sanity check. Use the organization to its greatest advantage.

At this point you have completed strategic planning

and are ready to move forward. But before going there, I want to introduce an additional thought. The dynamics of the battlespace will never allow you to be satisfied with the status quo; you must find a way to gain continuous situational awareness.

SITUATIONAL AWARENESS

After developing battlespace understanding, the pertinent information will get pushed down through the continuum of leadership in various ways as part of the framework for action. What must then happen, dynamically, is maintenance of continuous situational awareness at all leadership levels. What is going on in the market place with respect to the customer and the competition must get communicated up the leadership continuum from those closest to the action, no matter where they are in the leadership chain.

The framework for action provides tools to accommodate the flow of situational awareness information; these tools include updated critical information requirements, changing centers of gravity, leader backbriefs and actions that shape the battlespace as well as routine reporting. All of these will be covered in detail in subsequent chapters.

The importance of situational awareness if that it provides leaders the information they need to make decisions as to how and when to move to the next phase of the campaign plan. Knowing when to move to the next phase is a key and difficult decision and will not always be intuitively obvious. Having all leaders operating in an environment of constantly updated situational awareness is another force multiplier in the journey from vision to execution.

The second rule of strategy is to keep it simple. Having said that, the execution of any strategy to solve a complex problem will be difficult. "Simple" in this context means that the strategic statement must be succinct and easily understood. If a leader cannot explain, in general terms, the strategy in about twenty five words, it may be too complex or worse yet not clear to the leader who is attempting to communicate it.

One more thought on the second rule, keeping it simple. There are advantages to being able to capture the essence of the strategy in a single word or phrase. It is a way of capturing the attention of everyone in the organization and continuously focusing them on how the organization is going to go about successfully achieving the vision. In the case of some airlines during the months following the terrorist attacks 9 September their revised strategy might have simply been "survive." In the case of ACME, the CEO has called his strategy, "reinventing the company."

Recall our Acme Corporation operating along the eastern seaboard in two regions. The vision is clear; expand coast to coast. The strategy decided on by the Acme Corporation leadership has three pillars. First, expand quickly while the product has a technological advantage over the competition. Second, the new national organization will consist of a series of regions that mirror the success of the existing northeast and southeast regions. Finally, confine the expansion to the continental Unites States. It is essential that everyone at the operational level understands this strategy. They are the ones who bring the core competencies to bear on a daily basis and will cause the organization's strengths to be maximized during this operation.

The strategy to carry out a major operation may require policy changes or shifts in emphasis. For example, at the Acme Corporation it had been the policy that the leaders in the northeast and southeast regions do their own hiring and training of subordinate leaders. The strategy for expanding across the nation will include centralizing hiring and training at corporate headquarters. Leaders at the operational level will be instrumental in making this happen. Not only does the senior leadership structure the strategy, they must build consensus and get the operational leaders in line. This is not the place for compromise or trying to please everyone; it is a time for team building and selling ideas. Recall Colin Powell's Rule Number One, "Good leadership involves responsibility to the welfare of the group, which means that some people will get angry at your actions and decisions."43

Building a strategy can be lonely business, but because of their unique perspective, the most senior leaders must formulate the strategy for operations involving multiple elements of the organization. Leaders at different levels have different views of the world. In chapter four we saw the relatively well-defined, structured environment of the direct leader. The operational leader has a larger playing field but it is still primarily internal to the organization. The strategic leader, on the other hand, is the one who must constantly take into consideration and deal with forces external to the organization. Dealing with an expanded environment gives the senior leader a perspective not available to the other leadership levels. It is this perspective that will facilitate alignment of the organization's competencies against the challenges to be faced during the operation. Use the kitchen cabinet, the war council, involve selected operational leaders, or have the staff prepare some preliminary estimates, but do not think for a moment that building a strategy is an action that can be delegated.

There are instructive lessons to be learned from the Civil War in general but particularly the Battle of Gettysburg. The Battle of Gettysburg took place July 1-3, 1863, in and around Gettysburg, Pennsylvania. All the senior leaders from the Army of the Potomac and the confederate's Army of Northern Virginia briefly faced off at Gettysburg. Constrained in time and space, the events provide a laboratory for the study of enduring leadership principles. Looking back on the build-up to the Battle of Gettysburg will lead us to the third rule of strategy. Recall the first rule is to have one; the second is to keep it simple.

General Robert E. Lee was tiring of war, the casualty rates were high and the resources to sustain his Army of Northern Virginia were dwindling. The rich agricultural areas of Virginia had been picked clean. During the winter months of 1863, there were long debates about the strategy for the summer campaign.

The alternatives were to concentrate against Union forces in the west and south or take the fight to the Army of the Potomac. General Lee believed the will of the North to continue the war was waning and he prevailed with his arguments to undertake a bold stroke; his vision was to end the war with an 1863 summer campaign in Maryland and Pennsylvania.

Lee undertook an extensive external and internal analysis; he understood the enemy and his own organization. His internal strength was his three subordinate commanders, James Longstreet, Stonewall Jackson and J.E.B. Stuart; one of the most effective senior combat commander teams ever assembled. One internal vulnerability however was his bench of subordinate leaders which played a decisive role. The strategy was well reasoned and played to his force's core competencies.

Unlike the Army of the Potomac with its huge slow organic logistics operation that was an impediment to movement, Lee's Army was light, agile, lived off the land and moved relatively fast. The strategy was multifaceted but simple in its concept. First, the Army would move north by swinging west into the Shenandoah Valley thereby using the north-south mountain range to protect his right flank. Second, he would maneuver in the Maryland and Pennsylvania farmland, the breadbasket of the North and thereby sustain his forces. Having his entire force deployed and well supplied, he would then be able to threaten Harrisburg, Baltimore and Washington. There was, of course, a huge psychological factor associated with threatening the seat of government. The Army of the Potomac was stationed in close proximity to Washington, D.C. Whenever the Army had previously taken to the field to confront Lee's forces in Virginia, Lee had out-thought, out-maneuvered the Union leaders and generally been successful in a series of engagements. Therefore, the third pillar in Lee's strategy was to cause the Army of the Potomac to be drawn away from Washington.

In preparation for the summer campaign, General Lee had sent his cartographers north to map the area. What he saw was terrain he could use to his advantage. His strategy was for his forces to occupy favorable terrain giving him the advantage as the Union forces attacked. He could then fall back, regroup, pull the Union further from their supply lines, all the time inflicting significant casualties. Having weakened the Union forces he would then swing his cavalry around the Union flank positioning themselves between the Union forces and Washington, D.C. This, Lee believed, would defeat the will of the North to continue the war

It is easy to visualize the phases of the campaign; planning phase, prepare the force, movement north, position the forces on dominant terrain, engage the enemy, fall back to engage again, flank the enemy with cavalry to threaten Washington D.C. and end the war.

Lee had a strategy, the concept was sound and it was easily understood. It keyed on their strengths and capitalized on the vulnerabilities of the Army of the Potomac. It could have been successful. Lee had completed the first phase of the campaign by successfully moving up the Shenandoah Valley, winning engagements along the way, in order to begin positioning the Army of Northern Virginia in northern Maryland and southern Pennsylvania.

An obvious key to success in land warfare is to know where the enemy is located, their strength and intentions. During this era, responsibility for obtaining this information fell to the cavalry, the eyes and ears of the Army. Lee's most trusted subordinate was J.E.B. Stuart, a brilliant cavalry commander who had served Lee well and been successful in the past. Two unanticipated factors came into play, both of which had a dramatic impact on Lee's strategy. First, inexplicably, J.E.B. Stuart did not report in. He was out of touch, circumventing the Army of the Potomac as it moved north to engage Lee. By the first of July, Lee had not heard a word from Stuart in more than a week, he had no idea where the Union forces were, their strength or their intentions. Lee was blind. He was at a critical phase in the campaign plan and was lacking situational awareness, that all-important ingredient that enables a leader to make critical decision at critical points in the campaign.

Second, the town of Gettysburg was between the two armies and all roads led to Gettysburg. There was a convergence of ten major roads at Gettysburg. As forces on both sides maneuvered in northern Maryland and southern Pennsylvania, there was by happenstance a meeting engagement between Union and Confederate forces in the vicinity of Gettysburg. Lee made the decision to converge his entire Army on Gettysburg, the Union forces, however, were able to occupy the commanding terrain on the first of July. Having lost the advantage, Lee made the decision to attack on the second and third of July. During those momentous three days, history records horrific casualties, unimaginable bravery and sacrifice, brilliant application of enduring leadership principles as well as catastrophic failures in decision-making. On the third of July, the Union Forces repulsed Pickett's charge and the following day a defeated Lee began the long march back toward Richmond.44 That brings us to one of history's best illustrations of *the third rule of strategy; if the strategy is sound and being successfully executed, do not abandon it.*

Lee was where he wanted to be. His forces were better provisioned than they had been for months, the Army of the Potomac was being drawn into battle and the strategy was on track. The next step was to occupy dominant terrain of his choosing, conduct a tactical defense and wear down the Union Forces. But, he allowed himself to get sucked into a battle at Gettysburg where the advantage was on the side of the opposing force.

A footnote to the Battle of Gettysburg is that while Civil War fighting continued for nearly another two years, it could possibly have ended in July of 1863 had the Union Forces leader, General Meade, pursued Lee as he retreated. But, you see, Lee went north to win the war while Meade maneuvered only to win a battle. On the third of July as the Union forces retained the high ground in victory; there was no vision or strategy to propel them forward into the next phase of the operation wherein they could in all likelihood have totally defeated General Lee. There was no next phase and there was no sequel to their plan. It was a failure of leadership in victory.

What happened at Gettysburg can happen in any organization today. When working a complex project there will always be times when essential information is not available; there will be alternatives courses of action with strong proponents for each; external circumstances may have been altered and pressure is building to abandon the project all together. This is when senior leaders get very lonely. They must look at all the issues; assure themselves that they have a sound strategy; that the way ahead is feasible and doable; provide strong leadership, build consensus and stay the course.

If we have a vision of where we want to take our organization and a strategy has been laid out to get us there we have completed charting a course. This is the point in the process of getting from vision to execution where senior leaders all too often bow out of direct involvement. But there is an enormous amount of space between deciding on a strategy and actual execution. Somehow that gap must be filled. If the visionary, the strategist is no longer a part of the action, the operational planning can spin off in unintended directions. That is where the remaining elements of the framework for action come into play. The leader must remain involved and find a way to capture everyone's imagination, talent and energy. He or she begins filling the gap by declaring expectations.

RECAP

1. Strategy is the alignment of assets to their greatest advantage.

2. The first rule of strategy is to have one. Strategy brings the operational leaders into alignment.

3. The way you get a strategy is to create it by conducting an exhaustive external analysis of the market place (the customer and the competition) thereby building battlespace understanding. Then take an honest look internally at your organization's strengths and vulnerabilities. Armed with facts and assumptions, conduct an analysis of alternatives.

4. The second rule of strategy is to keep it simple, that is, succinct and easily understood.

5. The third rule of strategy is to not abandon it if assets are being brought to bear to their greatest advantage

6. A critical ingredient during execution is continuous situational awareness.

FRAMEWORK FOR ACTION

CHARTING A COURSE

Vision

Strategy

Next is declaring expectations; mission

CHAPTER FIFTEEN

MISSION: THE LAUNCH POINT

Mission Is The Beginning Of The Process Of Communicating Throughout The Entire Leadership Continuum.

Mission is a good word. Goal will also work but we all have personal goals and the word is generally overused. Objective is an alternative but in many cases is short term in nature, monthly sales objectives for example. But mission portends something larger in scope, longer range and can grab the attention of the entire organization. It is a declaration of a leader's expectations.

Organizations use the word mission in two distinct ways. First there can be an overarching, permanent statement of the enduring mission of the organization. For example the mission of the United States Army is to fight and win the nation's wars. This statement is simple, direct, descriptive and useful to continuously focus the Army. Every organization should have a mission and use it to indoctrinate its members and sustain focus.

The second use of mission is for launching individual projects. That is, describing to some segment or perhaps the entire organization what it is the leadership expects to accomplish during a specified period of time; downsize by twenty percent, increase sales by ten percent, merge with another company, expand the product line, etc. It is this second context that is the subject of this chapter.

Articulating the vision may have been the work of a single senior leader perhaps with the assistance of the war council to define the end, ways and means. Also constructing the strategy was in all probability an individual or small group effort. The mission statement is the part of the framework that takes the project public. Everyone in the organization should see it and understand it. Mission is the beginning of the process of communicating through the entire leadership continuum.

The purpose of this chapter is to determine what mission is, what it does for us, where it comes from and how is it used.

The boss writes the mission statement; it is his or her charge to the organization. The vision is *where* the leader is taking the organization, the strategy defines about *how* it will be carried out; now the mission will transmit to everyone in the organization *what* it is that needs to be accomplished and that everyone involved need to get on board.

There are two measures of merit for a mission statement. First and foremost is clarity. While it may take only seconds to craft the mission statement, it is helpful to always run it by a couple confidants to ensure it makes sense to them. Remember, if something can be misunderstood it will be and a mission statement that sends conflicting messages can be a formula for failure.

The second measure of merit is brevity. Effective mission statements are one or two sentences. It needs to capture the essence of what is to be done in a few words for all to grasp. A mission statement that runs to a paragraph or more is subject to interpretation, can be misunderstood and tends to go beyond the *what* and get into exactly *how* and *why*.

The mission statement is a tool for leaders at every level to declare their expectations. But as we work our way through the continuum of leadership, the mission statement means different things to different people at various levels of the organization. To explain how the mission statement gets transformed into action, let's return to the Acme Corporation. The CEO provides the following missions statement:

> **Our mission is to expand this company's operations throughout the continental United States and dominate the market. Increase annual sales from the current $30 million to $250 million in the next 36 months.**

The CEO called all of his senior employees together to fully explain his vision, strategy and to personally present his mission and intent. After answering a few questions and content that everyone clearly understood the mission, all principal subordinates head off to do their part.

Their first action for subordinate leaders is to restate the mission. This is an important and essential part of the framework, making the mission relevant. The Acme Corporation's chief financial officer clearly understands the overall mission but it lacks the specificity needed to get his group working. Having played a part in the end, ways and means review, the CFO is aware that about $200 million will be required to finance the expansion. Therefore, the CFO's restated mission statement is simple: raise $200 million. Based on the assumption that overall success may depend on expanding while their product has an advantage over the competition, the CFO could make that additional point in the mission statement by saying: quickly raise $200 million or raise $200 million by July. Another layer down from the chief financial officer are leaders whose expertise is in banking or stocks. A further restatement of the mission by a subordinate leader might be: by June first determine the feasibility of borrowing $200 million for company expansion. You see now what is happening throughout the Acme Corporation: the Director of Human Resources is working up a mission statement having to do with hiring, locating and training new personnel. The Vice President for Advertising is preparing a restated mission statement that will get her organization working on a national ad campaign. The sales manager is now truly a national sales manager and will prepare a statement to that affect.

Mission facilitates establishing a relevant framework for action in every part of an organization. Going one step further and conducting a mission analysis can further enhance this formula for action. Again, this is applicable at every level. Mission analysis is a tool for systematically sorting out what needs to be done and will thereafter facilitate assignment of actions. Mission analysis is a simple process of identifying the specified, implied and essential tasks. Perhaps a leader will grab a yellow legal pad, find a quiet place and jot down the tasks in a few minutes. An alternative is to gather a small group and conduct a brainstorming meeting to identify the tasks to be performed. It is critical that an organization not allow itself to get a few weeks or months into the project only to discover something important has been overlooked. This is analogous to a family planning their annual two-week summer vacation. The preparations are routine: tune up the car, research the best routes, stop the mail, make hotel reservations, etc. The departure day arrives, they are on schedule to get an early start, the car is loaded, but as they back out the driveway little Johnny looks out the window and says, "What about Fido?" Mom and Dad stare daggers at each other sending signals, "I thought *you* would make arrangements for the dog!" Mission analysis simply lays out the critical tasks to be performed and then identifies who is responsible.

Three mission analysis headings, specified, implied and essential, serve different purposes and make the process more complete. Under *specified,* the list will be short and perhaps taken directly from the mission statement. For example the Acme Corporation's chief financial officer's specified task is to raise $200 million. The specified task or tasks serve the purpose keeping what is most important in focus.

The *implied* task list is longer and its development is designed to identify the entire spectrum of possible actions to be undertaken. It facilitates innovative thinking by those who otherwise are comfortable with the status quo. Without heretofore being stated, it is implied that the CFO will look at alternative means to secure the $200 million needed for the Acme Corporation expansion. The list of implied tasks will include, for example; 1) borrow the money, 2) issue stock, 3) sell something, 4) use cash reserves, 5) combinations of 1-4. The list of implied tasks should initially be long and uninhibited, as it is easier to prioritize a complete list than to play catch-up as unidentified tasks are discovered later.

Finally, the *essential* task or tasks. As with the specified list, this will in all likelihood be only one or two items. The primary purpose of the essential task is to identify critical elements without which there will be a high probability of failure. The essential tasks add emphasis and facilitate prioritization of resources later on. The Acme Corporation CFO's essential task could simply read, "quickly" or be a specific date by when they need to have funds identified.

After contemplating moving forward from a vision and after some period of strategizing, there comes a time for action. The mission is the heart of the framework in getting from vision to execution. It is a declaration of leaders' expectations and a call to action.

RECAP

1. The boss writes the mission statement.
2. The measures of merit are clarity and brevity.
3. Mission is the beginning of the communication process through the entire leadership continuum, whereby the boss declares expectations.
4. The mission must be restated at every level and made relevant.
5. Conducting a mission analysis facilitates early identification of the specified, implied and essential tasks that must be performed.

FRAMEWORK FOR ACTION
CHARTING A COURSE

Vision
Strategy
DECLARING EXPECTATIONS
Mission
Next is intent

CHAPTER SIXTEEN

COMMUNICATING INTENT

Intent Is A Powerful Leader Tool Used To Declare Expectations And Provide Clarity Of Purpose.

While the mission statement is clear, concise and spurs everyone to action, it is not enough of a framework to support an operation over the long haul. The mission needs to be expanded upon and the vehicle to do so is the boss's statement of intent, the second element in declaring expectations. Intent is the most powerful tool available to a leader.

If the mission is the heart of a project, intent is its soul. Intent personalizes the mission statement and provides connectivity between the mission and a concept of operations. Intent is the part of the framework that lets all the subordinates into the leaders mind, gaining an understanding of how he or she feels about the project. Successful leaders are great simplifiers, having the ability to cut through the detail and make issues understandable. Intent is a tool for leaders to provide that clarity of purpose.

The purpose of this chapter is to identify the uses for a leader's intent and the key elements in its format.

In defining the characteristics of intent, it is foremost singular possessive; that is, it is the boss's personal creation, at every leadership level. Writing the intent is not the duty of a committee. Those who are going to work on the issues and execute the final plan have to believe the intent came from their leader. Second, just as with the mission statement, intent is public information; everyone in the leadership continuum must understand their leader's intent.

The third defining feature of intent is its relative brevity. While the mission statement is a couple short sentences, intent should consist of a few short paragraphs. There is an important reason for brevity; while intent is a vital piece of the framework, it must not preclude or inhibit initiative and inspired thinking by talented subordinates as the details of the project unfold. An intent statement that rambles on for pages will tend to articulate a solution, a specific set of alternatives or a complete concept of operations; it is too early in the planning process to risk articulation of the how-to.

The boss's intent statement serves two central purposes. First, as the organization progresses toward execution, a myriad of issues will arise and be dealt with. Leaders are often called away for periods of time, become incapacitated, or depart the organization in the midst of a project. In those instances progress must not come to a standstill. In the absence of specific guidance, a clear understanding of their leader's intentions will allow subordinates to use their initiative and continue toward mission completion.

I spent a couple decades of my career embroiled in the Cold War, wherein there was intense focus on the potential to engage the Soviet led Warsaw Pact in central Europe. One of the key elements in the intelligence preparation of the battlespace was an understanding of how the Soviet forces operated. The Soviet armed forces did not have a professional noncommissioned officer corps nor did their junior officers have the authority to make decisions and act on their own initiative; their station in life was to carry out specific orders. On the other hand, U.S. forces are led by intent with the clear understanding that winning campaigns and wars is the cumulative outcome of a multitude of small engagements. It was always clear to me that in spite of their numerical superiority, the Soviets could not prevail over a force wherein leaders at every level were trained to make decisions and take action in the absence of specific orders to accomplish what they knew their commanders intended.

The second purpose served by the boss's intent is to begin the process of binding together the leadership in a commonly understood endeavor. Recall that each successive leader is going to take the mission statement and make it relevant to their particular operation. Restating the mission will bring a more focused statement of intent. Remember, as an inviolate rule, mission and intent are inseparable and keys to creating conditions for success at every leadership level. When a subordinate leader is crafting his or her statement of intent, the rule of thumb is to capture the essence of the intent received from the leader one layer up. Imagine a thread running through the leadership continuum beginning with the strategic leader and ending at the direct leaders. But this intent thread is not a taught line; at each level after leaving the most senior leader it loops back to capture intent one level up and then continues. This simply and efficiently binds the thought processes of all the leaders in the continuum together just as a seamstress would hem the jagged edge of a piece of cloth to give it strength and lasting stability.

Along with mission, intent is a vehicle for leaders to declare expectations. Writing an intent statement is neither difficult nor time consuming. This is another part of the framework that will just take a few minutes of a leader's time. As a guide in writing the intent, there are four elements that need to be included; they are end-state, vision of the operation, why and keys to success.

Senior leaders are not necessarily any smarter or more talented than their subordinates but they do have the advantage of perspective. As one proceeds up through the leadership levels the view of a larger landscape becomes clearer. Leaders should never assume their subordinates have the same view of the end-state and the obstacles to be encountered along the way. The end-state must be described to ensure clarity of purpose. In the military the end-state is described in terms of friendly forces, enemy forces and terrain. For example, the intent may be to probe the enemy without becoming decisively engaged at this time (friendly forces); in order to determine his (enemy forces) strength and disposition (terrain). Or uses all forces available (friendly) to destroy his force (enemy) and seize a certain piece of terrain. In the business world this translates to your organization plus perhaps outside contract work aligned for this project as the friendly force, the competition as the enemy and the operating environment as the terrain.

The second element in the intent statement is to provide a vision of the operation. Recall earlier one of the measures of merit of an intent statement is brevity. This is the part where a leader who believes they have a monopoly on the good-idea market can get carried away and writes an entire concept of operations. That is a formula for failure. What the leader wants to do with this section is bound the problem and point his or her people in the right direction. Based on experience and perspective, the leader can build efficiency into the project by telling his subordinates where to focus their efforts.

Skillful leaders all have immense respect for their subordinates. A helpful rule of thumb is to believe they will do anything you ask as long as they know why they are being asked to do it. That is excellent advice for any leader at any level and the intent statement is the perfect vehicle to articulate why an operation is being undertaken. Including the why in the intent gets that question answered early in the planning cycle. Explaining why brings additional clarity and a sense of purpose to the project. Do not underestimate what your subordinates can accomplish when they understand why they are being asked to do something.

One of the greatest heroic feats in U.S. military history occurred during the Civil War at the Battle of Gettysburg in July 1863. Confederates were attacking Union forces that occupied a critical piece of high ground. General Winfield

Hancock observed an opening develop in his defensive line and knew that within minutes the Confederate forces would begin pouring through the breach, seize the initiative and the battle could be lost. General Hancock turned to the commander of the First Minnesota Regiment and told him to charge his entire 262-man force into the breach because he needed to buy five minutes of time to bring up a reserve force and reestablish the integrity of the defense. Knowing why, the need to buy five minutes of time, the First Minnesota charged into the face of a 1500 man offensive force and sustained 200 casualties within 15 minutes.45

General Hancock got his five minutes, the line was shored up, the battle was won and perhaps the course of U.S. history changed. The outcome of charging that line would have been intuitively obvious to the commander of the First Minnesota and his soldiers, but they understood why the attack was necessary, believed in their leader and executed the mission. Leaders in every type organization will from time to time ask employees to make sacrifices in order to move forward and be successful. While they will likely not have the same dire results as the First Minnesota Regiment, employees will be willing to make sacrifices if they know why they are being asked to do so.

The final essential element in a leader's intent statement should be a short list of keys to success. In virtually every operation there is going to be something upon which success will hinge or some actions that will enhance the chances for success. These may be obvious to the leader but leaders should never assume their subordinates have that same perspective. An example of a key to success could be the element of surprise; it may be speed in order to get to the market ahead of competitors; it could be a bold, audacious move; or adherence to core competencies. Whatever the keys, articulating them is another tool available to a leader for knitting the leadership together, keeping a project on track and declaring expectations. Recall in the previous discussion of mission analysis (specified, implied and essential); in all likelihood you will find linkage between the essential tasks in the mission analysis and the keys to success in the intent statement.

The Acme Corporation CEO's intent:

We are going to expand nationally. Eighteen months from now I intend for this company to be conducting operations in new regions across the continental United States that mirror current operations in the northeast and southeast regions.

We will accomplish this by establishing lean, efficient regional centers in key areas.

We can expect intense competition but that will not deter our efforts. We will develop procedures to enhance our competitive advantages so that thirty-six months from now we will have captured at least forty percent of the market and $250 million in annual sales.

We are making this move now because we have a better product than the competition.

While we have been successful recently, the environment is changing and we cannot assume today's processes and procedures will continue to serve us as well in the future. During the expansion, I intend to conduct quarterly reviews of operational procedures and make adjustments necessary to sustain a competitive advantage.

Success of this expansion will depend on speed of execution. Therefore, simultaneous planning at all levels will be a critical element.

Did the CEO cover the bases for an effective statement of intent? First, *end-state and territory:* "Eighteen months from now

I intend for this company to be conducting operations across the continental U.S." *Vision of the operation:* "We will accomplish this by standing up lean, efficient regional centers in key areas." *Enemy forces:* "We can expect intense competition..." *Why?* "We are making this move now because we have a better product than the competition." *Keys to success:* "...conduct quarterly reviews...make adjustments...success will depend on speed... simultaneous planning at all levels will be a critical element."

As subordinate leaders in the Acme Corporation receive the mission/intent package from the CEO, they should be able to develop a common picture of where the company is going and generally how it will get there. They should have a sense of what the boss expects of them and what the timetable will be. The mission and intent are linked, brief and concise. It is now the responsibility of the second level leadership to take a few minutes to make the mission relevant to their operation (recall the chief financial officer's restated mission is to raise $200 million) and provide more specific intent.

Each successive leader, from vision to execution, should work from intent. With this piece of the framework in place, what the most senior leader intended will be communicated as a consistent message throughout the organization to the point of execution. Intent is the vehicle upon which clarity of purpose rides and provides every leader an opportunity at the most appropriate time to declare expectations.

The chief financial officer's intent:

The Acme Corporation is going to expand to a multiple-region company operating across the entire continental U.S. It is my intent to provide the most advantageous financing arrangement for the $200 million expansion of this company. We will look at the entire array of options available to us: borrowing, selling, stock issue, using cash reserves and combinations of them all.

The Acme Corporation's product line is highly

competitive and our profit margins are small. Therefore, it is imperative that we find a financing solution that minimizes short-term risk to the company. The keys to success are speed and our best efforts. I want the first review of options in two weeks. Dig out the best possible data to preclude false starts or unfulfilled expectations when we begin the expansion.

Few organizations are blessed with a line-up of strong leaders from top to bottom. This is where mission and intent play such an important role. Weak leaders can cause initiative to stall out when they lose their nerve or focus. But the mission and intent provide three reasons for them to be more aggressive and productive. First, they have been given authority to act; they know their actions are part of an approved operation. Second, they know the organization works from a framework for action designed to make them active participants and to keep the communications flowing. They will feel some pressure to not break the flow of intent. Finally and perhaps most importantly, the weaker leaders know that eventually a follow-on piece of the framework is going to hold them accountable.

RECAP

1. Intent is the most powerful tool available to a leader. Properly used, it can transform an organization and become a culture in and of itself.
2. Intent is inexorably linked to mission.
3. Intent serves two purposes:
    *   In the absence of specific instructions subordinates will continue to perform because they understand what it is their leader intends for them to do.
    *   Intent binds the leadership and the organization to a commonly understood purpose as each successive leader's intent captures the sense of the intent one level up.
4. There are four essential elements of an intent statement:

- The end-state defined as friendly, enemy (competition) and terrain (operating environment).
- A vision of the operation to bound the problem and provide focus.
- Explain why.
- Keys to success.

5. Intent personalizes the mission statement, provides clarity of purpose and enhances communications throughout the leadership continuum.

FRAMEWORK FOR ACTION

CHARTING A COURSE

Vision

Strategy

DECLARING EXPECTATIONS

Mission

Intent

Next is boss' guidance

CHAPTER SEVENTEEN

BOSS' GUIDANCE

From Bounding The Problem to Pinning The Rose, Leadership Is A Hands-on Endeavor.

Recall mission and intent are for public consumption. Additionally mission and intent are a more formal part of the framework. Boss' guidance, on the other hand, is much more informal. This is straight talk directly from the boss at all levels, looking someone in the eye and telling them they have the lead. It is impossible to overstate the importance of this element of the framework. Leaders are communicators and boss' guidance is the vehicle for leaders at every level to set the tone for the way ahead in the third and final element of declaring expectations. There is no precise formula for the content of boss' guidance but effective guidance tends to answer who, what, when, where, why, and how questions.

SINGULAR POSSESSIVE. Issuing boss' guidance is not an act that can be delegated. Just as with vision, strategy, mission and intent, the boss may choose to confer with a select group of advisors in order to formulate the guidance. But when it is time to execute the boss has to gather the key players, address them directly and demonstrate commitment.

CONTENT. Putting together the boss' guidance is not a difficult task. Think of it as the marginal notes that accumulated while drafting the mission and intent statements. Mission and intent need to remain brief and focused; they are for everyone in the organization to see. Important bits of information and guidance that do not fit into mission and intent are natural additions to the boss' guidance. Who will have the lead? When do I need to see the first draft plan? Where will this take place? One note of caution, especially at the operational or strategic levels, do not provide too much guidance and end up outlining a complete detailed concept of operation, thereby negating the brainpower of the subordinates.

WHEN TO USE THE GUIDANCE. The short answer is early. Do not allow subordinates to become decisively engaged in a project only to discover they have to change direction after hearing the boss' guidance. You may choose to issue the guidance simultaneously with the mission and intent or an alternative is to issue the mission and intent and specify that boss' guidance will be forthcoming on Tuesday morning at nine o'clock in the conference room. This is a by-invitation-only affair. This latter approach provides subordinates with an opportunity to digest the mission and intent, to formulate questions and to think about the way ahead. Can I hire some outside consultants? Where does this stack up in priority? Do I cancel scheduled vacations? Timing for the boss' guidance is dictated by the nature of the project. If this is a crisis situation the guidance takes on greater importance and cannot be delayed.

VERBAL OR WRITTEN GUIDANCE. The boss' guidance can be either verbal, written or both. If this is a crisis situation and everything is happening on the fly, the guidance will, by necessity, be verbal. But even then someone should be taking notes for the record. Under normal circumstances as part of a deliberate planning process the boss should issue the guidance verbally. It is one of those occasions when you, as a leader, either fulfill your subordinates' expectations or fall flat on your face. Prepare your comments point by point because, just as with mission and intent, clarity is the measure of merit. These points should be delivered to a select group in a private setting. Perhaps at some point in the proceedings a memo is handed out with the key points listed. Regardless of how thoroughly you may have prepared your comments, if something can be misunderstood, it will be. This is not the time for individual interpretation; subordinates will be expected to depart this session and launch. Therefore, the forum must be open to questions and someone should be taking notes. This provides another answer to the question, verbal or written? The best of all worlds may be verbal guidance, followed by a question and answer period, with a memorandum for record forwarded to each attendee the following day that captures not only the points in the guidance but additional information that emerged from subordinates' questions.

BOUND THE PROBLEM. This may be the most important criterion for boss' guidance. Given any complex issue, it is possible to develop endless courses of action. This is analogous to an artist attempting to do a landscape painting of the whole world, an impossible task. To successfully complete a landscape painting the artist must set the left margin, perhaps a mountain, extending right to a tree, with a certain amount of sky down to the fence line in the foreground. Having done that, the artist's task is clear, fill in everything between the mountains the tree, the fence and the horizon. Similarly the boss has to identify the mountain, the tree and the fence, but then allow the subordinates to fill in the details. The boss knows the company must raise capitol for this project but the timeline is such that one piece of guidance is to disregard issuing new stock because it will take too long. Additionally there must be a national promotional campaign but television is not the preferred medium for their product and that option is removed from consideration. Time is a precious commodity for every organization; wasting it is not only demoralizing for subordinates but also it can lead to failure. Setting the boundaries for the problem is a first step in insuring time and energy will not be needlessly wasted.

PIN THE ROSE. Your organization is nearing the first major milestone in a company-wide project. The chief of staff is quizzing two key subordinates about the status of one aspect of the plan. One subordinate responds that it is not his responsibility; John's group should be working that. John, with a panicked look on his face says, "Uhhh, I thought you had it." The boss, in his guidance, either forgot to pin that rose or just assumed John would pick it up. The issuing of boss' guidance provides the perfect opportunity for a leader to point a finger at someone's chest and fix responsibility, "Jim, you are in charge of this operation." Perhaps others in the room consider themselves to be senior to Jim, but that issue has just been set aside. Jim has just been given tasking authority and is a decision-maker.

ESTABLISH A TIMETABLE. Firm, clearly articulated milestones emanating directly from the boss is a blow to the bureaucrats, procrastinators and weak leaders. When the boss establishes the end-state and the end-date, subordinates tend to act positively. Setting milestones is one of the simplest and most effective tools available to a leader. The milestones from the boss' guidance will identify key events thereby providing subordinate leaders the opportunity to further identify additional milestones to be issued in their own boss' guidance. As mission, intent and boss' guidance get restated and bind the continuum of leadership together in a common cause, they are also binding the organization together on a common timeline. This is vital because it facilitates necessary horizontal interaction among the numerous elements engaged in solving the problem, sales, production, finance and advertising. Whenever leaders interact along the leadership continuum, they should never pass up the opportunity to go over subordinates' milestone schedules. This can ease a leader's anxiety by knowing the subordinates are working inside the bounds established for the project as a whole and that they are on schedule. Laying out milestone schedules for complex problems is more than calendar work; it actually involves thinking through a synchronization matrix. You are a subcontractor responsible for putting in the foundation for a new house and you are ready to deliver sand, cement and bricks. The problem is, the lot has not been cleared and is covered with trees and undergrowth. It is also obvious that the electrician, roofer and plumber cannot begin until the framer is finished. The general contractor for the house must have a synchronization matrix outlining the order in which jobs will be tasked. In the development of a new product line there is the synchronization of milestones for finance, product development, market research, advertising, production, distribution and sales. The milestones for these critical events must get sorted out early in the framework to avoid confusion, inefficiency and finger pointing.

PRIORITIZE. There are only so many productive hours in a workday. If everyone is gainfully employed and they are expected to take on a new mission, where does this project stand in importance? What will get less attention? The boss cannot leave this important issue to chance. One subordinate may see this as number one priority while others have it further down their respective lists. This will result in an imbalance in workflow and milestones will get out of synch. The subcontractor has a dozen lots to clear. He needs to know which lot is his first priority because the foundation crew is standing by to begin work.

HOW THE ORGANIZATION WILL OPERATE. The boss needs to establish perspective on this project at every level. Is this an unusual event that will proceed based on new operating procedures or should everyone work within the context of the current policy? In nearly every project the most important element in the equation is people. How will they be affected, how will they be treated, how will they be led? Rarely is there a constant list of key factors brought to bear from project to project. This is an opportunity for the boss to clarify some dos and don'ts. For example, on occasion, outside consultants have been brought in temporarily for projects; it may be important in the guidance to authorize, deny or leave the consultant decision to the discretion of the individual departments. A situation bordering on crisis may involve guidance to cancel all leaves, immediately recall every employee, set up 24/7 operations in every department and authorize overtime pay. Do not underestimate the potential for disaster if boss' guidance is incomplete. The company is working on a sensitive project and two department leaders are engaged in conversation at the coffeepot. Jim is asking John if he got the word that this is to be kept close hold until a prototype is tested. With a look of disbelief John confides that he just finished an interview on the project with a local reporter and the public will know about it in the morning. Rarely will large operations fit neatly into standard operating procedures; it is incumbent on the boss to define the playing field and the rules of the game. The boss' guidance is the ideal forum for accomplishing this. Let's revisit the CEO of ACME Corporation where he has gathered the principal subordinates in a private session to issue boss' guidance:

You have all read the mission statement and my intent. Let me provide a little more guidance before we launch. *(verbal presentation)* The chief operating officer has the overall lead *(fix responsibility)* on the expansion of our company across the continental U.S. I will clear my calendar next week to receive your initial staff estimates. *(first milestone)* We will complete the overall plan of action by the first of May. I expect planning to be centralized here at corporate headquarters. *(how we will operate)* Initially plan for one new production facility out west. *(bound the problem)* Execution will be decentralized with newly appointed regional leaders empowered to make necessary decisions. Upon approval of your plans, I will select regional leaders from within the company. They know our culture and will understand how we operate. Upon naming new regional leaders, we will conduct simultaneous collaborative planning. Regional headquarters will be lean. Corporate headquarters staffs exist to support down. Regional leaders will get their senior subordinates from this headquarters; we will

backfill and train replacements here. *(bounding the issue)* **I realize you all are busy, but this is now your number one project** *(prioritize)*. **We will do all the work internally with no outside consulting contracts. Use your own discretion on overtime pay. Get the word out at every level; everyone must be singing from the same sheet of music. If you have any question get back to me ASAP.**

GUIDANCE IN STAGES. You have a vision, the strategy is sound but for every complex undertaking the crystal ball will almost always be a little cloudy; it is virtually impossible to foresee every potential obstacle. So when a leader is issuing boss' guidance there is a high probability that this piece of the framework will be revisited. Boss' guidance provides every leader at every level an opportunity to demonstrate their commitment and declare their expectations.

RECAP

1. Boss' guidance is an essential element in the framework for getting from vision to execution.
2. Boss' guidance should not be delegated. Persons in leadership positions must lead and this is an opportunity that must not be passed up.
3. Bounding the problem, fixing responsibility and establishing key milestones are the principle components in boss' guidance.
4. Boss' guidance is part of the process of binding the organization together in a commonly understood effort; it must be executed at the strategic, operational and direct leader levels.
5. It may be necessary to revisit boss' guidance throughout the life of a project as events unfold and circumstances change.

FRAMEWORK FOR ACTION
CHARTING A COURSE
Vision
Strategy
DECLARING EXPECTATIONS

Mission
Intent
Boss' guidance
Next is creating conditions for success; leader backbrief

CHAPTER EIGHTEEN

CREATING CONDITIONS FOR SUCCESS

Being A Leader Is Not A Passive Activity; It Is Hands-On, Interactive And Intuitive.

Getting from vision to execution is a multi-faceted endeavor involving the use of a large toolbox. The key tools in the framework for action, vision, strategy, mission and intent, are designed to get us started, identify an end-state, declare expectations and get everyone on a common path. But even a perfect launch will not provide answers to key questions that every leader at every level will be asking. Do all the key subordinates understand what is required? Are they on the same track? Are they on the same time-line? Do they understand the priorities? These are critical questions and they must get answered at the strategic, operational and direct leadership levels. Being a leader is not a passive activity; one cannot sit back and hope everything will work out for the best.

Everyone in the continuum of leadership has expectations; for example, a subordinate leader looking up the chain expects guidance from which to work and the senior leader has expectations that subordinates will seek out innovative solutions. Another expectation is that all leaders will be fully engaged. When engaged, what exactly is it that leaders do?

The answer is they create conditions for success. Creating, in this context, means being proactive, guiding, mentoring and deciding.

The purpose of this chapter is to provide a working list of conditions for success that leaders at every level in any organization can use effectively.

As with the previous elements of the framework – vision, strategy, mission and intent – these tools are not complicated, time consuming, or difficult to use. Nonetheless, they are essential to successfully navigate from vision to execution.

LEADER BACKBRIEF

One question that has been repeatedly asked throughout this book concerning the necessity for a framework for action is how do leaders know their subordinates understand what it is they are to do. Did they get it; "it" being understanding the mission, intent, timetable and priorities? In his book *The Stuff of Heroes*, William Cohen quotes Dana Mead, CEO of Tenneco, on the subject of leader backbriefs. "I learned a long time ago that you do not make assumptions about what people understand or do not understand or are doing or not doing when they are under a lot of pressure."46 Dana Mead succinctly described a condition for success. A leader at any level who tends to assume everything is on track will eventually get caught short.

The point was made earlier that successful leaders are great simplifiers. This is the time to add a second characteristic to that list. Skillful leaders also understand and can read people. Without being prejudicial, they have a sense of individuals' strengths and weaknesses; they can identify who can be left alone, has a tendency to get sidetracked, needs a periodic pep talk and who needs an occasional kick in the butt.

Following the session when the CEO of our Acme Corporation issued his boss' guidance, he asked the Chief Operating Officer to remain for a minute. Recall the COO has the lead for the expansion project. CEO: "Jim, I suggest you might want to follow up soon with Smith, I just don't get the feeling that he completely understands where we are going."

WHAT IS THE LEADER BACKBRIEF? The leader backbrief is nothing more than a subordinate leader updating his or her boss. Some refer to it as an in-progress review. There are some keys to a successful leader backbrief that can be explained by exploring who, what, when, where and how. Keep in mind as we get inside the leader backbrief this is not bureaucracy, creating hierarchy or spending endless hours with key personnel tied up in long unproductive meetings. The leader backbrief is a simple, efficient element of the framework for getting from vision to execution.

WHO DOES THE BACKBRIEF? The leader gives the brief. This is his or her opportunity to demonstrate their grasp of the situation, that they are in charge and to send a message concerning commitment. Visualize a subordinate leader arriving for a scheduled backbrief and he announces that the brief will be presented by three of his people who are working the issues. The boss will immediately surmise that this project might be in trouble because it may be leaderless. In those first moments he begins to visualize a built-by-committee camel while expecting a racehorse.

Leaders must be held accountable. The leader backbrief is a leader function and should not be delegated. Every leader must answer to someone; even the President of the United States is accountable to the American people. Almost on a daily basis the President's press secretary is issuing statements concerning the President's position on a variety of issues. But when there is an issue of profound importance, the leader backbrief comes from the President, usually in the form of a short, televised address to the nation. The CEO of Acme Corporation will have to brief the board of directors. The first-line leader on the assembly line will backbrief his shift leader.

WHEN, WHERE, AND HOW DOES THE LEADER BACKBRIEF OCCUR. The leader backbrief can be formal, informal, spontaneous, private, a group effort or all of the above. Recall the Acme Corporation CEO said in his boss' guidance that he wanted staff estimates next week. That represents the first leader backbrief and was part of the milestone schedule. We can assume all the Acme executives in attendance understand the company's operating procedure and what the CEO wants. That is, they know the CEO prefers a one-on-one brief but will tolerate the leader bringing along a small team. They know the CEO prefers a desk-side briefing with a few simple black and white paper slides as opposed to an expensive, multi-media presentation that took days to prepare.

While it is more time consuming, there is also merit in a group backbrief. That is, those receiving the boss' guidance reassemble at a designated time and one by one present their backbrief. There is value in the interaction because it can lead to broader understanding of the problems and issues. This forum also provides the opportunity for every person to hear comments and further guidance from the boss. If you watch televised football you have doubtless seen the defensive line coach talking to his guards, tackles and ends assembled in a row on the bench. As he is providing guidance to the left tackle, it is beneficial for the others to internalize the instructions. The objective is to foster teamwork and create a synergistic affect. He wants to create the illusion by the opposition that the defensive line squad appears to be a platoon. Teamwork and synergism are just as important in every organization as they are in sports. Every leader should be constantly on the lookout for ways to enhance teamwork. Taking the time to assemble key leaders and allowing them to feed off each other can be a force multiplier.

Keep in mind these are not rules that apply exclusively at the senior level. Imagine the shift leader on the assembly line with a span of control of six or eight first-line leaders. The mission was to institute some new procedures. The shift leader may call a five-minute stand-up meeting where he asks each first-line leader to describe his or her implementation plan. Each does so in a few seconds and everyone is back to work. But in the process, one of the first-line leaders hits on an ingenious idea that would be beneficial to all. The shift leader, seizing the opportunity to expand his boss' guidance, directs that everyone integrate that one aspect into their individual plans. Leader backbriefs are essential and valuable at every level.

WHAT DOES THE LEADER BACKBRIEF CONSIST OF? An organization that embraces some formula for getting from vision to execution in all probability has an operating procedure in place, preferably written, that spells out the minimum essential elements for the leader backbrief. Normally, these procedures are adjusted from time to time primarily to fit the boss's personal desires. Some bosses are office-bound, some prefer to get a sense of the environment at the subordinate level, some favor simple one-on-one desk side briefings, while others choose the group effort. Whatever the venue, whatever the audience, there are some key and essential elements that must be included in the leader backbrief and these should be well known and understood operating procedures.

The leader backbrief must begin with a statement of the mission. Recall the first act by every successive leader in the continuum is to restate the mission, to make it relevant. CEO: "The mission is to expand the company..." chief financial officer: "The mission is to raise $200 million...." By hearing the restated mission, this is every leader's opportunity to determine if their subordinates have their people concentrating their efforts on the correct problem. It also provides an opportunity to grade the paper. Does the restated mission meet the criteria of clarity and brevity? The briefer may have the mission statement displayed on a screen in the conference room or perhaps places a paper copy in front of the boss at his desk and opens the leader backbrief by saying, "Sir, my restated mission." The boss reads the sentence, nods in agreement and in about fifteen seconds the first element of the backbrief is completed.

Next is intent, a powerful tool available to every leader. This will take more than fifteen seconds. Recall this is the vehicle for knitting together every leadership level in the continuum. Is the intent statement clear and crisp or does it begin to get into details better left to later staff work? Does it capture the essence of the intent statement at least one level up. If not, the process of binding the organization together will be broken and the problem compounded as successive leaders issue their intent statements. Finally, the boss will want to get a sense from the intent that the subordinate leader sees where the project is going, that he or she visualizes the correct end-state and that the requisite sense of urgency and commitment are there. At this point the backbrief may have lasted only two or three minutes, but the boss is getting a clear sense of where his subordinate is headed.

If the mission and intent are not right, this is the time for some mentoring. If the boss simply gives a thumbs down and sends them off to rethink their mission and intent, it is doubtful they will see the light as they walk out the door. Use the backbrief to wordsmith the mission and intent until you are comfortable they have a clear understanding of where the organization is going and the part they will play. This is leader development 101.

There is another reason why the boss should not dismiss the presenter after hearing only the mission and intent, no matter how far off track they may be. Irrespective of what has transpired to this point, the boss must see the third element of the backbrief, a statement of assumptions. Take it on faith that in working a complex, multifaceted problem you will never have the luxury of knowing all the facts. Therefore, early in a project leaders at nearly every level will be working from a set of assumptions. As time goes on and new information becomes available, the list of assumptions will get changed. At this point it may be assumed that some things are not possible and listing them as such appears to be valid. Later on when more light is shed on the problem and more data is developed, the assumption may be discarded and a new course of action considered. Or at the other end of the spectrum some avenues we assumed would be available are no longer viable. The boss should carefully study the list of assumptions not only for what is there but also for what is missing. The higher up a leader is in the continuum, the broader their perspective is on the organization's operations. Therefore, they routinely see interaction of multiple operational elements, have a greater feel for the art of the possible and are in a position to comment on the validity of the assumptions.

The list of assumptions will be a key determinant in sorting out the courses of action. A great deal of time and effort can be wasted chasing a solution based on an invalid assumption. It is possible, at this point in the leader backbrief, that the boss could terminate the session, provide additional guidance and send them back to reconsider where they are headed with the project. Two circumstances could cause a termination of the backbrief. One, a subordinate leader involved in a complex issue claims there are no assumptions. It is difficult to fathom such a situation and if there are some key assumptions that will drive course of action development the boss has reason to worry and question this subordinate's ability to lead his group through this difficult task. The second circumstance that could terminate the briefing is a major invalid assumption that is driving the direction of the effort. The Acme Corporation's Director of Production gets to this point in his leader backbrief and the number one assumption is that new production plants will be constructed somewhere in the Midwest and on the West Coast. The boss realizes that everything following in the briefing will flow from that assumption. The boss also knows Acme Corporation has neither the capital nor the time for construction of more than one new plant. At this point the boss needs to provide additional guidance, reestablish the sense of urgency and reschedule the leader backbrief.

Another possible outcome from a review of the assumptions is that the boss' guidance was not complete, the mission and intent lacked clarity, or both. The boss may realize that the entire lineup of subordinates is hard at work but laboring under a false assumption. What if, for example the Acme Corporation CEO had failed to convey a sense of urgency for the nation-wide expansion of operations? This would become obvious in the first round of backbriefs and the CEO would have to backtrack and rework the mission, intent and boss' guidance.

In 1995 at the NATO headquarters located in Naples,
Italy, responsible for Southern European Operations, we were
working hard on the contingency plan for NATO ground
operations in Bosnia. My boss, Admiral Leighton Smith and I
had carefully worked through the mission statement and intent
and were satisfied with their clarity. Soon after issuing those
documents, we assembled a group of senior officers from several
countries throughout Europe for battle staff training. We were
surprised at the number of questions that began, "Admiral, what
did you mean by....?" If something can be misunderstood it will
be, particularly when dealing with multiple nationalities and
cultures. That battle staff training session was invaluable, if for
no other reason than to discover early on that the intent needed
to be reworked.

Mission, intent and assumptions are the three essential
elements of the leader backbrief. What follows depends on
where the project is on the timeline. If this is the initial leader
backbrief there may be a presentation of staff estimates and
a description of courses of action the subordinate leaders are
planning to develop. Subsequent leader backbriefs may go as
follows: "Sir, no change to the mission and intent; one new
assumption I mentioned to you the other day; the purpose
of this backbrief is to lay out the details of three courses of
action...." Circumstances and project timeline will dictate the
center section of the backbrief following mission, intent and
assumptions.

There are two final essential elements in leader backbriefs.
First are conclusions. All of what came before in the backbrief
is leading somewhere. The boss cannot assume everyone is
on track to take the right turn at the fork in the road. The
boss needs to hear it. The subordinate leader needs to clearly
articulate what conclusions he or she has come to at this
point in time. It may be bad news, but better now than later.
Perhaps the conclusion is that the timeline is not achievable,
the available capital is insufficient, or the timing is out of synch
with economic conditions. Also, the conclusion reached by the
subordinate leader may be contrary to where the boss thought

the briefing was headed; it may cause them to collectively reexamine the assumptions.

If there are no conclusions in the backbrief the boss may reach some of his own; the subordinate does not have a grasp of the situation, or has not sufficiently worked the problem, or lacks the fortitude to publicly state conclusions. Whatever the case, the leader backbrief has served its purpose. The boss knows this group needs additional guidance, mentoring, more time or perhaps a new leader.

The final piece of the leader backbrief is a recommendation. Everyone has a boss. Everyone is accountable. At some point they are looking for approval for whatever it is they intend to do. Recommendations are the logical ending to a leader backbrief. All the rules for conclusions apply to recommendations; they need to be stated, they should make sense in light of the mission and intent and beware if there are no recommendations.

In today's global economy, in which many organizations are dealing with diverse nationalities and cultures, the importance of clear and concise communications cannot be overstated.

LEADER BACKBRIEF RECAP

1. The leader backbrief is a condition for success and a force multiplier. Equally important is the timing of the backbrief.

2. The leader presents the backbrief. This is not committee work.

3. Leader backbriefs take place at every level in the continuum.

4. Hearing a subordinate's restated mission statement provides valuable insights into where the project is headed.

5. Ensure that the statement of intent captures the intent from leaders at least one level up in order to bind the continuum of leadership together.

6. At least in the early stages of complex problem solving, there will be assumptions. Every leader must review their subordinates' assumptions carefully.

7. Leaders are expected to tell their bosses what conclusions and recommendations have been reached.

CENTERS OF GRAVITY

Identifying centers of gravity can be difficult. The more comprehensive the problem the more complex is the task of identifying focal points. If you do not identify centers of gravity, does it follow that you will fail? Perhaps not, but correctly tagging them can save a lot of trial and error, time and resources. Therefore, identifying centers of gravity may not be a pure condition for success but can surely enhance the chances of success.

Center of gravity can be defined as a thing, a person, a place, a belief, a condition, or a circumstance that is central to success. Generally, centers of gravity are referred to in the plural because there is generally at least one identifiable center of gravity for both sides. In every business endeavor there is your center of gravity and that of the competition; on the battlefield those for friendly and for enemy forces.

Defining centers of gravity may be a subject you, as a strategic or operational leader, take up with the kitchen cabinet or debate with your war council. You may ultimately find you missed the mark but that does not mean the exercise was completely futile.

Whenever a staff begins to work a large complex problem there is the ever-present danger they will be broad based but lack the depth of knowledge necessary to get at the heart of the issue. Identifying a center of gravity is a way to focus effort, particularly when time is the constraint or limited numbers of personnel can be committed to a project; .boss' guidance can be an excellent time and venue to suggest or declare the centers of gravity. It follows that for subordinate elements – advertising, production, finance, etc – their centers of gravity will be unique. The leader backbrief becomes an excellent time to present centers of gravity and, if not presented, the perfect opportunity for the boss to quiz the subordinate leaders on the issue. In every endeavor leaders are seeking force multipliers and synergistic effects. To get there, they need to commit to an effort that will have a payoff out of proportion to the investment in time and effort.

During the Civil War, the Union's Army of the Potomac went through a succession of commanders (McClellan, Burnside, Hooker and Meade) all with their individual leadership strengths and weaknesses. That line up of commanders who preceded the appointment of General Ulysses S. Grant all had three things in common. First, President Lincoln appointed and ultimately fired them all. Second, Robert E. Lee, commander of the confederate Army of Northern Virginia, generally out-thought and out-maneuvered them. And finally, they all considered Richmond, capital of the confederate states, to be the center of gravity of the confederacy. It was not a completely absurd notion. One could easily build a case that says if you capture the seat of government, the government ceases to exist. On the other hand, one could argue that the confederate government was simply a handful of leaders in a few offices who could have packed up in a couple days and departed for Charlotte, Atlanta or wherever to reestablish the confederate capitol. The point is that a succession of commanders sustained tens of thousands of casualties while focusing on a place as the confederate center of gravity.

Enter General U.S. Grant, a person who had to this point in his life failed at every venture he had undertaken. But unlike his predecessors on the Civil War battlefields, he did not fail, he was not fired and he was successful. Of course there were multiple complex reasons for his success but central among them was that General Grant correctly identified the confederate center of gravity. It was not a place or a thing; it was Lee. Go after, stay after and fight General Robert E. Lee wherever he and his army are maneuvering; defeat him and his army and the war will come to a conclusion. Was it easy? No. General Grant's army sustained tens of thousands of casualties. Was it quick? No. It took many months. Was it correct? One hundred percent. Upon appointment as commander of all Union forces, General

Grant went to the field; completely abandoned his office in Washington, D.C.; stayed in the field and focused his personal attention, his army and all his subordinate commanders on one thing, the confederate center of gravity, General Robert E. Lee.

On a completely different note, if you did a case study of Federal Express you might conclude their center of gravity is time; getting the package to the recipient in the least amount of time creates customer satisfaction. Or if you looked at a small skunkworks operation the center of gravity might be scientific expertise and in turn that could lead to a conclusion that one condition for success is to hire from a limited pool of scientists.

For those of you old enough to recall the debacle we called the Vietnam Conflict (where I spent two years of my life), the center of gravity was not the hearts and mind of the South Vietnamese people where we toiled for years and years. I was too junior at the time to be in a position to know who (the Administration or the Congress, or senior military leaders, or all of the above) was responsible for making the center of gravity assessment. But after several years and little progress it seems in retrospect that it might have been intuitively obvious the U.S. had misidentified the center of gravity. But no, we slogged on for years and finally gave up. Conversely, the North Vietnamese clearly identified their center of gravity as patience and commitment. Additionally, from their viewpoint the enemy's (the U.S.) center of gravity was a lack of commitment (citizens, press, Congress) and a failed doctrine. They called it exactly right on both sides.

Looking at our Acme Corporation and noting the emphasis on selecting new regional leaders and their senior staffs from within the Corporate headquarters, I believe the Acme CEO sees his center of gravity as the strength of his bench and his confidence they can take the ball and run with it. On the other side of the line the CEO sees the competition as formidable but yet unable to match Acme Corporation's speed in reaching the customers with a better product.

Identifying and articulating centers of gravity can be a dicey proposition. If you call a bad shot you should see the signs quickly and adjust. If you are right, harnessing the talent and focusing the effort can pay huge dividends.

CENTERS OF GRAVITY RECAP

1. There are multiple centers of gravity for complex issues.
2. A center of gravity can be a thing, a person, a place, a belief, a condition or a circumstance.
3. Identifying centers of gravity will be difficult. If you are wrong, adjust and move on.
4. Avoiding the issue for fear of failure may cause you to loose an opportunity to properly focus an organization's efforts.

CRITICAL INFORMATION REQUIREMENTS

Overloaded with information, starved for knowledge, the lament of nearly every leader. The needle is in the haystack but the haystack is getting bigger every day. Finding a way to sort it all out is one of a leader's key conditions for success. This is true at the strategic, operational and direct levels in the continuum of leadership. For most problems there is a list of issues that are usually time sensitive in nature and which directly impact on the success or failure of the mission. It stands to reason that these problems can be solved if brought to the attention of the appropriate person in a timely manner. Most crisis scenarios center around a situation wherein a problem was not expeditiously reported to someone who is in a position to do something about it before the issue got out of control. Creating a list of critical information requirements early in the planning process creates a banner board that will light up when certain factors come into play.

Who creates it, where does it come from, what does it look like and who needs to know its contents? It is the boss' list and it is important that subordinates understand it came from the boss and has the weight of the behind it. The initial list of issues will be natural fallout from the attention given to mission, intent and boss' guidance. The first cut at the critical information requirements list may even be included in the boss' guidance; for example the CEO informs his subordinates to be especially alert to a specific situation and if they hear anything about it they are to let him know immediately.

In constructing the boss' critical information requirements list, first and foremost it must be short, three to five items, with critical being the operative word. Second, recognize that the list is dynamic. As the project progresses from initial staff estimates through courses of action development to decisions, a factor that was once critical will become a non-issue and new ones will emerge. Therefore, every time there is a gathering of players for any reason the critical information requirements list needs to get exposed, reviewed and revised if necessary. This serves a number of purposes; it places renewed emphasis on the list, keeps the issues fresh in everyone's mind and ensures the items on the list are relevant and timely. However the leader backbriefs are handled, one-on-one or as a group, they will be a key source of issues for the list.

Our Acme Corporation CEO has made the decision to establish two new distribution centers, one in St. Louis serving the Midwest and a second in the San Francisco Bay area for west coast operations. Heretofore, all Acme Corporation operations have been non-union. In the leader backbrief the subordinate charged with developing the courses of action for distribution raised the issue of possible union intervention in the west coast operations. The CEO tied a red flag on this issue and added it to the critical information requirement list. Additionally, the chief financial officer who was working a bank loan to finance the expansion reported some negative vibes he was receiving from a mid-level bank official. The CEO responds by telling the subordinate if any aspect of the bank loan transaction looks as if it is getting off track he is to let the CEO know immediately in order that he may personally call the bank president. There will come a point in time, perhaps within a few days, when the loan is formally approved and this item falls off the critical information requirement list.

Establishing the existence of the list is common sense. The issues to be included on the list just naturally tend to rise to the top. The hard part is insuring the list becomes common knowledge and that subordinates will react properly. A problem is analogous to a rotten egg, the longer you delay in dealing with it, the worse it will become. The whole purpose of the critical information requirements list is to get to that egg before it gets too bad and stinks up the whole operation. You have a continuum of leadership with information flowing both up and down; this is where it has to function. The critical information requirement list must flow down as far as necessary to wherever the eggs are. Then the person who is watching over the eggs must clearly understand how and when to report a problem. Whether the existing hierarchy is three or twenty layers it must be understood that those in a position to first identify the problem have both the responsibility and authority to immediately communicate to whoever is in a position to do something about it.

The direct leader on the assembly line noticed a slight vibration when inspecting one of the machines. He knows that if this machine becomes non-operational the line will completely shut down and it could take weeks to replace it. The critical information requirement to the operators is that if they hear a clicking sound, turn the machine off immediately, let him know and he will call in the maintenance crew for some minor repairs.

Prior to the initiation of fighting at the Battle of Gettysburg when forces were maneuvering into position, General Lee did not know the disposition of Union forces. At one point General Lee was informed that Union cavalry had been observed near the town of Gettysburg the previous day. Lee immediately concluded that if the cavalry scouts had been there the infantry would not be far behind. It was a critical piece of information but received too late for him to properly react because subordinates had concluded the information was not important enough to bother the boss with.47 General Lee's single most vexing problem preceding the Battle of Gettysburg was determining the location of the enemy, yet he either did not establish a list of critical information requirements or failed to properly communicate it to his subordinates. The results were catastrophic. Lee missed the opportunity to establish a defense on the critical terrain and that ultimately led to his defeat and tens of thousands of casualties.

The critical information requirements list is the quintessential big bang for the buck; low to no cost, little time involved putting it together, easy to do, yet represents a home run every time the call comes in.

CRITICAL INFORMATION REQUIREMENTS RECAP

1. The critical information requirements list emanates from leaders at every level.
2. It is a short dynamic list and should be continuously updated.
3. Items on the list must become common knowledge down the continuum of leadership to the level where the potential problems will first become apparent.
4. Everyone in the organization must be sensitized to the importance of passing information up the continuum to whoever is in a position to take appropriate action.

SHAPING THE BATTLESPACE

Every problem has a defined battlespace and every battlespace is configured such that you either have the advantage or are in a disadvantaged position. There are two ways to approach the issue; one is to just let it play out, take whatever comes and roll with the punches. In this scenario leaders will constantly find themselves surprised by unfolding events, will tend generally to be in a reactive mode and their thinking will dissolve into defensive survival.

The alternative is to be proactive and set conditions such that they play to your strengths and core competencies. In other words, shape the battlespace. Leaders at every level have his or her own battlespace; therefore, this tool for creating conditions for success is applicable at the strategic, operational and direct leadership levels.

In 1990 when Iraq invaded Kuwait, President Bush quickly set about shaping the strategic battlespace. The centerpiece was a coalition of leaders around the world who openly condemned Saddam Hussein's actions and sent resources and forces to Saudi Arabia to assist in the successful effort to force Iraq's invaders out of Kuwait. President Bush further shaped the strategic battlespace by gaining the will of the American people; there were few if any anti-war demonstrations and his approval rate was in the ninety percent range. Following from this was the near unanimous will of the U.S. Congress in support of the Gulf War effort.

A decade later in 2001 President George W. Bush similarly shaped the strategic battlespace following the terrorist attacks of September 11. His address before a joint session of Congress, beamed around the world by CNN, clarified the task at hand and his intent. It was critical that the war on terrorism not be viewed as the U.S. versus the Muslim world. The immediate positive response from the American people and nations around the world gave a clear indication that he had successfully shaped the battlespace thereby preparing the way for actions across the spectrum at the operational and direct levels. Following that speech there were numerous actions and activities at the operational level to include pulling together world-wide intelligence networks, the multi-nation agreements to freeze the terrorist organization's assets and military operations to shut down support of terrorist by Afghan leaders. Finally, at the direct level there was support for the Afghan Northern Alliance that was engaging our common enemy, the Taliban Government forces. The battlespace was shaped by leaders at every level.

The CEO of our Acme Corporation was intent on moving operations into areas of the country where they had no operational experience. One low-cost solution was to determine the optimum location for regional headquarters, distribution centers or production plants by simple map inspection. But this solution would provide zero insights into local culture; how would they be accepted, would they be viewed as a competitor to an existing long-time highly regarded company, would local unions be a factor? Recognizing the need to shape the battlespace for his subordinates, the CEO hit the road, met with city councils and union leaders, spent time with the editors of the local newspapers, made himself available to radio talk show hosts and television reporters. He got in touch with the States' industrial expansion agencies to obtain their blessing. By the time the Acme Corporation's subordinate leaders arrived on the scene to take up permanent residence the battlespace had been shaped and the potential negatives minimized.

Sam Walton who built the merchandising giant WAL-MART was obviously a genius at shaping the battlespace. When he brought a WAL-MART to the outskirts of small towns across the Untied States with its enormous range of products, one of the outcomes was that some number of small owner-operated stores on Main Street were in all probability going to fold in the face of WAL-MART pricing competition and product choice. Many of these small retail operations had been in business for decades, made Main Street vibrant and their owners were long-time civic leaders. There is an enormous downside in this battlespace. If Sam Walton was to achieve his vision for WAL-MART those issues had to get worked one at a time, on site, in order to shape thousands of battlespaces.

Not every battlespace is external; some poorly led organizations are in a constant state of turmoil with every project seeming to deteriorate into a crisis situation. Subordinate leaders frequently get off track or drop the ball in the middle of an important operation. In part one of this book we looked at how to use the continuum of leadership; how to define what strategic, operational and direct leaders do; the importance of optimizing span of control, delegation and empowerment; how to organize for action; the criticality of a positive corporate culture; and the necessity for a strong organization-wide leader development program. These are conditions for success on a continuing basis. But in exploring these issues we concluded that in order for them to be positive, leaders have to be proactive; in other words leaders have to shape the internal battlespace on a continuous basis as well as shape external events to get a particular project from vision to execution.

There is always a battlespace and there is always the option to do nothing. Occasionally, a person in a leadership position will get lucky with a do-nothing policy but that is not what leadership is all about. The road from vision to execution is full of potholes, using a framework for action to fill a few of them ahead of time can make the ride a whole lot smoother.

SHAPING THE BATTLESPACE RECAP

1. Every problem has a defined battlespace and it can be either a friendly or hostile environment.
2. While doing nothing is an option, the downside potential is enormous.
3. There are few if any measures of effectiveness for shaping the battlespace, but the outcome of doing nothing may eventually become painfully apparent.
4. Shaping the battlespace is a condition for success at the strategic, operational and direct leadership levels.
5. An organization's internal battlespace needs to be continuously shaped.
   FRAMEWORK FOR ACTION
   CHARTING A COURSE
   Vision
   Strategy
   DECLARING EXPECTATIONS
   Mission
   Intent
   Boss' guidance
   CREATING CONDITIONS FOR SUCCESS
   Leader backbrief

Centers of gravity
Critical information requirements
Shaping the battlespace

There you have it, all the tools in the framework for action. You can begin using them immediately. Here is a technique to get you started. I know this works because I have used it repeatedly during Vision to Execution leadership seminars. The boss calls in the war council and gives them his or her vision; then in open forum, using large chart paper, walks everyone through the framework. Engage everyone in the room and cause them to spit out all the external factors related to customer and the competition that will have to be researched. Ask them to be brutally honest as you walk through the underpinnings and assess the art of the possible. Of course not all the strategic planning can be done in that one short session but it will provide the initial roadmap of what needs to be worked. Follow that with a mission statement, clear and brief. As each chart is completed, hang it on the wall so everyone can continuously cycle back to insure they are staying with the vision, aligning assets to their greatest advantage, etc. Do the first draft of the intent statement covering all four elements. Outline the boss' guidance on bounding the problem, priorities, how the organization will operate, milestones and who will be in charge. Finally, begin the process of creating conditions for success by identifying the centers of gravity, critical information requirements and what will need to be done to shape the battlespace. The first time through the framework, there will be a tendency for members to want to jump ahead; take it one element at a time. There will also be a tendency to want to do too much with the mission statement, it will get too long and begin to describe the whole campaign.

To do this most effectively, follow a few simple rules. The boss should not lead this exercise; select a facilitator to do it. Also designate someone to be a scribe to capture every scrap of information flowing from the group (the facilitator who is working the room and putting key thoughts on the large charts will not be able to record every thought).

Finally, set a time limit. In my experience, one hour to work the entire framework is sufficient. Beyond one hour the session deteriorates into side discussions and arguments over details. The other reason for setting a one hour time limit is to give everyone confidence and understanding that a viable, usable, first-cut framework for action can be constructed in that short period.

CHAPTER NINETEEN

DEALING WITH CRISIS

During A Crisis, The Culture, The Character, The Discipline Of An Organization Get Laid Bare For All To See And Every Leader Gets Tested And Graded.

At some point every organization is going to find itself in a crisis. How that crisis is dealt with speaks volumes about its leaders. Nothing gets hidden during a crisis; all strengths and weaknesses are exposed. The culture, the discipline, the character of the organization are laid out for all to see. Additionally, every leader in the continuum gets tested and graded.

A discussion of how to deal with crisis may be the most appropriate conclusion to this book, because every element is brought to bear during a crisis. When time is not the critical factor issues get dissected, analyzed, reviewed and corrected if off track; there is time for discovery, mentoring, discussion and deliberation. But during a crisis, simultaneity is of the essence; leaders have to believe in the discipline of the organization and in the competence of leaders at every level.

The purpose of this final chapter is to go back and look at the underpinnings from part one, the framework for action in part two and see how it all applies during a crisis.

By its nature a crisis situation is time-constrained; the thesis here is that an organization that can touch all the bases while working through a crisis will out-think and out-perform the competition.

THE TWENTY-FIRST CENTURY OPERATING ENVIRONMENT

As mentioned in chapter one, during a conversation in 2000 with a regional director of one of this country's largest financial services institutions, he opined that it is hard to get people to compress time and all opportunities today are time sensitive. The word all is a bit of an overstatement, but in the context of the conversation, he was revealing a frustration that his subordinates were unable or unwilling to step forward when it counted and too much of his organization's activity dealt with crisis. The sheer volume of information leaders must deal with in a 24/7 environment, coupled with the ever-accelerating pace of play, has the potential to overwhelm individuals and groups of employees collectively and thereby significantly increasing the opportunities for crisis situations to develop.

These two factors alone, volume of information and pace, make timely recognition of an issue more difficult often resulting in a late start. It is relatively easy to determine when an action or a project needs to be completed, the crisis occurs when we are time-late in recognizing that it has to be initiated. As has always been the case, leaders find themselves constantly looking for the proverbial needle in a haystack. While the size of the needle has remained the same, the size of the haystack has continued to increase gradually over the millennia. But when society recently entered the Information Age the haystack grew exponentially in a very short number of years, thereby contributing to a crisis environment.

THE LEADERSHIP CONTINUUM

Once a crisis has been identified, the single most essential component in dealing with it successfully is strong leadership. Recall our bottom line leader definition, a leader is someone who takes the organization elsewhere; during a crisis that leader not only has to take us elsewhere, they have to do it quickly.

There is a continuum of leadership in every organization. The continuum facilitates communications both up and down through the strategic, operational and direct leadership levels. These channels of communication need to be recognized and exercised in a day-to-day operating environment. During a crisis one of the keys to success will be rapid, clear, concise communications among leaders throughout the continuum.

SPAN OF CONTROL, DELEGATION AND EMPOWERMENT

At no other time will these factors (span of control, delegation and empowerment) be more relevant than during a crisis. Recall the rule of thumb for span of control is to command one echelon down and have a clear understanding of what is happening two levels down. Crisis has a tendency to bring out the best and worst in leaders. Some will believe they have to gain and maintain control of the entire operation in order to be successful and in doing so violate span of control limits. If, during a crisis, subordinate leaders two or three levels down are made to wait for a senior leader to issue directions, the resulting inefficiency will doom the project to failure.

Hand-in-hand with the proper use of span of control is delegation and empowerment. Simultaneity of actions is key and essential during crisis situations; but will not occur unless leaders have routinely delegated responsibilities to their subordinates and recognize the ones who willingly accept the challenges. It follows that delegation, in and of itself, is meaningless unless accompanied with authority to act. Subordinates must be empowered to act. Only through delegation of responsibilities with the requisite authority will leaders of any organization be able to effectively deal with the inevitable crisis situation.

ORGANIZE FOR ACTION

Recall in chapter eight we looked at a number of organizational tools available to a leader such as the war council, the kitchen cabinet and the mobile command post. These can be especially valuable during a crisis because by their existence they consist of persons in whom the boss has trust and confidence. During a crisis the boss may make a quick call to a couple members of the kitchen cabinet to get an opinion on the actions about to be taken. The war council, if properly constituted, is ready-made for crisis; they are bright action people who have been tested in time-constrained, back-of-the-envelope actions and are people in whom the boss has trust and confidence.

If an organization has a mobile command post in place to assist subordinate headquarters through a troubled period or to conduct training, the chances are the team membership is a cross section of the entire organization. With the required expertise already in place, a mobile command post team may be instantly transformed into a self-contained crisis-action team. Envision a scenario wherein the crisis-action team is called up, perhaps augmented in certain critical disciplines and work directly for the senior leader until the crisis is resolved. Taking this a step further the boss may reach into the organization, pull out a trusted vice president and appoint him or her the crisis action team chief of staff with responsibility and authority to initiate organization-wide taskings. This type of solution may provide the fast, focused action necessary to deal with a crisis and at the same time avoid disrupting important on-going routine actions. If a relatively small crisis situation that could be contained and dealt with surgically is allowed to permeate the entire organization, take it out of its rhythm and drag down overall productivity, the smaller crisis can end up inducing a crisis of major proportion.

CULTURE

There is a culture in every organization; it is a powerful

and pervasive force. By far the most important cultural trait is an organization's character. Dealing with crisis involves cutting corners and moving fast. One of those corners available to be shaved off is honesty and integrity. Doing so may facilitate resolution of the crisis but the long-term ramifications can be catastrophic. A deep-seated cultural addiction to uncompromised character must be present and prevail even in the darkest hours of a crisis. Organizations with a strong value base will survive crisis situations not in spite of their honesty and integrity but because of it.

LEADER DEVELOPMENT

Your leader development policy has been put in place, the organization has a solid institutional program, high achievers with promising potential have been tested through multiple assignments, the company is supportive of a number of self-development programs and the company finds itself in a crisis. This is when all the hours, effort and resources dedicated to the leader development program pay off as decisions are made in compressed timeframes and execution is by necessity decentralized. Senior leaders have faith that the entire leadership continuum is staffed with leaders who know how to and are not afraid to lead. During a crisis is when an organization comes closest to being able to measure the effectiveness of its leader development program; the measure may simply be success or failure. Without a bench of solid leaders, no organization is likely to perform well during a crisis. If the objective is to out-think and out-perform the competition there is no substitute for strong leadership throughout the organization.

FRAMEWORK FOR ACTION

In part two, framework for action, we worked our way through an extensive tool kit containing tools for vision, strategy, mission, intent, boss' guidance and other elements associated with creating conditions for success. We saw the interaction and linkage among these elements in the Acme

Corporation over a period of weeks and months. But during a crisis, the time-line for action may be minutes, hours or days rather than weeks or months. How does the framework for action tool kit function during a crisis? It is a time when you will not only want to touch the same bases, it will be even more important to do so. During a crisis, utilizing the elements in the framework is simply accelerated.

A key ingredient during crisis is discipline; discipline in the context of operating from a set of rules and standards that result in controlled efficiency, or perhaps better characterized as controlled chaos. If an organization has no commonly understood framework for action, it is difficult to believe they will do anything except flounder through a crisis. Some employees will be working ninety miles an hour, but on the wrong things; some will be way out in front, but in the wrong direction; others will be bewildered, standing by waiting for specific instructions while a few talented ten percent will be doing eighty percent of the productive work. A commonly understood framework for action provides a disciplined approach to communicating problems, issues, milestones and solutions throughout the continuum of leadership. Expectations flow in both directions in the leadership continuum; subordinates expect to receive mission, intent and guidance and leaders expect subordinates to make the guidance relevant to their part of the problem and quickly develop viable courses of action.

Another factor present in successfully dealing with crisis is the role leaders play. Leaders will tend to be more hands-on, even at the strategic and operational levels. The boss will stay more closely tuned to details, weigh in more frequently with guidance and cut off marginally productive staff work.

The Los Angeles riots of April/May 1992 resulted in 52 dead, about 2,400 injured, and an estimated $1 billion in damages to approximately 15,000 structures. At the time I was the commander of the Seventh Infantry Division at Ft. Ord, California, about 350 miles north of Los Angeles. When the police officers accused in the beating of Rodney King were acquitted, all hell broke loose in about one hundred square miles of south/central Los Angeles. While local police departments, LA county sheriff's department, the California highway patrol and some California National Guard units were doing all they could, California's Governor, Pete Wilson, began to believe more was needed. At the time, the Seventh Infantry Division's readiness status (defined as training status, personnel strength and equipment readiness) was at a high level. The Seventh Infantry Division was designed to be light and the most rapidly deployable infantry division in the world.

Along with the rest of America, we were watching with shock and horror as events unfolded on the streets of Los Angeles. The first phone call came to the Seventh Infantry Division about 2 a.m. from Forces Command in Atlanta, Georgia. Forces Command was my senior headquarters two layers up and essentially in command of all ground combat forces in the continental United States. The 2 a.m. call was a warning order that federal military forces may have to be sent to Los Angeles but the staff officer at Forces Command further instructed us not to do anything yet. The first thing we did was to disregard that instruction. The chief of staff assembled key personnel and we began thinking through the problem. The next call from Forces Command came about 8 a.m. and essentially we were told that it was still unclear exactly what forces would be involved, but it was definite that the Seventh Infantry Division was no longer a candidate. Throughout the early morning hours we had been tuned to CNN watching events unfold. About thirty minutes following the 8 a.m. call from Forces Command, CNN provided live coverage as President Bush walked into the White House press room and announced that he had decided to send the Seventh Infantry Division to Los Angeles to assist in restoring order. None of my chain of command, I Corps, Forces Command, Army Pentagon staff or the Joint Chiefs of Staff had prior knowledge of the President's announcement. We all heard it simultaneously; it may be an understatement to assert that this falls nicely into the dealing-with-crisis category. Before noon that day I was on-scene in Los Angeles with a crisis action staff and the deployment of soldiers aboard U.S. Air Force C-141 aircraft was underway. Simultaneously marines, to be under my command, were deploying overland from Camp Pendleton. By nightfall, thousands of soldiers and marines were deployed throughout the Los Angeles area. Using the Los Angeles situation as a case study in dealing with crisis, let's walk through the framework for action and see how the pieces were applied. The most important point is that the framework does apply, all of it.

VISION

By its nature, crisis does not portend a grand, long-range vision of where the leadership will take the organization. But in the first minutes of a crisis a leader must create some vision of an end-state that can be quickly articulated through the continuum of leadership. The picture in everyone's mind must have a set of common elements. It is analogous to someone attempting to describe a painting of a landscape by only articulating the colors used. From the description, one person visualizes a beach scene, another a mountainous landscape and a third an urban environment. The leader has to quickly get everyone oriented in the right direction with the most complete picture available at the time.

In the case of the Los Angeles riots the vision came out of discussions held in the early morning hours before the President's surprise announcement. In describing how we would operate, all subordinate leaders were able to see in advance how events would unfold in Los Angeles. The Seventh Infantry Division was a "light" division. The way it was organized and equipped distinguished it from "heavy" divisions that contain hundreds of tanks and mechanized tracked troop carriers. But even a light division has field artillery, mortars, machine guns and attack helicopters. The vision of the operation was thousands of light fighters, with only M-16 rifles, operating in squad and team-sized elements over an area several times larger than that of a division employed on a conventional battlefield. My decree of "no crew-served weapons" were four words worth a thousand pictures because they had such profound meaning to that particular organization by defining what the force would look like and what they would be doing in a few hours once deployed on the streets of Los Angeles.

Vision is the first step in taking an organization elsewhere and the Seventh Infantry Division was, in fact, going elsewhere. By looking at the end, ways and means we quickly arrive at a vision and to have confidence that it was in fact an operable vision. *End* was to assist in restoring order. *Ways* was not to inflict damage and kill people, but to establish a presence. *Means* was to get there the fastest with the most force and that was to fly soldiers and what they carried with them rather than ship thousands of tons of cargo and equipment. Vision, even if it is viewed through a soda straw versus a wide-angle lens, is an essential start point, even during a crisis.

STRATEGY

Recall from chapter fourteen the first rule of strategy is to have one. From the definition that strategy is the alignment of assets to their greatest advantages, what does alignment of assets mean in the context of a crisis? It means to take a realistic look at your organization, assess its strengths and take stock of its core competencies. Having done so, build a strategy around what you can do best. Crisis is no time to run a play you have not practiced. Imagine you have just marched eighty yards on the football field using a good mix of basic running and passing plays; it is fourth down on the one-yard line; there are thirty seconds remaining on the clock; and your team is behind by four points. Does the coach call together the second string players on the sideline, draw up a new play in the dirt and send them in to execute? Not if he wants to keep his job; go with what has made you successful.

For Los Angeles, ours was a two-part strategy; part one getting there and part two how to operate once on the ground. Recall General Robert E. Lee's strategy for the 1863 summer campaign was to move north quickly, live off the land use the mountains as a screen for his right flank. Once into Maryland and Pennsylvania, use the terrain to give him the advantage over a numerically superior force. Brilliant. Recall, however, he broke the cardinal third rule for strategy, if you have a good one, do not abandon it.

The Seventh Infantry Division was the most capable organization of its kind in the world when it came to rapid deployment. This was no accident. That particular light division had been especially designed from a blank sheet of paper and fielded over the previous ten years as the premier rapidly deployable force in the U.S. defense establishment. Being trained and ready to rapidly deploy on a moment's notice was one of the four specified responsibilities of every first-line leader. So the strategy to get there was simply to designate the units that would deploy, establish the order, get sufficient Air Force transport aircraft and let the subordinate leaders execute.

Once on the ground in Los Angeles, the second part of the strategy was to establish as wide a presence as possible, a soldier-on-every-street-corner concept. Small units such as platoons and companies would headquarter in parks, shopping malls or schools and disperse from there. This dictated the make-up of the force, soldier power without heavy equipment or a huge logistics tail. In other words, invoke the second rule of strategy, keep it simple. Since division-wide training consistently emphasized light decentralized operations, there was never a doubt that we had a strategy that emphasized our core competencies and was immediately executable. And we did not forget the third rule of strategy; that is, we did not abandon it because we were confident that our assets were being brought to bear to their greatest advantage.

MISSION, INTENT, BOSS' GUIDANCE

During a deliberate planning process where time is not necessarily the driving factor, the implied task list may be initially developed, revisited after receiving the boss' intent and then perhaps reviewed again following boss' guidance. With time as the defining factor in a crisis it is almost imperative to issue the mission, intent and boss' guidance simultaneously. There simply is insufficient time for subordinate leaders to recycle back through these three critical elements of the framework. Take your best shot and move on.

MISSION. When you have an entire organization using one commonly understood framework for action, they will eagerly anticipate the mission statement when a crisis occurs. The mission statement is a call to action and authority to move forward at every echelon in the continuum, clarity and brevity being the measures of merit.

What we received from President Bush could not have been more clear and concise, deploy to Los Angeles and assist in restoring order. The continuum of leadership swung into action by restating the mission to make it relevant to their areas of expertise. For example, the commander of the third brigade (not designated to deploy to Los Angeles) restated his mission to immediately set up and operate the departure airfield control center while the division's logistics commander directed his command to deploy and sustain a light infantry force.

Following the restatement, every leader at every level was immediately and simultaneously into mission analysis, identifying specified, implied and essential tasks to be performed. The specified tasks were easy, deploy and restore order. There are three points to be made concerning the implied task list. First, keying off predetermined standard operating procedures can save precious time. For example, it was implied that every soldier would deploy with their pre-determined rucksack load; departure airfield control orders would apply; pre-determined marshalling areas would be used; commanders were authorized to cancel approved leaves of absence and recall those already gone; family support group rules would go into effect immediately, etc. Secondly, the completeness of the implied list is important from the standpoint of also identifying what it is that will not be done. For example, the day-to-day over-arching mission of the division was to train to close with and destroy the enemy. This of course was not what was going to happen in Los Angeles. So that implied task was taken off the list. Additionally, it was a normal implied task to bring all the combined arms elements (infantry, artillery, engineers, air defense, air attack) to bear on the enemy. This was to be a light infantry only operation. The third point to be made about the implied task list, and why it is so important to take the time to brainstorm the implied tasks, is that during a crisis the implied task list becomes the plan. It was implied that we would need more aircraft; "John, work that." We would need a headquarters location in LA; "Jim, work that." Literally hundreds of actions were identified within a few minutes, all of them needed to be worked, all were assigned to someone for action, the Chief of Staff was pulling it all together and the plan was emerging while we simultaneously went into execution. Finally, identifying the essential task in our mission analysis was easy, do it all quickly.

INTENT. Intent is the most powerful tool available to a leader and in the event of a crisis, the single most important element in the framework for action. Getting every single leader knitted together in a commonly understood cause is absolutely essential because if a well-intentioned leader unknowingly heads off in the wrong direction the time lost can be catastrophic.

Recall that intent serves two purposes; first, as stated above, it binds the leadership together. The second is to provide some assurances that as events unfold and the fog of war sets in, individuals will, in the absence of specific instructions, execute based on what they understood their leader intended. In Los Angeles we visualized decentralized operations to the extreme. We could easily conjure up a scenario involving a couple soldiers, at 2 a.m., separated by several hundred yards from their first-line leader, being confronted with a situation requiring some type of action. With this in mind it became obvious that as the division commander, my intent had to permeate the entire continuum and be understood by every individual soldier and marine. The measures of merit for intent, clarity and brevity were never more applicable than during this particular mission.

Intent is the vehicle for declaring expectations. In the case of Los Angeles perhaps the most important part of the statement was what we did *not* intend to do, that is we were not going to engage the enemy. There was no enemy per se although there were numerous encounters with heavily armed gang members.

Thinking through the four elements of intent, the *end-state* was to create a safe and secure environment in order for life to return to normal. The *vision* of the operation was to use widely dispersed teams. *Why* we were going was because the organizations on scene lacked the manpower necessary to control the situation. The *keys to success* were speed and disciplined, decentralized light force operations.

BOSS' GUIDANCE. In a crisis the guidance will, by necessity, be more focused and contain some specific taskers. In order to optimize the limited time available, the number of courses of action to be considered will be limited and may in fact be a single way ahead; time available and circumstances will dictate.

Bounding the problem, fixing responsibility, establishing the timetable, setting priorities and getting the organization right all come into play during a crisis and must be dispatched quickly.

Putting the right faces in the right places can be a critical task; the old saying a chain is only as strong as its weakest link is most applicable during a crisis. A leader who says, I hope Jim can handle this, may be on a slippery slope during a crisis. Remember hope is not a process; therefore, tailoring the organization to meet head-on the demands of a crisis may be the most important element of the boss' guidance.

Organization took center stage during the early minutes as the Seventh Infantry Division prepared to deploy to Los Angeles. I had two world-class Brigadier General Assistant Division Commanders ("executive vice presidents" for operations and for support), Buck Kernan and Ken Simpson. Complicating the situation was the fact that General Simpson, with a handful of key individuals, was already deployed to

Guantanamo Bay Cuba dealing with another national crisis involving tens of thousands of Haitian refugees.

Recall we had a two-part strategy for Los Angeles, one was to get there as rapidly as possible and the second was how we would operate once deployed throughout the Los Angeles area. A third key player on my team was the chief of staff, John Walsh. It was like cutting off my right arm but the first critical organizational decision was to leave Colonel Walsh at Fort Ord to push the division out, thereafter keeping us sustained and to look after the home front and all the myriad of issues that emerge when several thousand "employees" deploy from home base. That settled, I needed a chief of staff in Los Angeles for the joint task force command. As previously mentioned we were going light and therefore did not need field artillery systems. The division artillery commander, Colonel John Ryneska was another strong leader and was immediately tagged to be the task force chief of staff.

What we were undertaking involved acting now and getting all the pieces rolling simultaneously; my division operations officer could best be used by remaining at Ft. Ord as part of the push package. Therefore, I now needed an operations officer for the Los Angeles task force.

On an on-going basis, 24/7, we had one of the three infantry brigades packed up and on alert for worldwide deployment. While they were the most ready to go, the force was configured too heavy for this mission, individuals' gear was palletized for shipment and all of this was a hundred miles north (in the wrong direction) at McCord Air Force Base. We neither had the time to break down and reconfigure this deployment package nor did we have the time to transport several thousand soldiers to that base. We needed to begin deploying now and do it from home base using the local Monterey airport. So, while the third brigade would not go to Los Angeles, their key personnel were available; the brigade commander, Colonel Mike Canavan, became my operations officer for Task Force Los Angeles. General Kernan would be my key number-two guy in Los Angeles.

Having put the key players in place, the final piece of organizational guidance was to keep the forward division headquarters small. I told the task force chief of staff to hand pick a few top notch majors and have them on the first transport aircraft. By the way, all the key persons mentioned above by name continued to be promoted, all retiring as General Officers.

Having a framework for action deeply rooted in an organization facilitates the fulfillment of expectations in both directions. My key subordinate leaders expected to get a mission statement, my intent and boss' guidance. Once dispatched, I had well grounded expectations that they knew exactly what to do with the information.

The deployment Gods were smiling on us that day in that we had previously scheduled two Air Force C-141 transport aircraft into the local airport for deployment training that was to begin that morning. They became the lead elements of the full deployment, which began within a few hours.

There was more to the boss' guidance including the critical issues surrounding logistics (keep it light, live off the land), reconfigured tactical transportation (transfer trucks from units not going to the infantry), communications (need all small unit radios), etc. The important point was to touch all the bases and do it quickly. Mission, intent and boss' guidance were on the street being acted upon in about thirty minutes after the President Bush's announcement. I had at my disposal a twin engine, nine passenger aircraft. Having selected key advanced party personnel, the final point in my boss' guidance was, "We will be wheels up in sixty minutes." We were on the ground in Los Angeles before noon setting the stage for operations that would begin that evening.

CREATING CONDITIONS FOR SUCCESS

Being successful in a crisis situation is more tenuous than during deliberate operations. Leaders must use every tool available to enhance their chances to out-think and out-perform the competition. They must also be proactive and decisive, guiding and mentoring their subordinates. Let's briefly recap the conditions for success outlined in the previous chapter.

LEADER BACKBRIEF. During a crisis we will cut some corners and seek ways to streamline our progression through the framework for action. But the leader backbrief must not be eliminated from the equation. During a crisis the backbrief may be a quick phone call or a few comments to the boss as you are walking down the hallway. Whatever the circumstances it is important that everyone recognize that the backbrief is even more essential during a crisis because if some element of the operation gets off track there may not be enough recovery time available, thereby putting the entire outcome in jeopardy. The leader backbrief, however and whenever it is delivered, must still capture the restated mission and intent. It is imperative for senior leaders to quickly get a sense that the continuum is bound together in a commonly understood cause.

After issuing mission, intent and boss' guidance, the one area I was most concerned about was logistics. The intent was to go light, use the city's water, contract for meals if necessary (which we did, "I'd like 200 Big Macs to go") and use schools' shower facilities. No competent logistician and we had a good one, wants to get caught short; their inclination is to exercise what I call, "just in case" logistics. That is, take everything just in case we might need it. Speed was essential to mission accomplishment and nothing will bog down an operation as much as excessive logistics support. Therefore, I forced a quick backbrief from the logistician before I departed for Los Angeles, scaled him back considerably and instructed my chief of staff to watch the logistics activities carefully as he pushed the division forward.

CENTERS OF GRAVITY. A center of gravity can be a thing, a person, a place, a belief, a condition or a circumstance. During a crisis, when everything is moving quickly and bordering on chaos, it may appear justifiable to pass over the consideration of centers of gravity. While you may be successful without identifying them, it is possible you may lose an opportunity to focus the organization at a point in time when focus can be a force multiplier.

The point was made in the previous chapter that there are frequently multiple centers of gravity, usually at least one on the positive side and one that is a challenge. For the Los Angeles operation, our positive center of gravity was our ability to rapidly deploy and operate in a decentralized mode with responsibility and authority delegated all the way to the direct leadership level. Identifying this as a center of gravity was a simple way of reinforcing core competencies and communicating confidence in junior leaders.

We identified two challenging centers of gravity. One was the size of the area. A one hundred square mile area of operations is several times larger than that assigned to a division for conventional combat operations. Furthermore, urban areas are by orders of magnitude more difficult to operate in than any other type of terrain. The problems associated with tactical communications, transportation, intelligence and command and control would severely challenge us. What flowed from the identification of this center of gravity were taskers:

- We need a thousand city maps for our first-line leaders, today.
- We need cell phones for more reliable urban communication and a task force phone book, today.
- We need drivers who know the city. Get the city buses out of their storage areas and running, today.

A second challenging center of gravity and one we instinctively know could be our Achilles heel, were the rules of engagement. In the military there are rules of engagement for every operation; that is, given a set of circumstances, what action can be taken. The challenge in drafting rules of engagements is three-fold. One is to identify all the realistic scenarios applicable to a particular operation; second prevent the lawyers from interpreting the laws of war in such a way as to completely tie the commander's hands; and finally how to put it all on one 3x5 card in language that every soldier and marine can carry in his or her pocket, understand and execute.

The first and ever-present rule of engagement is the inherent right of self defense. Beyond that it gets difficult. All of the division's training was oriented on how to close with and destroy the enemy; Los Angeles was obviously a very different situation. Having identified rules of engagement as a center of gravity, my first instruction to the newly appointed task force operations officer, John Ryneska, was to get a pad of paper, find a quiet place and begin drafting the rules and we would review them on the flight to Los Angeles in an hour. We did so, I approved them, radioed the changes back to the chief of staff, they were printed by the thousands and given to every soldier to study.

Through years of experience, senior military leaders know if some element of the rules of engagement can be misunderstood it will be; the results can be catastrophic, create political turmoil, inadvertently antagonize an adversary or cause needless casualties. Hoping everyone would understand the rules of engagement was not a course of action; we had to get this right.

Upon arrival in Los Angeles, everyone was first transported to a staging area. From there, subordinate commanders received their assignments; linked up with transportation, drew some rations and checked communications. The staging area was a marine air base with large hanger bays and space to simultaneously accommodate thousands of troops. Upon approval of the rules of engagement, a team was formed to create scenarios that the soldiers and marines would likely face on the streets of Los Angeles. At the staging area, every first-line leader and his subordinates were coached through the scenarios. When every leader was certified in the minds of those conducting the training, the unit then and only then, was issued ammunition and prepared to deploy.

One final point concerning centers of gravity, the fog is usually thicker during a crisis. Many factors come into play rapidly and it is often difficult to see at the outset what later on may become an obvious center of gravity. It happened to us upon arrival in Los Angeles. After some hours on the ground, having met with the chief of police, the Los Angeles county sheriff, Governor Pete Wilson and the commander of the California National Guard, it became painfully obvious that there was not any one person in charge of the entire operation.

I should have seen this coming because it is a normal characteristic of a crisis; everyone has good intentions, everyone wants to be a part of the solution but all too often the combined actions of several diverse elements are, at least temporarily, leaderless. Governor Pete Wilson was on the scene continuously with a small staff; about a thousand California highway patrolmen were in hotels on the outskirts of Los Angeles awaiting orders; the FBI's Los Angeles agent in charge was involved; the FBI sent in their disaster expert, Buck Revell; the Bureau of Prisons sent a reaction team; the California National Guard was in the process of deploying; the area of operations encompassed a number of police departments beyond the LAPD; the Los Angeles county sheriff's deputes were everywhere; fire departments from throughout the greater Los Angeles area were engaged; and the Los Angeles mayor's office was working on various issues. Furthermore, what actually made matters worse was that while no one was in charge, every element mentioned above had a leader, decisions were being made and actions taken. It was analogous to handing a group of talented musicians each a sheet of music for a different song. They were making noise, it was not pretty, was going nowhere and had no identifiable melody.

There is an old adage on the subject of leadership: when in charge, take charge. Since I was the only leader expressly sent by the President of the United States, we set out the next morning to get control of the operating environment. I became the self-appointed CEO with vice presidents in charge of politics, law enforcement, fire, etc. The decision to take this unilateral action was reinforced by three events all-occurring within hours of arriving in Los Angeles. First was a meeting with the governor and his staff. While obviously the senior state executive on scene, neither he nor his staff had a strategy, a plan or the command and control means to execute them even if they did exist.

The second event occurred at 6 p.m. Pacific time. President Bush had gone on national television at 9 p.m. eastern time to discuss the events in Los Angeles. One of his first statements was to declare that he had decided to federalize the California National Guard. With that single verbal executive order, I became, at that instant, the commander of the California National Guard, thereby expanding my responsibilities, authority and capabilities. The National Guard now worked for me, not the governor. What President Bush did during that address substantiates another inevitable element of a crisis situation: prepare to be surprised. Again, my entire chain of command and I heard the President's declaration at the same time, for the first time.

The third event influencing my decision to take charge occurred that first evening when I went to the combined Los Angeles police department /Los Angeles county sheriff's department crisis center. There I met with LAPD Chief Darrel Gates and Sheriff Sherman Block. Without even an exchange of pleasantries, Chief Gates entered the room, took his seat, looked across the table at me and said, "General, we do not need you and we do not want you!" My previous suspicions were immediately confirmed; Chief Gates was a bigger part of the problem than the solution. My response was something to the effect that he was entitled to his opinions, but having been ordered to Los Angeles by President Bush we needed to focus on finding a solution and doing so quickly. All this is by way of making the point that a condition for success is to identify centers of gravity at the outset and be prepared to be confronted with others as events rapidly unfold. An additional observation for senior leaders is that during a crisis when a team is dispatched, be it a handful of individuals or an infantry division, they will not always be met with open arms and may need support from up the leadership chain.

Discovering that no one person was in charge caused me to cycle back to organization and issue additional boss' guidance. I called my chief of staff at Ft. Ord, told him to dip into the stay-behind units and immediately send me a dozen "iron majors." He knew exactly what I wanted; bright, mid-level, think-on-your-feet, articulate, officers. Upon arrival and after personally informing leaders of all the key organizations in the city that liaison officers were on the way, these officers were dispatched as my personal liaison, 24/7. Having a clear understanding of my intent, the liaison officers were to stay inside the decision cycles of the various leaders and inform me if something was getting off track. Furthermore, they assisted in clarifying my intent for those with whom they were working.

SHAPE THE BATTLESPACE. Every problem has a defined battlespace and every battlespace is configured such that you either have the advantage or are in a disadvantaged position. There are two ways to approach the issue: one is to just let it play out and take whatever comes, or the alternative is to be proactive and set conditions such that they play to your core competencies.

It occurred to me that the residents of Los Angeles would be rightfully apprehensive. Was this martial law? What role would the troops play in enforcing the curfew? What authority did I have from the President? The use of federal military forces in U.S. cities had precedent, but it had not been necessary to employ them since the 1960s and early 1970s during the Vietnam War protests. In the natural course of events the citizens of Los Angles would be getting their information from the evening news and the following morning's newspapers. Given the time lag of a couple decades since anything similar had occurred, I was sure the legions of young television personnel and newspaper writers would be researching files for background information and in doing so would land on the Kent State stories. I did not want any reference to the shooting of students at Kent State and all the negative connotations associated with the Vietnam War protest era. I needed to shape the battlespace and do it quickly. The city was completely shut down, schools, public transportation, every store, post offices, everything. People were running low on groceries, no one was working and the police were attempting to enforce a curfew. I wanted Los Angeles to look for some positives. Therefore, I tried to assure them through the media that the United States Army troops, the marines and federalized California National Guard, all under my command, were there to create a safe and secure environment wherein the citizens could feel comfortable getting commerce up and running and returning to some semblance of normalcy. It worked.

Rarely are there measures of effectiveness for being proactive in shaping the battlespace. There was no way to know how much influence I had in those early interviews over what the media reported or what might have been reported without access to me and the troops. But doing nothing when your gut is telling you the potential for negatives is high is not what leadership is about.

CRITICAL INFORMATION REQUIREMENTS. Among the elements in creating conditions for success, the boss' critical information requirements list is the tool that is especially applicable during crisis situations. Time, or the lack thereof, drives everything in a crisis. If initiatives get off track during a crisis, the time it takes to recoup may defeat the organization. The critical information requirements list may only be verbal during a crisis; it may be initiated by a phone call from the boss directly to the person most likely to see the problem emerge. Recall the criteria for the list is that it be short, specific and dynamic.

In Los Angeles, the first two critical information requirements were shots fired, a crowd gathering, or both. The third relates to the realization that no one person was in charge. After getting the liaison officers in position with leaders of all the key organizations, the charge to them was to immediately report any decisions made relative to what that organization was proposing to do that was not in concert with the direction we had set for the force as a whole.

Because the Seventh Infantry Division, as an organization, had a framework for action, because leaders at every level were familiar with the elements of the framework and because using the framework was a part of the division's daily operating procedure, the rapid response to the crisis in Los Angeles was successful. The greater Los Angeles area environment was back to normal within a few days and the 13,000 soldiers and marines packed up and returned home.

RECAP

1.   It is inevitable that in every organization from time to time there will be an unexpected call to action. Even in the best organizations there may be a few moments of chaos, but organizations with uncompromising character and possessing a framework for action will quickly fall into line and begin to work through the predicament.

2.   During a crisis the leadership underpinnings of an organization will become exposed for all to see. Subordinates' expectations of their leaders will be realized or leader deficiencies revealed.

3.   An organization whose leaders immediately visualize an end-state then proceed to touch all the bases will consistently out-think and out-perform the competition.

ENDURING LEADERSHIP PRINCIPLES

Great leaders:
Get out front during a crisis

CHAPTER TWENTY

SUMMARY

Leaders Command The Present, Advance Ideas And Shape The Future.

A friend of mine once commented that the framework for action is analogous to a fine orchestra with everyone playing from the same sheet of music. My response was that I do not subscribe to that example and do not believe successful organizations are structured to that extent. In an orchestra every member is expected to hit a particular note at a precise time without variance in order to produce the desired product. Utilizing the framework for action is more analogous to a group of talented jazz musicians who come together to play. They recognize there has to be a leader; they all recognize and follow a melody that is their framework for action but within that framework each player is thinking, improvising, innovating and applying individual expertise. They all visualize a common end-state, are working within their core competencies and moving in a common direction to accomplish the mission.

This has been a book for leaders, leaders at the strategic, the operational and direct levels. Leadership is an art with an endless learning curve and a demand for continuous self-development for those who accept the challenge. Leadership principles are timeless and serve leaders at all levels in every type of organization in every segment of society. It has been my intent to convince you of the wisdom of Helmuth von Moltke who concluded a century and a half ago that one cannot rely on natural genius for the development of senior leaders.

It takes a lot of tools to build a house; it also takes a lot of tools to lead an organization, whether your organization is a team of six or a cast of thousands. We have opened the various leadership toolboxes and exposed you to the tools of the trade.

There is an old adage in the United States Army concerning teaching that says, I'm going to tell you what I'm going to tell you, then I'm going to tell you, then I'm going to tell you what I told you. In the concluding portion of the introduction I suggested what I was going to tell you by outlining nine areas related to leadership. Then we opened all those toolboxes and took a look at the individual tools available to leaders at all levels. The only task remaining is to tell you what I told you. This book has provided you with an opportunity to:

- Assess a short list of enduring leadership principles relevant to the challenges of the twenty-first century's operating environment.
- Gain a better understanding of the varying responsibilities of direct, operational and strategic leaders and why/how leaders at different levels must lead differently.
- Recognize the value of using a chief of staff, kitchen cabinet, war council, mobile training team, crisis action team, or skunkworks to enhance personal leadership skills.
- Understand that building a bench may be every leader's second most important responsibility.
- Comprehend the power and pervasiveness of a corporate culture.
- Recognize that an organization without values and lacking goodness will, in all probability, fail in the long run.
- Appreciate the importance of the after action review and how it can transform an organization.
- Become familiar with a methodology for optimizing

leadership skills by using a time-proven framework for action.

- Put into practice rules for how to declare expectations in clear, succinct terms.
- Learn the techniques of tracking an operation from vision to execution and get positive results.
- Understand that intent can be a leader's most powerful tool and how and when to use it.
- Understand the importance of creating conditions for success.
- Deal more effectively with crisis situations.

Now it is time for you to choose the tools that are right for you, assemble your own leader toolbox, go face the challenges of leadership in the twenty-first century, take your organization elsewhere and make 2 + 2 = 5. Good luck.

CHAPTER TWENTY ONE

MY ENDURING LEADERSHIP PRINCIPLES

Built, Changed, And Used Over A Lifetime Of Leadership

This is my set of enduring leadership principles that have evolved over the years through experience, mentoring, study and observation. But, as pointed out at the end of chapter one, the important task for you as you grow as a leader is to develop your own set of principles. They will serve as a guide to daily activities as well as a list of subjects you can use to mentor subordinates as you continue to build your bench.

I believe great leaders:

1. Understand their changing environment.
2. Motivate subordinates.
3. Build consensus.
4. Seek solutions without compromise.
5. Act decisively.
6. Insure their subordinates understand how they intend to lead.
7. Understand that leadership is not about power.
8. Use the continuum of leadership to enhance communications up and down the leadership chain.
9. Recognize that direct, operational and strategic leaders lead differently.

10. Understand the difference between leading people and leading organizations.
11. Optimize their span of control.
12. Delegate operational duties.
13. Empower subordinates.
14. Optimize the talent in their organization.
15. Establish and cultivate a positive culture.
16. Continue to study the art of leadership.
17. Know their subordinates.
18. Mentor subordinates.
19. Build a bench.
20. Set a proper example in both their private and public lives.
21. Are accountable for their actions.
22. Communicate with clarity and brevity.
23. Know how to plan.
24. Use a framework for action.
25. Get out front during a crisis.
26. Act with agility.
27. Recognize that change is inevitable and they must take the organization elsewhere or preside over the funeral.

GLOSSARY

After Action Review: A professional discussion of an event, focused on performance standards, that enables leaders and employees to discover for themselves what happened, what did not happen and why it happened. It is not a critique.

Backbrief: A subordinate leader updating his or her boss after having received mission, intent and boss' guidance. It is a leader's tool to confirm that subordinates are on the correct track.

Boss' Guidance: Verbal or written direction from a leader to a by-invitation-only group of subordinates. It is the vehicle for leaders at every level to set the tone for the way ahead. Boss' guidance expands on mission and intent in order to fix responsibility, prioritize, set milestones, bound the problem and describe the operating environment.

Campaign: A series of organized actions aimed at accomplishing a stated purpose and typically focused on a path toward an identifiable end state

Center Of Gravity: It can be a thing, a person, a place, a belief, a condition, or a circumstance. Center of Gravity identifies that which is key and essential to your success or the success of your adversary.

Chief Of Staff: Leader of the staff elements of an organization at the operational or strategic leadership levels. A close confidant of the boss, the chief of staff's principle duty is that of integrator.

Continuum Of Leadership: The relationship among the leaders of an organization's elements between the direct leaders at the point of execution to the organization's most senior leader. There is a continuum of leadership in every organization.

Corporate Culture: A culture exists within every organization: it is a powerful and pervasive force that defines an organization's reputation, its operating style or its relationships among the members of the continuum. An organization can have either a singular or multi-faceted culture, which can have a positive or negative overall impact. The most powerful and essential cultural trait is character.

Critical Information Requirements: A short, dynamic list of issues that have the potential to significantly influence success or failure of an activity. It is the boss' list and it must be understood to the level where the issue is most likely to be first detected.

Delegation: The art of sharing operational responsibilities with subordinates in order to maximize efficiency and effectiveness. Establishing a set of values for an organization cannot be delegated.

Empowerment: Having delegated responsibility, empowerment is the act of additionally delegating the authority necessary to carry out required actions.

End-State: What a leader perceives the organization will be or where it will be after having institutionalized a new order of things or a new way of doing business.

Intent: A leader's further declaration of expectations beyond what is contained in the mission statement. Intent provides connectivity between the mission and a concept of operations. Intent is the part of the framework that lets all the subordinates into the leaders mind. The intent statement should provide insights into a vision of the end state, why the action is necessary, an outline of the operation and the keys to success.

Kitchen Cabinet: A small group of individuals selected by a senior official in any type organization to provide advise and to undertake special assignments. The members are normally well known to the person they advise; are from outside the organization and therefore not encumbered by day-to-day operations. They have a wide range of experience and expertise.

Leaders: Those who focus on their organization's purposes and end state; someone who will take the organization elsewhere.

• **First-Line Leaders:** A direct leader whose subordinates are at the first level of execution.

• **Direct Leaders:** Leaders at the lower end of the continuum of leadership whose primary function is to execute. They demonstrate how to accomplish tasks, leading by direct example.

• **Operational Leaders:** A leader who brings diverse capabilities to bear on a problem in the accomplishment of strategic objectives; they seek synergistic effects. Operational leaders ensure subordinates understand what needs to be done. The principal distinction between the direct and operational leaders is in the how and the what. Operational leaders are integrators.

• **Strategic Leaders:** With a vision of the end state, strategic leaders confront issues beyond the organization's operating environment, shape the battlespace and provide direction to operational leaders. At the strategic level coordination may be protracted, have a wider impact and be conducted under uncertain conditions with persons external to the organization.

Leader Development: A basic responsibility of leaders at every level; build a bench of potential replacements by using the three pillars: institutional development, assignments and self-development.

Manager: An indispensable part of an organization's operations; one who looks after the organization's processes, integrating the day-to-day utilization of people, time and resources.

Military Grades (U.S. Army):
• Second Lieutenant: leader of a platoon
• First lieutenant

- Captain: leader of a company
- Major
- Lieutenant Colonel: leader of a battalion
- Colonel: leader of a brigade
- Brigadier General
- Major General: leader of a division
- Lieutenant General: leader of a corps
- General

Military Organization:
- Squad: 6-10 soldiers lead by a Staff Sergeant
- Platoon: 3-5 squads, 20-30 soldiers lead by a Lieutenant
- Company: 3-4 platoons, 75-125 soldiers lead by a Captain
- Battalion: 3-5 companies, 300-700 soldiers lead by a Lieutenant Colonel
- Brigade: 3-5 battalions, 2000-5000 soldiers lead by a Colonel
- Division: 5-7 brigades, 12,000-18,000 soldiers lead by a Major General
- Corps: 3-5 divisions, 50,000-75,000 soldiers lead by a Lieutenant General

Mission: Mission is a declaration of expectations, to some segment or perhaps the entire organization, of what it is a leader expects to accomplish during a specified period of time. It is the launch point in moving from vision to execution.

Mobile Command Post: A small, specially selected, trained, team of experts available to relocate on a moments notice to a subordinate organizational element and provide emergency assistance and/or training.

Planning: Proactive thinking at another level.

- **Campaign Planning:** Articulation of a series of synchronized actions aimed at accomplishing a stated purpose and typically focused on a path toward an identifiable end-state. Campaign planning uses the organizational structure, applies a framework for action and links the continuum of leadership (strategic, operational and direct leaders) in a common purpose.

- **Branches:** Branches are contingencies off the approved plan in the event things do not unfold as expected. Branches are developed by asking, what if......?
- **Sequels:** Sequels are subsequent operations based on alternative outcomes of the base plan.

Shaping The Battlespace: Proactively setting conditions such that they play to your strengths and core competencies; a tool for creating conditions for success applicable at the strategic, operational and direct leadership levels.

Skunkworks: A few people in a single place taking a project from concept to prototype, good, fast and cheap. The key to a successful skunkworks is to operate in a controlled environment wherein all the participants interact and are empowered.

Span of Control: Exercising authority over a number of subordinates that maximizes efficiency and effectiveness not only of the leader but the subordinates as well. The rule of thumb for span of control is that a leader should sustain close contact with what is taking place one echelon down and have a clear understanding of what is happening two levels down.

Strategy: Strategy is the alignment of assets to their greatest advantage. Articulation of a strategy informs subordinate leaders how, in general terms, they will collectively go about getting to an end-state.

Vision: Seeing the organization as it will be after institutionalizing change. What the leader "sees" is an identifiable, attainable end state.

War Council: A small, select group of action people pulled from throughout the organization to serve an operational or strategic leader under special circumstances.

NOTES

1 *Encyclopedia Britannica,* http://www.britannica.com/search?qu ery=helmuth%20von%20moltke&ct=&fuzzy=N

2 *Publishing and Printing Technology,* http://www.ssc.cc.il.us/acad/ career/depts/technology/ppt/whatsup/trivia/gutenbrg.htm

3 *Encyclopedia Britannica,* http://www.britannica.com/search?qu ery=alexander%20graham%20bell&ct=&fuzzy=N

4 Steven Brown, Katie O'Donnell, Cayman Seacrest, Dave Maloney, Kathleen Albonese, Todd Bassion, *Generation X,* http: //www.cc.colorado.edu/Dept/EC/generationx96/Genx/

5 *Webster's New World Dictionary* (New York: Simon & Schuster, 1982), p. 801.

6 Colin Powell, *18 Lessons From Colin Powell,* http:// dir.yahoo.com/Government/U_S__Government/Executive_ Branch/Depa.../Powell__Colin

7 *Webster's New World Dictionary* (New York: Simon & Schuster, 1982), p. 859.

8 *Webster's New World Dictionary* (New York: Simon & Schuster, 1982), p. 859.

9 Harold S. Geneen, *The Book of Leadership Wisdom,* ed. Peter Krass (New York: John Wiley & Sons, Inc., 1998), p. 3-21.

10 Field Manual 22-100, *Army Leadership* (Washington, D.C.: department of the Army, 1999).

11 Colin Powell, *18 Lessons From Colin Powell,* http:// dir.yahoo.com/Government/U_S__Government/Executive_ Branch/Depa.../Powell__Colin

12 General George S. Patton Jr., *The Patton Papers, Vol I,* ed. Martin Blumenson (Boston: Houghton Mifflin, 1972).

13 Robert W. Galvin, *The Book of Leadership Wisdom,* ed. Peter Krass (New York: John Wiley & Sons, Inc., 1998), p. 415-419.

14 Frederick W. Smith, *The Book of Leadership Wisdom,* ed. Peter Krass (New York: John Wiley & Sons, Inc., 1998), p. 211-223.

15 Selected Speeches and Statements of General of the Army George C. Marshall, *The Infantry Journal,* 1945.

16 *Great Quotations By Winston Churchill To Inspire and Motivate You,* http://www.cyber-nation.com/victory/quotations/authors/quotes_churchill_winston.html

17 Dwight D. Eisenhower, *At Ease: Stories I Tell to Friends* (New York: Doubleday & Company, 1967).

18 General Mathew B. Ridgeway, *The Military Review,* June 1987.

19 Colin Powell, *18 Lessons From Colin Powell,* http://dir.yahoo.com/Government/U_S_Government/Executive_Branch/Depa.../Powell_Colin

20 Alan Axelrod, *Patton on Leadership: strategic Lessons for Corporate Warfare* (New Jersey: Prentice Hall, 1999), p. 23.

21 Alan Axelrod, *Patton on Leadership: strategic Lessons for Corporate Warfare* (New Jersey: Prentice Hall, 1999), p. 23-24.

22 Frederick W. Smith, *The Book of Leadership Wisdom,* ed. Peter Krass (New York: John Wiley & Sons, Inc., 1998), p. 211-223.

23 Gordon R. Sullivan & Michael V. Harper, *Hope is not a Method* (New York: Broadway Books, 1997), p. vii.

24 Gordon R. Sullivan & Michael V. Harper, *Hope is not a Method* (New York: Broadway Books, 1997), p. viii.

25 Niccolo Machiavelli – *The Prince,* Translated by W. K. Marriott of The Gutenburg Project, http://www.the-prince-by-machiavelli.com/

26 Petronius, *Satyricon,* Translated by P.G. Walsh (UK: Oxford University Press, 1999).

27 *Webster's New World Dictionary* (New York: Simon & Schuster, 1982), p. 778.

28 *The American Heritage Dictionary of the English Language, Fourth Edition* (Boston: Houghton Mifflin, 2000).

29 William Cooper Procter, *The Book of Leadership Wisdom,* ed.

Peter Krass (New York: John Wiley & Sons, Inc., 1998), p. 176-187.

30 *Nordstrom,* http://about.nordstrom.com/aboutus/?origin=hp-leftnav

31 Training Circular 25-20, *A Leader's Guide to After-Action Reviews* (Washington, D.C.: department of the Army, 1993).

32 *Elton Mayo's Hawthorne Experiments into Employee Motivation and Workplace Productivity,* html://www.accel-team.com/motivation/hawthorne_02.html

33 *The Chief Executive,* http://www.bestofbiz.com/briefings/default.asp?p=193

34 William H. Pinkovitz, Joseph Moskal, Gary Green, *How Much Does Your Employee Turnover Cost?,* http://www.uwex.edu/ces/cced/publicat/turn.html

35 Rushworth M. Kidder, *How Good People Make Tough Choices* (New York: Fireside, 1995), p. 49-50.

36 Gary Strauss, "Recruiters Cast Covetous Eyes at GE Execs," *USA TODAY,* 28 November 2000, sec.B, p1.

37 *Defining the Moral Crisis,* http://www.iath.virginia.edu/cecmpe/defining2.html

38 Rushworth M. Kidder, *How Good People Make Tough Choices* (New York: Fireside, 1995), p. 8.

39 Thomas A. Edison, *The Book of Leadership Wisdom,* ed. Peter Krass (New York: John Wiley & Sons, Inc., 1998), p. 125.

40 Marcy Carsey, Tom Werner, *Father of Broadcasting David Sarnoff,* http://www.time.com/time/time100/builder/profile/sarnoff.html

41 *Executive Bios,* http://www.intel.com/pressroom/kits/bios/moore.htm

42 *Civil War Biographies,* http://www.civilwarhome.com/biograph.htm

43 Colin Powell, *18 Lessons From Colin Powell,* http://dir.yahoo.com/Government/U_S__Government/Executive_Branch/Depa.../Powell__Colin

44 Michael Shaara, *The Killer Angels* (New York: David McKay Company, Inc., 1974)

45 Joseph Flowers, *The Fight of Their Lives* http://www.gettysburgguide.com/fight.html

46 William A. Cohen, *The Stuff of Heroes* (Marietta, GA: Longstreet, 1998), p. 92-94.

47 Michael Shaara, *The Killer Angels* (New York: David McKay Company, Inc., 1974), p. 88

ENDURING LEADERSHIP PRINCIPLES:

1._____

_____

_____

_____

_____

_____

_____

_____

_____

_____

_____

_____

_____

_____

_____

_____

_____

_____

_____

_____

_____

_____

_____

_____

_____

_____

_____

_____

_____

_____

Made in the USA
Lexington, KY
31 December 2009